A BOOK ON
PRACTICAL MANAGEMENT

THE MANAGEMENT AND THEIR EXPECTATIONS

Written by
Kashinath Jha
M.A., M.B.A., P.M.I.R., P.G.D.C.A.

Edited by
Seema Jha
M.Sc.

Himalaya Publishing House

MUMBAI • NEW DELHI • NAGPUR • BENGALURU • HYDERABAD • CHENNAI • PUNE • LUCKNOW • AHMEDABAD • ERNAKULAM • BHUVNESHWAR • INDORE • KOLKATA

First Edition : 2011

Published by : Mrs. Meena Pandey for **Himalaya Publishing House Pvt. Ltd.,** "Ramdoot", Dr. Bhalerao Marg, Girgaon, **Mumbai - 400 004.** Phone: 022-23860170/23863863, Fax: 022-23877178 **E-mail: himpub@vsnl.com; Website: www.himpub.com**

Branch Offices :

New Delhi : "Pooja Apartments", 4-B, Murari Lal Street, Ansari Road, Darya Ganj, New Delhi - 110 002. Phone: 011-23270392, 23278631; Fax: 011-23256286

Nagpur : Kundanlal Chandak Industrial Estate, Ghat Road, Nagpur - 440 018. Phone: 0712-2738731, 3296733; Telefax: 0712-2721215

Bengaluru : No. 16/1 (Old 12/1), 1st Floor, Next to Hotel Highlands, Madhava Nagar, Race Course Road, Bengaluru - 560 001. Phone: 080-32919385; Telefax: 080-22286611

Hyderabad : No. 3-4-184, Lingampally, Besides Raghavendra Swamy Matham, Kachiguda, Hyderabad - 500 027. Phone: 040-27560041, 27550139; Mobile: 09848130433

Chennai : No. 85/50, Bazullah Road, T. Nagar, Chennai - 600 017. Phone: 044-28144004/28144005

Pune : First Floor, "Laksha" Apartment, No. 527, Mehunpura, Shaniwarpeth (Near Prabhat Theatre), Pune - 411 030. Phone: 020-24496323/24496333

Lucknow : Jai Baba Bhavan, Church Road, Near Manas Complex and Dr. Awasthi Clinic, Aliganj, Lucknow - 226 024. Phone: 0522-2339329, 4068914; Mobile: 09305302158, 09415349385, 09389593752

Ahmedabad : 114, "SHAIL", 1st Floor, Opp. Madhu Sudan House, C.G. Road, Navrang Pura, Ahmedabad - 380 009. Phone: 079-26560126; Mobile: 09327324149, 09314679413

Ernakulam : 39/104 A, Lakshmi Apartment, Karikkamuri Cross Rd., Ernakulam, Cochin - 622011, Kerala. Phone: 0484-2378012, 2378016; Mobile: 09344199799

Bhubaneswar : 5 Station Square, Bhubaneswar (Odisha) - 751 001. Mobile: 09861046007

Indore : Kesardeep Avenue Extension, 73, Narayan Bagh, Flat No. 302, IIIrd Floor, Near Humpty Dumpty School, Narayan Bagh, Indore - 452 007 (M.P.). Mobile: 09301386468

Kolkata : 108/4, Beliaghata Main Road, Near ID Hospital, Opp. SBI Bank, Kolkata - 700 010, Phone: 033-32449649, Mobile: 09910440956

Guwahati : House No. 15, Behind Pragjyotish College, Near Sharma Printing Press, P.O. Bharalumukh, Guwahati - 781009. (Assam). Mobile: 09883055590, 09883055536

DTP by : HPH, Editorial Office, Bhandup

Printed by : Shri Krishna offset Press Delhi-93

PREFACE

This is a Practical Management Book, based on my personal experiences, observations, day-to-day practical working systems of the Management & the Common Problems being faced by the employees at their workplace.

I have tried to explain the various types of expectations of the Management, seniors, H.O.D., which they expect directly or indirectly from their subordinates. This Book also explains the weak points of the Manager, workers along with their probable solutions.

I hope this Book will prove its worth to all the employees working in any type of Establishment to make a good relationship with their Employers, Seniors & H.O.D., so that they would get their promotion, increments and other benefits on time and their superiors at their workplace would not ignore their work.

I acknowledge to my friends, colleagues & seniors with gratitude and sincere thanks who had provoked & inspired me to write this Book.

Suggestions for the improvement in the Book are welcome and will be gratefully acknowledged.

Kashinath Jha
Author

FROM THE AUTHOR'S PEN

- At the workplace, there is a big gap between the workers and the management, incharge, heads of the department, middle management and the top management. The systems made by the top management only works on paper and the middle management or the seniors of the concerned department make their own systems for the organisation as per their convenience and benefit. This is one of the main reasons for loss in any organisation. The middle management and the respective seniors manipulate or give wrong information to the top management. They make different groups at the workplace for their own benefits. They give promotion and increment to their own group of workers. Most of the seniors/heads of the department/middle management are corrupt and they misuse the resources of the organisation for their own benefits. They even settle their personal score thereby leading the company towards doom.
- The true employees or workers expect from their management that they should seek the list of all the workers (in all cadres), from time to time, who have been or have not been given promotion, In some cases it has been seen that a worker works in the same cadre and department for as many as 8 to 10 years, thereby stagnating and feeling helpless. The names of such workers should be sought out every 5 to 6 years, so that they can get their due benefit.
- After reaching a certain point, the Higher management being the supreme boss should divert their mind (apart from bigger responsibilities and challenges) on humanitarian grounds towards the poor and humble workers who are in dire need of being uplifted (Like Mr. Narayan Murthy did to his personal staff and driver) than giving donations to big political parties and smartly dressed cheats or spending lavishly on weddings and parties.
- The joy of having wealth is in sharing it. As we all know charity begins at home, so why not upgrade the living conditions of our own brood (here workers)
- This book would be very helpful for the workers/employees working at any level in an Organisation. Through this book the workers / employees or seniors / the management could develop good understanding among themselves and could evaluate each other at the workplace.

This book would also be beneficial for the freshers or new recruits who are on the brink of starting their career..

I have tried to communicate the message to the top management about the practical happenings of the workplace where honesty is ignored and dishonesty is rewarded.

CONTENTS

CHAPTER 1

INTRODUCTION

In the present days, there is a huge gap between the workers / employees and the Management. The workers do not know what type of expectations, their Management/ seniors, expect from them. They do not know how they should work, so that the Management would love them and their work. In general, all the seniors/ managers are seen to be very calculative. If, we are a car owner and are sitting on the back seat of the car and the driver is driving it, in this situation, we expect from that driver that he should drive the car assuming that he is the owner of that car and handle it with care. If we are planning to go out, we expect from our driver that it is his duty to check the oil, brake, water, engine etc before leaving the station. If the driver does his homework before leaving the station, we love him and his work. We will continue his service, otherwise, there may be a problem between us. We also expect from him that he should have full knowledge of the mechanical parts of that car. We also expect that he should know the roads, directions and the destination where we are going to visit.

For example, if in a family, there are four daughters in-law. What does the mother in-law or head of the family, like the management, expect from them? In due course, one daughter-in law from them becomes more faithful to the head of the family and the rest of them were unable to get that position. While the family is one and the head of the family is one, the rest of the daughters-in-law could not understand what their mother-in-law is expecting from them.

At this situation, the head of the family / management desires from them the following points:

- They should know the rules and regulations of the family / Organisation culture.
- The main motto of the head of the family is to develop the family and keep them united.

- The daughters-in-law should develop themselves in such a way that they can take whole responsibility of the family. They would run the family with full coordination & cooperation as per the desire of the head of the family.
- They should follow and respect the in-laws religion by being very tolerant towards their faith.

They should first know the rules and the regulations of their in-laws family. The head of the family would never like that any one of the family members disobey the norms of the family. Similarly, at the workplace of any Organisation, the Management never expects from their workers that they would disobey the rules / regulations of the Company. If a worker disobeys the rules of the Company, the Management always tries to punish him by any means. The Management always likes only those workers working in their Organisation, who follow the rules and the regulations laid down by the Company.

Similarly, the Management expects from their workers that they should know the main motto of any assigned work / objectives / mission / target etc. Without knowing the motto, the workers would never do their work or discharge their duties / performance in a good way. They should know the importance of the assigned job. They should also know the technique, which the Management have planned for their Organisational development. The worker should be very familiar with the books, write-ups and the published matters of the Organisation, so that the communication gap could be minimised.

Likewise, a father desires from his son that his son should know about the family business very well. He should have keen interest in his father's business / job. He should know about each vicissitude and the viable strategies related to the business. If the father has faith in a particular religion, he also expects from his son that the son should also have faith in that particular religion etc.

Sometimes, if the son does not obey the father's religion or his rules / regulation at any given situation, the father does not give his son the benefit of his property and does not want to give the facilities, which a son deserves. Therefore, if we are working in an Organisation, which follows a particular religion / system / rules and regulations, then the workers / employees should also follow the same religion / systems / rules and regulations. If they do not want to do the same, the Management will not give benefits to such workers.

In another way, we can take the example of a domestic servant, who works in our house. The same logic will also be applicable in the servant's case. Here the Management is the head of the family and the worker / employee is the servant. Here, what we expect from that poor servant is honesty, faithfulness, dedication, loyalty, hardwork, good behaviour, and knowledge of the rules and the regulations of the family / household.

It means the servant should be very honest towards his duties. He should be very obedient to his master. He must discharge his duties as per the given schedule of the master; otherwise, the head of the family would be unhappy. Another example we can quote here is from the Hindi film "Bawarchi". The servant handles the family members, very tactfully, politely and respectfully. Every family member likes the servant due to his good behaviour and hard work, dedication, devotion, emotion, interest with which he does his assigned work, inspite of the adverse nature of the family members. The family members like the servant because he delivers his duties without asking anybody anything or without questioning. He provides the entire requirement of the concerned members as per their desire. He does the work in the interest of the family. He follows the rules and the regulations of the family and never tries to escape from the new assignment or responsibility or ignores the instruction of any family member. Thus, the head of the family is very happy with his behaviour and work. They also want this servant to benefit so that he gets his proper due or reward.

Generally, it is inherent in human nature that they want something extra from their servant or worker. The head of the family or the concerned members want everything done properly from that servant, without giving him any instruction. Here they expect that the servant should know what type of service his master or members are demanding or expecting from him or require from him.

More or less, the same logic is also applicable or seen in any Organisation. The Management at various levels desire that the subordinates should give extra care to the Organisation and they should take care of their likes and dislikes. They should devote some extra time apart from the official work schedule, so that the subordinates would have faith on their boss.

One thing more that the Management always desires from the employees is that they should always be attentive to their orders. They want that as much time and energy as they are devoting to the Organisation, the subordinates should also be ready for this in the same way. In short, full dedication is needed from all sides.

I have emphasised the several situations of an Organisation where a person wants to prove himself or a fresher wants to do something new and prove himself as the best among the rest of the people under the guidance of seniors / supervisors / in charge or head of the department to fulfil the common goal.

Through this book, I wish to clear the several points that the superior / boss / head, in charge, expects from their subordinates at the workplace. What type of performance the subordinates, should perform, so that their boss, head, in charge, Management could appreciate their work and it would be recognised, appreciated in the Organisation. How a worker would get recognition in the Organisation by doing good work. I would try to clarify my thinking through various common practical examples, which we are facing every day in our life.

I will try to emphasise on the various expectations of an employee & employer, which may vary from person to person. As different persons, have different equations, circumstances, logic, and strategy in their life. This also influences the seniors, head or the in charge.

In general, it is observed that management means, the employer, but in my opinion:

The employees working in an organisation, who are responsible or answerable for any assigned job, in charge, supervisor of any division /unit, is known as the management.

If any organisation is growing well, then it means the management as well as the whole workforce are also responsible for that growth. Therefore, when they are responsible for the growth then definitely the whole workforce is also responsible for the loss. Thus, the whole workforce also can be called the Management. Each workforce is directly or indirectly a part of the Management. They are all mutually interlinked and inter-dependent.

❖❖❖

CHAPTER 2

A BRIEF NOTE ON THE MANAGEMENT

THE MANAGEMENT

Management is a process. It is a process of getting things done by working with the people of work and resources applied with a view to accomplish the task set for within the framework of the policies and programmes.

"MANAGEMENT is an art and science of preparing, organising and directing human efforts to control the forces and utilise the material of nature for the benefits of men."- **American Society of Mechanical Engineers.**

Objectives of any business activity are to be achieved through organised and co-operative endeavour. For this, a group of people are to be assigned jobs according to their knowledge and skill. Their activities are to be planned, directed & co-ordinated so that pre determined objectives might be achieved. This gigantic effort of planning, directing and unifying the good efforts to achieve common goals is called Management.

As per Satya Saran Chatterjee: "Management is the activating element of any enterprise for getting things done through its personnel."

The management also entails the best possible utilisation of available physical resources to the satisfaction of all those whom they are meant for.

According to KIMBALL AND KIMBALL: "Management is the art of applying the economic principles that underline the control of men and materials in enterprise under consideration."

Elmore Peterson & Grosveno: "Management may be defined as a technique by means of which the purpose and objectives of a particular human group are determined, classified and effectuated."

Keith and Gubelline: "Management is the force, which integrates men and physical plant into an effective operating unit."

Oliver Sheldon: The term management is commonly used to cover the formation of policy, its execution, the designing of the organisation and its employment."

Appley: "Management is the attainment of pre-established goals by the direction of human performance along pre-established lines.

E.F.I. Brech: "Management may be defined as a social process entailing responsibility for the effective, planning and regulation of the operations of an enterprise. Such responsibility involving (a) the installation and maintenance of proper procedures to ensure adherence to plans; and (b) the guidance, integration and supervision of the personnel comprising the enterprise and carrying out its operations."

James L Lundy: "Management is principally a task of planning, coordinating, motivating and controlling the efforts of others towards specific objectives."

Mary Cushing Niles: "Good management... achieves a social objective with the best use of human and material energy and time and with satisfaction of the participants and the public."

TYPES OF MANAGEMENT

The whole Management can be divided into three categories.

(1) Top Management:

Top Management is responsible for planning. It lays down the policies and programmes for the enterprise. It thus provides a framework within which the entire enterprise works. Top Management is responsible for providing leadership, guidance and supervision for the whole Company / Organisation. Under this Management, the shareholders, Board of Directors and the Chief Executives are associated. The overall functions of the top Management can be divided into the following:

(1) Preparation of Different Policies in the Organisational interest &

(2) General Administration

In the other wards, the main functions of the top Management can be divided into these three categories, like wise:

(1) Overall Management

(2) Overall Operation

(3) Overall Relationship

OVERALL MANAGEMENT

The whole probable functions of top Management can be categorised under the overall Management, like this:

(1) Purpose of the Enterprises

(2) Broader Policies of the Enterprise,

(3) Nature and size of the Organisation

(4) Planning, objectives, methods and procedure regarding the work to be accomplished

(5) Mode and procedure of appointment of personnel including appointment of personnel of the top,

(6) Controlling procedure to be adopted and

(7) Leadership and direction to be provided.

It means, the top Management is responsible to take all type of major decisions related to the enterprise/organisational benefits, or their future growth. They decide how the enterprise works smoothly. The top Management do not bother about the day-to-day routine work or their daily problems. The top Management silently monitor all such activities, which give the direct impact on the growth, brand, image and overall development of the workforce engaged in the enterprise. Whenever they feel that, there is any shortcoming or something is lacking which may hamper the whole organisation, they immediately try to change them.It is the top Management, which is finally responsible for all the activities of the enterprise.

OVERALL OPERATION

Under these categorical functions of top Management, it includes all types of issues of instructions and directions to the entire workforce at every level in order to get the assigned work done. In this way they look after the entire task/ responsibility assigned to the different groups. of workforce in a manner which satisfies them and helps the enterprise in achieving the objectives according to the prior fixed and scheduled plan.

OVERALL RELATIONSHIP

The most important functions of all level Management, especially the Management seating on the top level is to see the harmonious relationship between all the levels of work force through good co-ordination, without which it is very difficult to run the enterprise. The top Management is the only one responsible for any liaison work in the enterprise. Apart from the other important work, they try to establish a cordial relationship between shareholders, workforce, society and the Government for smooth sailing and better results. In other words, it can be said that the top Management works like a representative for their enterprise with the outside world. If in spite of having all the resources, the Company / Enterprise in not doing well due to any circumstance, the persons sitting on the top Management are only responsible for those defects. It means they have not given proper guidance to their personnel of the enterprise.

2. Middle – Order Management

It comes just below the top one. Such a Management is responsible for the execution of the Policy made by the top Management. It tries to implement all the instructions, rules and regulations laid down by the top Management in the interest of the Company or the Organisation. Middle Order Management is answerable to the top Management. Its main functions are:

(1) To provide plans,

(2) To Guide

(3) To Supervise

(4) To Co-ordinate and

(5) To exercise control over the lowest level of Management.

Middle-Order Management also works as an advisory capacity. Such type of Management, generally gives advice to the top of the Management but on the other side, it also guides to the lowest Management. It tries to make a good and successful link between the two Managements of any Organisation.

FUNCTIONS OF MIDDLE-LEVEL MANAGEMENT

The main responsibility of this type of Management is to make a powerful relationship with the top Management and the supervisory level Management. They must make a good co-ordination between them. The work of middle Management is not fixed for all the enterprises as it differs from one Management to another. They take all the responsibilities assigned by the top Management on their own shoulder and make the top Management free from all routine directions, supervision or co-ordination responsibilities.

The Middle Management generally makes them free from all-small things and lets them make plans for the entire enterprise or organisational level. The Middle-Level Management should make schedules in such a way that the top Management should be totally left free to make plans and administer the whole enterprise in the best interest of all who are related directly or indirectly with the enterprise.

They should also establish a co-ordination between the activities of different wings of the enterprise. The Middle Management also makes harmonious human relations based on human psychology within the framework of the policies.

Apart from the above, the middle management also prepares the workers for future work and progress and creates a spirit among the workforce.

3. Supervisory Management:

The Management, which works under the control and the direction of the Middle-order Management, is called or known as the Supervisory Management. This Management takes the orders from the Middle – Order Management and explains it to the workers at operating level, through a systematic way, provide plans, guide, supervise, co ordinate and take control over the lowest level of Management. This type of Management is responsible as well as answerable to the Middle-order Management.

The following are the main functions of supervisory management:-

(1) To supervise and control the work of the operating staff.

(2) To distribute the work among the workers.

(3) To see that plant's and tools are in working conditions and every worker is in possession of acquired plant's, tools and equipment.

(4) To see that the work is going on according to schedule and policies, plans, etc.

(5) To provide adequate training to the work force.

(6) To make security arrangement for material, men, plant, tools and equipments.

(7) To develop harmonious relationship among workers.

(8) To explain to subordinates the working procedures clearly, so that they could understand.

The Lower Level Management

Such type of management is responsible for the execution of the plans, Policies and programmes. This level is directly involved in the operation of job while the middle-order management, second tier, is indirectly responsible for the execution.

Shareholders
Board
Chief Executive
Departmental Heads
Sectional Heads
Superintendents
Lower Command
Operating Command

Top Management

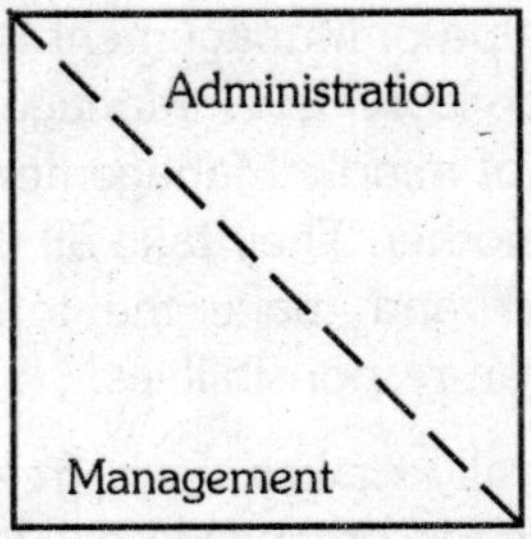

Lowest Level of Management

Overall the main functions or the main principles, on which the concept of management is based, can be divided into these areas, like:-

- Planning
- Organising
- Motivating
- Controlling
- Co-ordinating

PLANNING

According to **Koontz O' Donnell:** Planning is an intellectual process, the conscious determination of course of action, the basing of decisions on purpose, facts and considered estimates.

Alford and Beatty: "Planning is the thinking process, the organised foresight, the vision based on fact and experience that is required for intelligent action".

Theo Haimann: "Planning is deciding in advance what is to be done. When a manager plans, he projects a course of action for the future, attempting to achieve a consistent, co-ordinated structure of operations aimed at the desired results".

Billy E. Goetz: "Planning is fundamentally choosing and a planning problem arises when an alternative course of action is discovered".

Harold Koontz and Cyril O' Donnell: "Planning is the function of a manager which involves the selection from among alternatives of objectives, polices, procedures and programmes. It is thus decision making affecting the future course of an enterprise or a department."

George B Galloway: "Planning is the opposite of improvising. It is organised foresight plus corrective and hindsight."

Mary Cushing Niles: "Planning is the conscious of selecting and developing the best course of action to accomplish an objective. It is the basis from which future management actions spring. "

George R Terry: "Planning is a method or technique of looking ahead- a constructive reviewing of future needs so that present actions can be adjusted in view of the established good."

Planning is an intellectual process of taking decisions. It is a process of deciding the future course of actions. Managers would like to leave the future on the series of events to follow. Instead, they generally like to take concrete steps to safeguard against all future eventualities. Planning is a process of looking ahead.

Planning contributes positively in attaining the objectives of the business enterprise. Since plans are there from the very first stage of operation, the management is able to handle every problem successfully. Plans try to set everything right. A powerful, sound and effective planning process knows how and when to tackle a problem. This leads to success. Objectives thus are easily achieved.

If we act in right earnest and in proper perspective, we derive the following distinct advantages from planned course of action:

Planning Avoids Chaos: In general, we plan for only our future not for our past. If we take or make a proper planning before the start of any type of work along with their merits and demerits & prospective characters. If our objectives are, clear with proper flowchart of work schedule, aiming to achieve the target. We may definitely avoid the future problems. If we make production according to the market demand, make recruitment as per the genuine workforce requirement based on our programmes and make purchase of materials for the Company as per the needs. It is sure that we never have to face a chaos situation in the Organisation.

Planning Minimise Cost: Planning involves a lot of time, energy, patience and money for its formulation. Naturally, it is a costly exercise. Planning of any programme is very costly only for one time. However, once it is formulated and implemented in right earnest in every sphere and at every stage, cost of performance tends to decline. At the same time if we ignore procedure or any important step during the planning course of action for the planned programme, we would not help in minimising the cost. Therefore, we should always give the importance to every related step of planning, which can minimise the cost of production.

Purposeful and orderly activities: In planned course of action, everything moves according to pre-determined policies, programmes, procedures and schedule. If proper harmony, coordination & relations are maintained, we can achieve miracles through planning otherwise it is very difficult to achieve any type of target or goal. Proper implementation in a right way of any pre-determined work schedule is more important than making a planning for the same. It means we should have to maintain a planning schedule of action.

It guides business along with predetermined channel: If, we have planned for our future programme in a very scientific way, having clear instructions of procedure of actions, how to implement, how to work, what work to be done or what not to be done with clear remarks. It will be very helpful for all the workers as well as for the personnel involved in the work. They can easily achieve their target without having any problems. They can use this schedule as guidelines for achieving purposes.

Planning helps the performance of other managerial functions:

Each function as well as work of any Company is correlated with each other. If one schedule of any work will be delayed then automatically other related work or outputs will also be delayed. If the planning and their schedule of action are proper then it will be very helpful for all the managerial functions to execute their assigned responsibilities in a good and harmonious way.

No industry or for that matter commercial sector can think of success without a proper planning. Planning provides guidance for future. So it is necessary to have a good, positive, clear, transparent planning so that every one can understand and they can use the best of their efforts in achieving the organisational or assigned goal.

ORGANISING

Whenever our planning work in an Organisation is completely related to a particular assignment or business goal in company's interest, then immediately the second function of Management comes, which is organising. According to J.C. Massie, "An organisation is a structure and a process by which a cooperative group of human beings allocates its tasks among its members, identifies relationships and integrates its activities towards common objectives."

In other words, dividing and combining efforts of a work force for making such joint efforts more productive, effective and fruitful is termed as Organising.

In this stage, the Organisation or Company assigns a person who is known as an Organiser for a particular job, assignment, or business target or for common goal in company's interest.

An Organiser: Generally, an organiser divides the work, duties, and responsibilities as per the work schedule assigned to a particular work. During the assignment of work to the workforce, the organiser also considers the ability, capacity, knowledge, Interest of the person to be assigned to do a particular job.

A Definer: Secondly comes a definer, which means, one who defines the work, duties, responsibilities, and obligations, assigns the task, delegates the authority, establishes coordination, above all sets, and defines the mutual relationship.

MOTIVATION

The inducement to the people to contribute as effectively and as efficiently as possible is called motivation. In any organisation, the Management acts as:

An Inducer: who induces the people to put forward their best for achieving their given objectives is called an inducer. He stimulates to and gets response from the working force.

A Communicator: who communicates between the Management and the working force at the lower level are called a communicator.

A Leader: who directs guides and provides leadership to the working force until they get their assigned job completed.

CO-ORDINATING

As per S. S. Banerjee, "Co-ordinating is the integration, synchronisation or orderly pattern of group efforts in the enterprise towards the accomplishment of common objectives."

In the words of Terry, "Co-ordination deals with the task of blending efforts in order to ensure a successful attainment of an objective."

Co-ordination in the Management of personnel takes place at all levels, from top Management through to the supervisor and those for whom he is responsible. The personnel department has to co-ordinate the task of developing, interpreting and reviewing personnel policies, practices and programmes, such as safety programmes, employee benefits, job evaluation, training or development, and communication.

The main functions of any co-ordinator can be divided into the following categories:

A Harmoniser: Who harmonises all the activities of a concern in order to facilitate its working and its success.

An Organiser: Who arranges group efforts and provides unity of action in the pursuit of a common purpose.

A Promoter: Who promotes the unity of purpose for the achievement of the desired results.

A Consolidator: Who consolidates the activities of different parts of an organisation with a view to minimise the friction and maximise the collaborative effectiveness.

CONTROLLING

Controlling is the act of checking, regulating and verifying whether everything occurs in conformity with the plan that has been adopted, the instructions issued and the principles established. It is greatly concerned with actions and remedial actions.

Controlling: is an executive process involving three elements- standards, evaluation and correctives. Here the management functions in the role of:-

A Standard Setter: who works out a standard and sets it for those who are to work for the enterprise and accomplish the task assigned to them.

An Evaluator: who evaluates the performance of the work force based on the standards already set for?

A Corrector: who applies correctives and takes measures to set things right, when anything goes wrong.

CHAPTER 3

THE ORGANISATION

Dr Varma & Agarwal have written in their Book "Principles of Management that the Organisation is a process of dividing and combining efforts of a working group for making such joint efforts more productive, effective and fruitful. Organisation allocates duties to the managerial staff. It adds certainty and promptness to the work to be done. It avoids gaps and overlapping functions. It establishes a neat pattern of relationships among efforts to be put, job to be done and work to be performed. It ensures team- work. Organisation, thus, is a framework for the fulfilment of common aims.

As explained by Satya Saran Chatterjee an: "Organisation is not only a mechanistic structure of duties, activities and relationship but it is as well a human Organisation consisting of diverse social groups. Attitudes, aspirations, likes and dislikes of personnel play a great part in transforming the Organisation as an organ of productivity and creating." Thus according to him, Organisation does not provide only a mechanical structure but also takes due note of human faculties. By doing this, it encourages initiative and develops a responsible sense of duty in a personnel working for the Organisation."

As per Mr. A. P. Strong: "Organisation is the process of integrating into a coordinated structure of activities required to achieve the objectives of an enterprise; stating this structure with qualified; competent personnel and supplying them with physical factors necessary to perform their functions." Strong, therefore, clearly indicates that the Organisation is nothing but a process of integrating and coordinating the efforts of men and material for the accomplishment of a set objective.

Louis A. Allen defines an Organisation as "the process of identifying and grouping the work to be performed, defining and delegating responsibility and authority and establishing relationships for the purposes of enabling people to work most effectively together in accomplishing objectives."

According to Sheldon: "An Organisation is the formation of an effective machine, the management of an effective executive and the administration of an effective direction. Administration determines the Organisation; the management uses it. An Organisation is a machine of management in its achievement of the ends determined by its administration."

James L. Lundy: According to him, an Organisation is a process of "welding together a frame work of positions which can be used as a management tool for the most effective pursuit of the goal of an enterprise."

McFarland, Davis, Spriegal and Breach: According to them, the Organisation is an expression of mutual rights, relationships and responsibilities of personnel working in an enterprise.

Chester I. Barnard: According to him, "when two men work together to move a stone, they are increasing their individual strengths by pooling them and that when they recognise this, they form an Organisation."

John M. Pfiffner: "Organisation is essentially a matter of relationship- man to man, job to job, department to department." The relationship may either be of formal or of informal type.

On the other hand, it can be defined: as, an Organisation is a mechanism with which a management directs co-ordinates and controls the activities of man, machine, money and materials- the 4 Ms. This mechanism may be linked to the steering mechanism of a motor vehicle. If the steering mechanism is faulty or is improperly operated, the vehicle is apt to go off the course. Similarly, if an Organisation is poorly designed; or if the management is lacking in personal leadership, an enterprise may fail in achieving its objectives.

Characteristics of Organisation

Organisation is an effective and necessary instrument for the attainment of pre-determined goals. The following are the main characteristics of an Organisation.

- A determination and an enumeration of the activities necessary for the achievement of the goals of an enterprise.
- A group of these activities and assigning authority and responsibility to a particular position like Manager.
- The carrying out of the functions assigned to the manager.
- A co-ordination of authority relationship so that the efforts of individuals may be directed towards the achievement of company goals.
- It Increases managerial efficiency.
- Ensures an optimum use of human efforts.
- Balances various activities proportionately.
- Facilitates coordination.
- Provides a better scope for adequate training.
- Helps in identifying the pitfalls.

- Develops the managerial growth and expansion of the enterprise.
- Prevents the growth of laggards, wirepuller, intriguers.
- Discourages and controls corrupt practices.
- It denotes a group of personnel whose positions, rights, responsibilities are well defined and classified according to the nature of assignments.
- It also denotes the process of classification and sub-classification of jobs, duties and authority on the one hand and methods and procedure of production and other performances on the other."

The Organisation can be divided into two parts.

(1) Formal Organisation, based on formal relationship, and

(2) Informal Organisation, based on informal relationship.

Informal Organisation, duties, responsibilities, rights and authority are clearly defined. Procedures are laid down. Methods are evolved, discussed and put before the personnel in clear terms. While on the other side *in informal Organisation,* nothing is clearly defined or laid down. It is a developing process, which develops, based on work performed and mutual relationship between different personnel, job, duties and authority. Out of cooperative behaviour, love for common good and social gain, courteous and affectionate relations and team spirit develops in an informal Organisation. This form of Organisation may help in being effective, lasting and a fruitful Organisation as compared to the formal one. This is why a good relationship is always there in an informal type of Organisation.

The formal type of Organisation is formally divided into three broad forms. They are-

(1) Line Organisation

(2) Line and Staff Organisation

(3) Functional Organisation

Line Organisation

In line Organisation, the authority descends from the top of the hierarchy to its bottom level, gradually, through downward delegation of authority. As a result all major decisions taken and orders given by the top executives is passed down to their immediate subordinates who, in turn, break up decisions in specific instructions for the purpose of their execution by another set of subordinates. When authority flows from the top to the subordinates at the lowest level in a more or less straight line, it is known as a line Organisation and the subordinates under it are responsible to their immediate superiors.

Merits of a Line Organisation

- Line Organisation is a simplest type of Organisation system in which, it can be easily defined and explained to the ordinary people.
- It is also economic and effective. Here, one individual controls all the activities affecting a department.

- Responsibilities assigned to any one are fixed hence, each individual knows to whom he is responsible and who is or are in turn, responsible to him.
- Such a type of system gives greater control and adequate control system to the Organisation.
- In Line Organisation, the concerned executive has sole responsibility in his own department or jurisdiction.
- It develops all round officers who are qualified to take over the higher position of the line of command in a department.

Demerits of Line Organisation

- On the other side, if we see the demerits of Line Organisation then we will see that here the executive/managers/workers are always over loaded or over burdened at their assigned workplace.
- As, all are experts of all types of jobs, this is the reason; no one has master knowledge on one subject. (Clear case of Jack of all trade, master of none)
- Since a single person takes the decisions, sometimes, it is feared that the decision taken by any authority, may be biased.
- The system is generally based on a one-man management and the decisions indicate the dictatorial operations.
- It does not provide any means by which a good worker may be rewarded and a bad one punished.
- The executive is overloaded at each level of Organisation. He has to look into too many jobs of diverse nature, so he cannot justify with only one assigned work, therefore efficiency level of the workers decrease due to the overload of work.
- Since one person has to look into the different types of assigned work, without having the prior experience and specialisation, for which they are working, they cannot give the adequate and required result to the Company.

Line & Staff Organisation

A line and staff Organisation combines the advantages of both and to a large extent tries to do away with their disadvantages. This is why today this form of organisation is widely acceptable and is recognised as one of the best. Under this form of Organisation two sets of staff are generally at work- the advisory and assisting staff technically known as staff executive and service staff that is line executive. The staff members concentrate their attention upon the research and planning aspects of business problems while the line officials are left free to devote their attention to the execution of the policy.

In the modern industrial world, almost all giant business enterprises have a line and staff organisation. Through this organisation, the goal of an enterprise can be achieved in a systematic and efficient way. The popular concept of line and staff is that "line functions are those which have direct responsibility for the accomplishment of the objectives of an enterprise:, and the staff refers to those elements of an organisation which help the line staff to work most effectively in the accomplishment of the primary objectives of the enterprise."

Merits of Line and Staff Organisation:

The following are the main advantages of this form of Organisation:-

- As it gives a clear-cut and undivided delegation of authority, responsibility, one can achieve their operating efficiency through specialisation easily.
- Here any decision can be taken very easily, as both the line and staff functions together.
- The system is very flexible.
- It provides an adequate opportunity for the advancement of workers.
- Both the productivity and profitability increases.
- Through this system, the efficiency increases at all level of all workers.

Demerits of Line and Staff Organisation:

- Lack of responsibility is seen at any level under this system and the carelessness develops within the workforce.
- Every time there is a possibility **of dispute** even on a minor issue.
- Advice rendered by anyone is generally ignored.
- Specialist of any subject feels very isolated and neglected.
- The staffs are unable to carry out its plans or recommendations because of lack of authority.

FUNCTIONAL OR STAFF ORGANISATION

In this form of Organisation, authority does not flow downward from top. In other words, single authority is done away with and multiplicity of authority is introduced. According to **Taylor,** each worker instead of getting orders and instructions from (eight) different bosses, every boss gives orders and issues instructions pertaining to his specialised function.

In this form of Organisation, authority becomes functional and specialised. The workers in this form of Organisation are responsible and answerable to all his superiors from whom he takes orders and instruction for each of his specialised jobs.

Here the supervisors are responsible for their specialised jobs and answerable individually to their superior under whom they are working. The authority here is divided and does not flow from one but from many in a diffused manner.

Merits of Functional Organisation:

- The efficiency improves at all levels of Organisation due to specialised services made available with the help of this form of Organisation.
- A distinction is clearly established between two types of work-mental and physical. This helps in better understanding of the problems.
- Due to availability of expert, specialised and technical knowledge, a good production is expected.
- As one gets full and sufficient time, to devote his entire energy to do one thing only.

- Mass production increases in this system.
- It gives more work satisfaction for specialised personnel because every one gets time to deliver his ability in front of others.

Demerits of Functional Organsation:

- It increases conflicts between two persons related to their responsibility.
- Action cannot be taken immediately because of divided control. It reduces the opportunities for the training of all around executives to assume further leadership in the firm.
- It increases the indiscipline and casualty.
- It raises problem of lack of coordination.
- Implementation of anything is very difficult.

THE PRESENT DAYS' ORGANISATION

Present days Organisations are those where all types of decision-making powers, whether negative or positive, in favour or against the Organisation, are totally centralised with a single person. The Organisation may be very big or small.

- In general, it has been observed that the Management of such type of Organisation expects the following from their workers/staff or personnel.
- Generally, they prefer to recruit female staff instead of male. As the male staff may sometimes oppose on any irrelevant subject/ issues or on any matter related to the job, while female workers, oppose less on any issue or on any official matter.
- The female workers/ staff are more hard working, obedient and courteous towards their supervisors, senior, of the Organisation than the male staff.
- They prefer female workers mostly below thirty years, and single because they have less responsibility.
- The female worker might be less educated, less efficient, less technically fit, but still the seniors like them, as it is very easy to boss upon them.
- Female staff can very easily be tortured or harassed by any of their seniors. By offering them sympathy, the seniors can easily satisfy their hidden bad habits and animal instincts.

Some Organisations, do not like qualified, educated or more skilled staff. They never want to face any opposition or negative natured worker in their Organisation.

In general, it is seen or observed that some persons sitting on high position in Organisational hierarchy, are very weak in their administration but they love loose gossiping.

They always want to know about the personal life of their colleagues and female staff working in the Organisation. They can give more time to listen to all the personal problems or grievances of the female staff but they do not want to listen to their official problems.

They expect from their subordinates or employees that they should not speak about any weak point of their department or the Organisation in any public place or in front of any person or in any meeting. They believe that if any one has any problem, they should meet them separately or privately. They should give information to their concerned seniors first then to anyone else. (In short, there is no transparency).

In short, they have vitiated the atmosphere of the office and some departments have become the den of corruption.

One more thing they never like is that they should never point out any mistake in front of others.

❖❖❖

CHAPTER 4

A BRIEF NOTE ON THE PRACTICAL MANAGEMENT

THE PRACTICAL MANAGEMENT

In an Organisation, there are different types of decision makers at different level of management, who give instructions to their subordinates to complete a particular assigned job or responsibilities. The concerned Management does not even want to know the situation of the workforce, and the facilities provided to the concerned worker, but they want only to give the instructions.

The instruction makers only like to give instructions to their juniors or subordinates but they never like to help them in the completion of the assigned job or responsibilities. The Manager will get very angry, if any one raises any question about the assigned job or the procedure towards its completion.

There are several systems at various levels, which are formed to make working environments at workplaces smooth, but in practice, the entire system does not work. All the systems work only on paper and verbally, in front of the higher management or seniors but as soon as the concerned seniors leave the office or workplace, the system goes in vain and no one follows them. At this situation, the concerned workers never stop their work because they have to work for their survival and they manage or tackle all the hurdles at their own cost and presence of mind or common sense. They try to complete the assigned job, inspite of having several hidden technical, administrative, financial, emotional, and physical problems.

Without getting any promotion, increment or any recognition, the juniors, subordinates and some seniors are also completing their assigned responsibilities, thinking that they are doing their own work and not for the company. Inspite of working hard with dedication, they sometimes, feel that they are totally ignored by the Management or by the immediate seniors. God knows the reasons behind it.

In Schools & Colleges, we take proper education and we think and hope that our future will be good and sound. We can earn money and fulfil the basic requirement of our family. We will get a good job as per our education and knowledge and our boss will highly appreciate our education and work. Some take up courses like Management, Medical, Engineering or other various technical courses depending on the aptitude, to make the future secure. We think that we have sufficient knowledge about the situation and can tackle any type of hurdles in future.

However, when we practically start working, the whole scenario what we had expected and had studied theoretically changes drastically at the workplace. What we had studied or the subjects we had taken in the Schools & Colleges, their theory is totally changed at our workplace during the completion of assigned responsibility. At the same time, the assignment, which we have been given by our seniors to complete, also varies from person to person. The same assignment, when it is with seniors, becomes different and when it comes to juniors or subordinates, its nature changes. The assignment, which the juniors have been assigned to do, never get any support or the basic requirement for that particular job. In such situations, the juniors or subordinates manage the work with co-ordination with other colleagues at their own contacts and personal relationships. The meaning of assignment changes, when it comes to the juniors/ subordinates from any senior person. Like a savage lion or tiger, the seniors are waiting to maul their juniors (like innocent preys) under their feet.

I would like to give an example of a *musician who thinks* that he has sufficient knowledge of his music. He can easily convince anyone by his music, and he can get a job easily in the market. However, in practice, it is not so easy to convince anyone with his views, work, and get work in the market. The present education system is very different from its real implementation at the workplace. We can only implement 10% of the knowledge, at the workplace, which we had studied in the past and rest 90% of our knowledge, we have to manage as per the situation based on our common sense and intuition. Therefore, what we had studied theoretically cannot be practically implemented at the workplace.

A person after his continuous and sincere efforts lands a Class -I, job. He studies Hindi, Sanskrit, Urdu, and different, subjects to compete the Class-I, examination but when the same person gets the job and becomes an I.A.S / I.P.S. / I.F.S officer, their work profile is very different from their studied subjects. Here they have to manage the situation according to their common sense and not based on their subjects, which they had studied in the past or for the examination. Therefore, the Management, we study, changes in its practical implementation.

A motor trainer trains his student to drive the vehicle, to control the steering, clutch & brake. They learn the basic rules of driving the motor vehicle but when the person drives his vehicle at his own risk, he controls the vehicle completely. As per the rules, we cannot overtake the car from the left side of another vehicle. We have to make the other vehicle alert by honking and signal light, if we are taking a turn or want to overtake. As per the rule, we have to move on the road only on the left side. We should never cross or ignore the red signal. We have to wear the seat belt during driving. There are several rules and regulations, which we have to maintain during driving.

On the other hand, when we practically come on the road and drive the vehicle, we follow only 10% of the rules & regulations, and rest we manage according to the situation followed by our common sense. During driving, if the vehicle gets out of order in running on the road in a lonely place, then all the theoretical concepts do not work and common sense helps in solving the problem at such a situation.

The Practical Management can be defined as under:

In the absence of maximum resources, facilities, specific instructions of seniors or Management, if workers complete their assigned task/work/job with the help of their common sense/knowledge, perform to their best of ability as desired by the seniors, is known as the Practical Management.

It means such Management is not predetermined or it cannot be a predetermined course of action because here actions are managed based on situational demand. For example, mishaps are not premeditated. At the workplace, due to any circumstance or reason, if fire breaks out, maximum so-called heavy weight seniors would, first try to leave the office and would not wait to give any right instruction to the concerned subordinates or juniors but always would try to know the result. At this situation, when a person does his duty selflessly with the available support in Company's interest or a common goal/interest, without harming any one is known as *practical management.*

In an Organisation, most of the instructions coming from the top Management are 90% Clear and the same instructions when are given to subordinates or the head of the department through the middle management are 40 % clear. At this situation, the subordinates or juniors try to perform their responsibilities. They take help of their common sense, past experiences and from other colleagues. With time, they develop their common sense and knowledge practically.

If a sales representative sells a product and collects money from the market based on any scheme/project. Here it is clear that, it is not necessary that the people give him, money or purchase a product from him, due to the brand name of that product but due to the good conduct of that particular sales representative. Here the salesperson has applied the theory of practical management and inspite of having several administrative problems, he manages the situation and achieves his target.

The Practical Management is associated with such type of management which a Manager / Person / seniors/ in charge, perform their daily routine work at their workplace, planning, organising, directing & co-ordinating, supported by available resources to complete the assigned responsibility in the organisational interest.

To tackle & manage all the hidden problems smoothly, silently, without making any noise/ opposition/demand and fulfil the requirement of the seniors or the Management as per their desire, can be called *Practical Management.*

Under *Practical Management* procedure, no work or assignment is impossible to solve but any type of impossible assignment can be solved through Practical Management, because here the workforce give the result and do not transfer the responsibility to another person. Here they do not wait for the facilities or support but they only wait for the right instruction of the Management. Through Practical Management, the work done gives more satisfaction to the higher authority and the individual, than the work done by the individual in a general case.

The worker and the subordinates will get more promotion and increments by the seniors or in charge, if they complete their assigned work, responsibility, or assignment through *Practical Management.*

❖❖❖

CHAPTER 5

MANAGER AND THEIR TYPES

INTRODUCTION

Manager literally means a person controlling, administering business or a person who manages money in a specified way, a person controlling the activities of persons, team etc.

A responsible manager should be like the guardian angel to his juniors and subordinates. He should always be ready to hear their grievances and help them during their time of need. He should also be ready to accept mistakes or faults on the behalf of his subordinates. In short, he should be like a father figure to his juniors/subordinates. He should guide and give right information & support. The managers who are able to conquer the faith of their subordinates are the true managers.

Based on Practical Management, the Manager of any Organisation can be classified into the following categories according to my observation /experience at the workplace.

Class One Manager (White Collared):

These Managers love their organisation as well as their subordinates. They have full sympathy and good feeling for their juniors. They never like any one passing comments on their subordinates, whether the comments are true or not. The Manager is always there to support his subordinates or juniors and guide them. No one can dare to say anything to his or her subordinates. These Managers want that whosoever have any problem with their staff, should first of all talk or discuss with them so that they can take some action, if necessary. In this condition, the subordinates or juniors have great faith on their seniors. They discharge their responsibilities as per the organisation needs or as per the instruction of their seniors and as a result, the Company gets progress. The seniors and the subordinates both get promotion and increment from the Management.

CONFUSED BOSS / MANAGERS

The role of Boss or Managers in any organisation is very important for the progress, of the respective companies. The Boss or Managers are the pillars of any organisation. If the organisation has sufficient fund, manpower, transportation, materials and all the required things for the smooth functioning but is not sure whether the company would get profit or would survive or succeed in the competitive market. Here the role of the manager is of paramount importance.

For success, along with the other required essential factors, the manager should be a dynamic leader, who is ready to take risks and challenges. Otherwise in spite of having all good qualities the leader / seniors / H.O.D. / Manager would not be able to guide his division and his subordinates and thereby would not succeed in his endeavours.

In several cases, it is found that the seniors, Boss, Managers are very confused. They are unable to guide their workers or juniors. There are several factors responsible for this. They are:

(1) Lack of Education
(2) Un-matched Education with their responsibilities
(3) Obligatory Service
(4) Depends upon others for their views / cant' take decisions.
(5) Having Inferiority Complex
(6) Lack of Confidence
(7) Family Problems

Lack of Education:

If the Boss, seniors are unable to guide their subordinates it means that the person is not very qualified as per the requirement of the assigned position. May be they got the job giving false information or fake certificates to the management. It is also possible that their education was totally different with their present job profile. If the person had Arts background, then they cannot guide the scientific missions of the organisation.

Sometimes due to some unavoidable circumstance, the management gives position to such workers whose interest or educational background is totally different with their assigned job. If, he takes the responsibility in which the seniors have no education or knowledge, then it would be very difficult for them to guide their subordinates or juniors. Such seniors cannot take any independent decision on any problems and due to this reason; they may always seem to be confused.

It means a sound education, skill, experience and to work as a team are a must for a manager heading any department. Then only they can guide their juniors or subordinates in company's interest. However, in the present market, people think it is not necessary to have a sound education. They believe that they can hypnotise their management with their smooth &

sweet talks. In the initial period, they can easily impress their management but after some time the same management may sack them when they come to know their reality. Such type of managers who are superficial and lack depth are of no use for any organisation.

UN-MATCHED EDUCATION WITH THEIR JOB RESPONSIBILITIES

The un-matched education with the assigned job responsibility is also one of the factors of a confused Manager, seniors, except for some exceptional cases. The respective Management assigns work to most of the workers working at their workplace exactly opposite from their interest. If a worker does not have any interest in his assigned responsibility then it is sure that such a worker would never give his best efforts to complete the work and as a result, the company would have to suffer. Similarly, when the workers responsible for a particular job, have no interest in that job, then the concerned persons would not try to learn more about the new job and will suffer consequently as their work would remain incomplete, unsatisfactory and would invite the senior's ire and he would suffer.

At this situation, if such seniors give any instruction to their subordinates, the instruction may be flawed and would not be followed, as it would be very difficult for their workers to understand what their seniors want from them. Such seniors after sometime become a liability for the organisation.

OBLIGATORY SERVICES

In most of the organisations, there are several posts which the management has to fill up by such workers or persons from different fields, who had helped them some times in the past when they were in dire straits, so they have to oblige their relatives or near & dear ones. The management does not see the educational qualifications or any other required factors for such persons. They have to engage them somehow. At such situation, the person, who has been given the job, has no idea about the work, which he is doing nor is he inclined to learn the work or work procedure. They have no fear of their job being snatched away as the management would not punish them for not fulfilling the requirements because they know that they have good relations with the top management who would not take strict action against them. Practically, when we observe such workers, we find that they do not know anything related to the work or have no idea of what they have to do or what they have to instruct to their workers. Inspite of having no knowledge of the work, they instruct their workers in such a way that they know everything and have full command on such subject. It takes some time for the workers to realise their half-baked knowledge or lack of understanding, which confuse them thus jeopardising the work and the progress of the company.

DEPENDS UPON OTHER'S VIEWS

It is also one of the main factors of confusion of the seniors. Sometimes, the seniors consult their workers, colleagues or seniors on a particular matter on which the seniors have to take a decision. If the person from whom the seniors are taking advice or consultation, are themselves confused on any particular subject, then how can one imagine that the concerned seniors would give the right instruction to their subordinates. Due to such reason the seniors, have a lack of confidence on their assigned work and when there is a lack of confidence then it is sure that the concerned person's instruction would be very confused and unclear.

INFERIORITY COMPLEX

Some of the Managers are very introvert and in spite of having other qualities, they do not feel comfortable to speak in front of others. They do not give instruction properly to their subordinates or juniors. They always think about themselves and gradually lose their confidence level and once the confidence level of any one decreases, the concerned persons become very confused. They do not remember what instruction they had given a few minutes ago and why. Sometimes, they give the same instruction to more than one person which creates confusion among the workers and the management.

PERSONAL FAMILY PROBLEMS

A person cannot work properly, if his stomach is empty or he is hungry. For a smooth working environment, it is necessary for all the workers to have a healthy diet and sound mind. A sound mind depends upon the emotional relationship between the workers and their families. When a worker is disturbed due to any unavoidable circumstance at his workplace or in the organisation, he cannot give his best efforts to the organisation or is unable to fulfil the desire of his managers.

His mind becomes over burdened with problems and he cannot take a proper decision. It means he is confused. One of the other reasons for a confused manager is his family problems. When a person is struggling with his family problems, he certainly cannot concentrate on his work. At this stage when he gives any instruction to his subordinates for any assignment in the company interest, the instruction is not substantial or is half-baked. The subordinates make fun of such seniors who are managers only for namesake.

Jealous Manager

It has been observed that a person recruited for any position in any organisation on obligatory basis is associated with the employers as a close or distant relative or a close family friend. In the beginning, the person works in that organisation very faithfully but gradually his mind, behaviour, attitude, thinking philosophy etc changes.

He may act bossy or think himself to be very superior or to be the owner of that organisation. He would start disobeying the rules and regulations of the organisation, and would start issuing false statements from time to time and would misguide the management in his favour.

Such type of managers gradually make the systems in their own favour and have no sympathy for the mother organisation and may split into a separate group within the organisation and misappropriate company's funds for their own benefits. Such people can never think about the betterment of the company. They have a hidden or stealthy competition with the higher management who had given them jobs or had obliged them. They will always try to misuse the company resources and try to pull it down. They always feel very uncomfortable with the progress of their own relative.

Inspite of having the proof of misappropriation, generally workers do not try to raise their voice or do not talk about it to others because they know that the concerned person or boss is the relative of the top management and they would not rely on what they say. Close relatives of the higher management, working in the same company, prove to be very dangerous for the organisational growth. In other words, they may become a liability for the company. In company interest it should be avoided recruiting close relatives in the same company but if due to any reason they have to be recruited then they should not be given any big responsibility otherwise the concerned person would misuse the funds as well as tarnish the image of the organisation.

Pomeranian Manager:

Such managers always try to copy the life style of their master and wish to get very close to him. They are superficial & may not have in depth knowledge about anything, which can help the management. They always try to please the management by any means. They try to show that they are always guarding the organisation and they are always present with the management. They show that they can do any kind of work, assigned to them under any circumstances. However, in practice, these types of managers are of no use for the management or the organisation. If God forbid hard days come in the organisation or if the company is going through a rough phase, these managers would leave the organisation without bothering for the company. They would safeguard themselves and not the organisation.

On comparing the behaviour of such managers, we will find that it is very much similar with the behaviour of a Pomeranian dog. A Pomeranian dog, tries to sit on his master's chair, walk together with his master and sleep together but during genuine requirement or when there is a genuine problem, he would not bark to alert people because he is timid by nature. However, he would bark when not required.

Alsatian Manager:

Alsatian Dogs are very faithful to their masters. He would first of all try to save his master than anyone else during any emergency. He does not bark uselessly like a Pomeranian, but no one can dare touch the master in the presence his Alsatian dog. He always sits, near the feet of the master, and tries to safeguard his master. He can face any problem coming to his master. He is a true servant of his master. In the long run, the Management likes such type of Managers who have inherent qualities like Alsatian Dog. viz are very faithful and trustworthy to their master.

Street Manager: (Having the characteristic of a street dog)

If, we talk about the Street Dog and its characteristics, we can say that such dogs have no moral. They have no fixed master and no one wants to take the responsibility of them. They devote their whole day for their survival and at night, the same dog gives protection to the society from anti social elements, without getting anything in return from the same society. No one gives them recognition or importance of their efforts.

If any of the dogs make more noise, whether they try to alert the people living nearby or give information about any mishap just happened or going on or otherwise. However, the persons living nearby throw stones on them, hurt or bash them up when they are giving them unconditional security. In general, hardworking managers are treated like street dogs by the middle management. (The manager having the qualities of Alsatian is the most favourable for the organisation who is always there to guide and protect the organisation and its master.)

Grey Hound Manager:

These managers are very raw and savage like the Hound. They would not think twice before seeing the opportunity to kill the boss or take over his position/ property/ organisation. If due to unavoidable circumstances they are given the power of attorney, they ditch their boss and takeover the company just like the ferocious Hound, who would strangle his master.

Managers who Shrug off their responsibilities (Palla Jhar):

These Managers do not want to take any responsibility and always divert their responsibilities to their subordinates with the instruction, **do the needful**. They do not give any instruction in writing to their subordinates so that they can do their work peacefully. If the Management is displeased with any of his subordinates, working, under such **Palla Jhar Manager**, the Manager immediately forwards the names of his juniors or subordinates to the management for taking necessary action against them. They never try to defend their juniors in front of the higher Management. They never have any feeling for their subordinates. If any subordinates make any mistake, they do not ask them to rectify it or whether they have proper facilities to complete the target or assigned responsibilities. They do not bother for the concerns of the subordinates but they support the management to issue a letter to his own subordinate to please the higher management. As a result, workers working under this type of Manager, have zero faith, regards, sympathy, and respect for such seniors. Due to their nature, workers want to leave the organisation frequently and the organisation does not make proper growth.

Swan / Swan natured Manager:

Swan is an aquatic bird which we all have seen. A Swan sitting on the bank of a river / pond or other waterlogged areas watches fish with concentration. This bird does not like to do any hard work for its livelihood except sitting at one place and watching the small fishes moving in the water. Fish is the main food of Swans. The bird survives on fish, which they swallow immediately after catching. If we correlate this bird with our managers working with us in the organisation, we would find that there are several characteristics which are similar to them.

Some managers do not like to do any work or any hard work. They do not want to justify their salary with their contribution to the organisation. They survive in this competitive market by catching the faults of other workers and passing on the information to their superior. They only like to point out the drawbacks or the weak points of others. These managers are very harmful for the organisation. They may be successful for a short period but truth prevails ultimately.

Indifferent Manager (Unconcerned Manager):

In every organisation, some workers are very indifferent. These people do not want to harass or give trouble to anyone under any circumstance. They are always neutral and live in their own sweet world. They do not bother about what is going on in the organisation or whether they had completed their assigned responsibility or whether someone is watching their work. They come to the office just to pass their time. They are very introvert as per my observation. They never indulge in anti organisational activities. They come to the office on fixed time and leave the office on fixed time or as per their schedule. In short they are good for nothing.

Termite Manager:

Some people are very laborious and hard working. They never try to show that they are tired and are unable to do anything. They do not like to work in the daytime in the presence of others but they prefer to work alone at night. (By nature, such people seem very good, so that no one can watch their activities. As they are very slow and steady workers). So most of the people like them but they are very selfish. They work only for themselves. They are very wily, clever and foresighted. They are basically white collared robbers who rob the organisation slowly. They conquer the faith of most of the superiors of the organisation with their sweet talk. They do not like to follow the rules and regulations of the organisation and try to convince others that the rules and regulations of the organisation are outdated. They are like termites who literally suck the organisation and make it hollow or rob its finances slowly and steadily.

❖❖❖

CHAPTER 6

A BRIEF NOTE ON THE BEHAVIOUR OF THE MANAGEMENT TOWARDS THEIR WORKERS

The behaviour of human beings varies from person to person. The organisation appoints several managers at different levels to look after the manpower to get the desired work from them. In this chapter, I have tried to explain the behaviour of the seniors at the workplace. How they treat their subordinates and up to what extent do they give importance to their sincere efforts and contributions, how they rule over the workforce in the company's interest and how they bend the rules for their own ego satisfaction and benefit.

I have tried to explain the different kinds of behaviour of the seniors with examples from our daily life so that it would be easy for common people to understand their mysterious/enigmatic managers.

IGNORE TO RECOGNISE THE WORK DONE BY THE SUBORDINATES

In any Organisation, some people work with their zeal /heart not for the monitory benefits but for their self-satisfaction and acceptance from their seniors for recognition for their work / creativity. They want only a small appreciation for their contribution to the Organisation.

For example: We have seen in our own family that a small child cries, when the child feels hungry. Here hunger may be for food, water, love, attention, fear of unknown people, uneasiness or something else happening against his/her wishes.

Here the child cries only to attract the mind / grab attention of others towards himself / herself. The little child wants 100% attention from others. The child also wants appreciation for his activities that he is performing at home or other place etc. If he does not get a proper response for his activities, it is very much possible that the child would get angry and would make noise just to attract other's attention on himself / herself.

Whenever, the guardian / head of the family ignores any work done by the small kid, the kid automatically reacts on the whole family, because he wants a little recognition, a little appreciation from his guardian / parents for his work, and creativity.

More or less, similar case is also seen in the Organisation and at the work place where we are giving our valuable lifetime. Some of the workers in any Organisation are found to be very creative and labourious but unfortunately they are not recognised or they are never allowed to come in the front of the Management. They never get any benefit like promotion or increments or other benefits by the Management only because the concerned seniors do not want to promote their creativity in front of the Higher Management. They try to overlook or turn a blind eye because of the following reasons.

(1) Lack of Security or Insecurity of seniors.
(2) Groupism of seniors.
(3) Fear of upgradation of juniors.
(4) Popularity of juniors.
(5) Commanding Authority.
(6) Fear of leakage of weak points of the Management as well as of the concerned seniors.
(7) Misguide the Management.

1. Lack of Security / Insecurity of Seniors:

In general, people work in any Organisation only to save their chair or service and not for the benefit of their Organisation. They do not like to disclose the weak points of the Organisation as well as they also do not want to forward or give suggestions to the Management, which may be in Company's interest. They never disclose such things because if they take the initiative, the Management will immediately give / assign the new work to them. This is the reason; they never try to disclose anything related to the intelligence or creativity of their subordinates.

On the other hand, if the Company's obedient workers give or forward any suggestions to the concerned seniors or do any work beyond their assignment, which may give the individual some popularity, the concerned seniors will ignore the good work of the workers because the concerned seniors know, that if they disclose the plus point of the workers or subordinates in front of the higher management or superiors, the higher authority would definitely appreciate such work (which they do not want to happen). They all are very insecure about their service. Hence, they fail to appreciate the productive work of their subordinates and the Organisation loses substantially.

It is their lack of confidence or the lack of losing their position, which forces them to overlook the good work done by their juniors. In a way, they show a lack of honesty and transparency in their work. This is the reason, they do not want to give any promotion or upgrade their subordinates and they always want to ignore their good work by all means.

2. Groupism / Cronyism Of Seniors:

It is also seen that at various stages, people / workers are making groups in any Organisation for various reasons. The reasons may be in the Company's interest or against it.

The groupism of seniors in the Company's interest is very rare but most of the employees make groups to save themselves from the management or to save themselves from the assigned responsibilities or any such work to be done or any mistake done by them. They make groups, so that the juniors, subordinates, or colleagues cannot make any complaint against them to the higher management.

Generally, after attaining a certain level of cadre/ designation, the seniors try to take their lunch, tea, snacks with their colleagues in a separate place or canteen where they gradually mix with each other in such a way that if one of them commits any mistake in their routine work/ assigned work schedule, the group members / seniors will try to cover up that mistake by all means. If other people who are not a part that group unfortunately do the same mistake, then it is sure that they will never leave them. They would try to get them punished as soon as possible.

The same seniors of that group will definitely issue a show cause notice, take action, or punish the concerned fellow. Due to such friendship or groupism, misappropriation of company's funds occurs because the culprits know that no one will raise his voice against them.

If anyone by mistake raises his voice and makes a complaint against them, nothing will happen to them as the person who had made the mistake and those who had raised their voice, are friends or part of the same group or are cronies. At this situation, I would like to say that groupism or friendship within the Company, among the colleagues is very dangerous for the company as well as for the individuals.

Thus, the members of such a group do not like to listen to any type of suggestions/progress/ good work done by any subordinates or colleagues. In any case, if they did, the concerned seniors or middle management tries to ignore their valuable work for the benefit of the Company.

3. Fear of Upgradation of Juniors:

One of the important reasons is the fear of upgradation of their subordinates / juniors. It is a very peculiar thing or it may be called natural behaviour of human beings that very few people in our society have the heart of appreciating other's good work. They are very jealous by nature and do not like to see others progress.

They do not like to see the upgradation or progress of the organisation. The whole group works to create obstacles in front of such subordinates by hook or by crook.

If their subordinates give a good output to the Organisation, the concerned seniors will ignore them or will not forward their message to the higher authority. They think that if they will boost up the morale of their subordinates, they may fall in trouble or the juniors may get promotion or other good assignment for their outstanding Work / performance. This is the reason; the concerned seniors always try to ignore the credit of their juniors in a normal circumstance.

Sometimes, if any subordinate performs outstanding work, the seniors take the credit themselves and simultaneously they pass on the message to the higher management in such a way that he(senior) has done the work and he is the only capable person in this Organisation, who can do such outstanding work in the company's interest.

4. Popularity of Juniors:

It is the truth that some people are jealous by nature. They do not like to see others progress. Even in our own family, one brother does not want to see the progress of his own kin. Our close relatives are also one of the most prominent oppositions or critics in our life. One enemy can tolerate another enemy but our close relatives cannot tolerate our progress in any circumstance.

In various organisations, the higher / top management, in good faith, generally appoints their own relatives for the various key ranks, so that they can take care of the organisation better than others but when we see their contribution, we find that they have not contributed positively, on the contrary they are not inclined to do positive work.

People having obligatory posts or positions make themselves busy in gossips/ plans/ programmes etc and try to pull the legs of their relatives sitting on the top position. It is because the persons appointed by the higher authority are jealous of their own relatives, who had given them good position & prestige in their Organisation.

In these circumstances, in extraordinary cases, if one does something good in company's interest, the management, inspite of having full knowledge of their contribution, does not like to give them weightage and generally try to ignore their contributions, because of their behaviour.

5. Commanding Authority:

Sometimes, the concerned seniors/Head of the Department ignore the work done by their subordinates in Company interest because they know clearly that if they promote their subordinates, the concerned seniors would get into trouble, as the subordinate may be more qualified and be a forward planner. In their own interest, the concerned H.O.D. never recommends or supports their work. They know that if they will support them, one day the subordinates will become their boss or H.O.D.

6. Fear of Leakage of Weak Points of the Company as well as of the Respective Seniors:

It is the bitter truth that no one is perfect in any Organisation or at the workplace. More or less very few people in the organisation are found to be very sincere, serious and accountable to their responsibility.

Most of them are working only to protect or save their job and not for the benefit of the Organisation. If, some workers are found working in favour of the Company, then such workers are targeted by most of the seniors in a negative way because they do not want that anyone should work directly for the company's benefit or progress.

The reason behind it is, if any one works in Company's interest through his own motivation, the respective seniors begin to think that their secret will be out and they may land into trouble.

As most of the seniors or middle management people are not very well versed with the company norms and they do not want to give any chance to anyone, to know about their working style as well as some times they also do not want to disclose the intention of the company. This is why; the seniors and middle management always tries to create obstacles in front of the genuine workers.

7. Misguide or Misleading the Management:

Most of the workers in any organisation are found to be very irresponsible and take all the work/task in an easy way. They try to do their assigned work in their own way or working style, whether the result may be in favour of the organisation or against the organisation. The seniors are always found busy in their work presentation in front of the higher management in their own way.

In rare cases, the presentation gives the actual result as per their calculation because maximum facts used in any presentation are found incorrect or manipulated which can never give the right result. In such situation, if a person works in company's interest, the concerned Head of the Department will never like or appreciate such workers and their work done by their juniors, but if their seniors by mistake appreciate their work then the concerned seniors may not be in a position to misguide the Management through their presentation.

There are several examples when the higher authority ignores the ideas / suggestions/work done/creativity of the subordinates, so that they could save themselves or their chair could be saved. They do not bother about the impact of their wrong message, on the public.

Every day we read in the Newspapers about several incidents/accidents, which take the life of, numerous innocent people. Sometimes, due to flood millions of people have to face an irreparable damage. Every now and then, some natural calamity takes place, which jeopardises the life of many people.

They know very well that such incidents may occur anytime but they do not give them importance because the information providers are junior people. They do not give importance to their suggestions.

They know that if they give importance to their suggestions their position may get awkward. They give importance only to any work /instruction, which comes from the higher authority. Thus, it can be said that such people misguide the higher management/authority by ignoring the suggestions coming from the junior/subordinates.

WORK PRESENTATION / POSSIBILITIES

Work presentation plays an important role in our life at various stages. Every one or every worker is devoting at least 8 hours of duty at his/her office / the workplace as per the job assignment and work schedule but at the time of work assessment to be done by their respective seniors, one gets a very good remark while other does not get so.

If we analyse this topic, we will find that the presentation of any worker on any assigned job, which does not directly involve its working procedure of that work but the presentation of that concerned work or assigned job, accelerates his activities of assigned responsibility. The work presentation also depends upon the kind of the instructed work/order given by the seniors/mgt. Sometimes, the seniors give such instructions to their junior, which is very difficult or which cannot be done by a single worker within a limited period then it is the presentation which can help the concerned worker to present it in a good shape in front of the Management before giving it its final shape.

When a senior wants to give punishment or wants to harass a particular person, he gives orders in such a way that the concerned worker will have to face problems to complete the specific work in a specific period. The senior knows very well that the assigned work is very difficult to perform and the worker assigned for this work will never be able to complete the assignment without having proper guidelines and proper work force but in spite of having knowledge, they give orders to do such work. This is just to harass him.

At this situation, the concerned worker will certainly fail to present or perform the assigned work, due to the lack of proper working environment and lack of co-operation from his senior. Here the work suffers immensely.

If the worker will not perform his assigned work, the senior will give a poor remark and he will forward a bad/negative report against that particular worker.

At the same time, if the worker is clever /intelligent, innovative and has good personal relation or rapport with all other concerned people in the department, then it is possible that the work which is really very difficult for a general worker, can be done with the co-operation and co-ordination of other colleagues within or outside the department.

A good presentation of work may secure a good remark by the immediate seniors; while confused presentation of the worker may secure a bad remark by the concerned seniors and the whole productivity of the workers depend only on such presentation performed by the subordinates.

The following factors, which are directly responsible for the work presentation of the workers.

(1) Instruction
(2) Possibility
(3) Skill
(4) Knowledge
(5) Facilities of technology
(6) Support

1. Instructions:

Any work presentation is never successful, unless the instruction for a particular job to be done is crystal clear. It means for a good work presentation, first, it is very necessary for all, the instructions, which one generally receives from the higher authority /immediate seniors/office in charge / H.O.D, should be very clear. It should be so clear that even a non-professional can understand it easily.

Sometimes, it has been observed that inspite of having all the facilities; workers find themselves unable to perform a good presentation as per the desire of the concerned seniors, due to the following reasons:

(a) Written Instruction
(b) Verbal Instruction

(c) Symbolic Instruction

(d) Confused / Half / Partial Instruction

(a) Written Instruction: In an Organisation, a written instruction gives a better result, authentic as well as a proof for the subordinates. No one can deny or refuse that they had not given a particular instruction to their subordinates. There are several qualities of written instruction, which help a person perform well and give a good presentation of their assigned work / job.

In our practical life / work place, 70 to 80% of the instructions of any organisation are based upon verbal or other methods but not in a written form. As everyone knows that a written instruction of any authority is an authentic proof for a person and no one can deny that they had not given the instruction to their subordinates for a particular work on a particular assignment. If the organisation has to face any problems due to the written instruction given by the authority, the concerned authority may get immediate punishment through the court of law.

On the other hand, due to written instruction, one can also get a reward from their Management. Inspite of having several qualities of written instructions, in practice or in general life, seniors do not like to give their subordinates any instruction in writing. If they have to give, in writing under any circumstance then they generally use such a language which confuses them or their instruction is vague which makes the subordinates directly responsible or guilty for the outcome and the seniors are not held responsible.

They generally remark / write, *"DO THE NEEDFUL"* which itself is very vague. Here, the workers will be responsible for any wrong thing, happening but if good things happen due to that instruction, then the seniors would directly take the credit for the work done by the subordinates / juniors.

If the instruction will be in writing and clear, then the presentation of any work assigned to the subordinates definitely will be good and fruitful in company's interest.

(b) Verbal Instruction: Having a good knowledge of the merits and demerits of the written instruction, people feel very comfortable and safe to give instruction to their subordinates verbally because if the instruction is verbal, then there is no authenticity that such instruction had been given by a particular senior. Here the instruction givers feel that they are on the safe side but on the other hand, the concerned workers will face a very embarrassing situation. The subordinates cannot name their seniors boldly, who had given the instructions; due to which huge damage occurs which the Organisation has to face.

Sometimes, when a person gives verbal instruction it may be possible that due to lack of clarity of words / sentence, will make, other persons / people forget or misunderstand the actual instruction. It is true that at least 30% of the conversation or verbal instruction automatically vanishes in thin air due to the communication gap. So when the instruction receivers will not be able to receive the actual instruction then how can they perform the desired work and when they put forward their presentation on the basis of their verbal instruction, it may be possible that the outcome may be wrong or in a different direction or misdirected completely.

Many times, the seniors pass on their instructions and responsibilities, deliberately to their subordinates / juniors, in such a way, that they cannot perform their duties well. They do not bother to ask them, how will they perform or how will they do it. Even they do not bother to ask them, if they require any assistance from them or, is there any confusion in understanding the instruction. If it is so, they may clarify but in reality, the concerned seniors will never ask such questions to their subordinates, but they will give instructions, in such a way that they themselves cannot understand what they had instructed verbally.

At this situation, the presentation and performance will definitely be affected due to such faulty instruction. When a person could not do well, due to the senior's fault, the same seniors will tell them that they are useless or burden to the organisation and that they took a long time to complete their assigned job due to which the company had to incur heavy loss in respect to brand and image.

The concerned workers do not get a proper remark on their work and they are unable to get promotion and increment because in the company's eyes or records such workers do not work. They are useless and a load or a burden to the company.

(c) Symbolic Instructions: In any organisation or in our general life, we find that most of the people use symbolic instructions to instruct the people standing on the other side / juniors to do a particular job / task.

When both the parties are used to understanding symbolic instructions and have faith in each other, then to some extent it is okay but as soon as one party is changed due to any reason then it will be very difficult for the new party to understand the symbolic language / instructions.

At this situation, it will be very difficult for a worker to give a good result and their work presentation will automatically deteriorate or suffer. The senior will ask what he had explained / instructed on the required matters. If one could not understand the fact, then it was his fault. As we, all know that the boss is always right, they are never wrong. We, workers shall have to follow their instructions. Both sides of the coin are reserved for the boss. We have no right practically to argue with him on any topic/ issues. If the workers argue then they might have to face various hidden problems. They might be handed over the suspension letter or may face termination in cases where the boss is hell bent upon demoralising his subordinates.

(d) Confused / Incomplete Instructions: Sometimes the seniors / H.O.D. deliberately gives a confused / half-baked instruction to their subordinates but expect from their juniors that they should do their job according to their instruction and understand it completely.

In many, cases the seniors give such a vague instruction that it would be very difficult for anyone to understand. The instruction itself sometimes is so confused or unclear that when the seniors want to instruct their juniors / subordinates, they are not clear themselves. If one instruction is associated with the other one, then only one assigned work might be completed. Otherwise, it will be very difficult to do the job.

At this situation, sometimes the seniors give instructions to their staff to stay in the office. And if they could not come back to the office on time due to any reason, to complete the assignment, it is the duty of the concerned seniors to inform their subordinates about their plans clearly, so that they could leave the office only after completing their work but they would not do so due to ego problem or to settle some score.

They think that it is not their duty to inform a junior about their programmes. At this, stage how can one expect a good performance from their subordinates? If the subordinates are not able to complete their duty well, the reason behind it, is, that the instruction coming from their seniors is incomplete and unclear.

2. Skills:

Worker's work presentation also depends upon the skill of the concerned workers. The skill of such workers depends upon their interest to deliver the assigned job. If a person has all the qualities but has no interest to deliver the assigned work, then no one can get the job done from such workers. Whether they are active or lazy, how their grasping power is, whether, they implement their own common sense or not, whether they know the benefits of time management or not? How fast they are doing their job, what type of circumstances they are facing, whether they will have to work long hours? From, how far are, they coming to the work place etc are the main factors which affect the worker's performance.

All these factors are responsible to deliver a good work-presentation for skilled workers. If a person has enough skill but does not have all other required qualities, then it will very difficult for him to give a desired out-put as per the management's wishes / requirement.

WELL VERSED WITH MODERN TECHNIQUES

If, a person / worker has all the qualities like skill, education, interest but is not well versed with computer and the Internet, then it is sure that he will have to face many problems in performing good result without their support or it is also possible that he will not be in a position to give the desired output.

If the management asks its workers to prepare a list of candidates, with particular qualities, where the number of candidates is around 10000. We are very sure that a single worker cannot do the desired work and then it will take at least 2-to 3 months to complete the work manually.

Inspite of having good qualities in the candidates, if the work environment is not favourable then in such situation the worker will be a wastage in the eyes of the management because they could not provide the required data / result / out-put to the management in a specific time frame.

It means, presentation of any work also depends upon the facilities, to be provided to the individuals to complete a particular job in a specific period. If a person gets all the necessary required facilities to present or to prepare a specific assignment, then it is possible that a mediocre worker can also present his work quite fairly or up to the mark to the management. Thus, the mediocre worker can also get good response by the concerned seniors or management.

Sometimes, some managers who are known to be sadists knowingly do not give or do not provide the technical help to their staff. This is why, inspite of having every quality, the workers could not perform to the best of their abilities in the company's interest. The reason behind, it is only that their seniors did not want to see the growth of their own subordinates. They always tried to humiliate them and gave work without any kind of technical support, so that they could be condemned / humiliated in front of other colleagues. By doing this, they are doing a great disservice to their subordinates.

The concerned seniors behave in such a peculiar manner even with their own juniors or subordinates so that at the time of appraisal they can put forward the message to the higher management, that these particular workers do not know anything and they should not be given any promotion or increment. They also want to show that they are not fit for the organisation, so, why should appropriate action not be taken against such workers.

TO IGNORE THE PROBLEMS

There are different types of people, found at any workplace. Every one has his/her own identity. They take their assigned work given by their seniors, in a different manner to get it completed. Some of them may do these things in the following manner:

(1) With great enthusiasm

(2) In a normal way

(3) Would take it lightly

(4) While some of the people will try to ignore the assigned work or problem raised by their workers / subordinates.

The whole phenomenon raises the following questions:

(1) Who will be affected?

(2) Who will bear the losses?

(3) Who has raised the problems?

1. Who will be affected ?

It has been observed that the brain of human beings gives instructions to the respective parts of the human body, to protect itself from any mishap or act accordingly as per the instruction given.

If the part "B" of our body is going to get affected due to any reason, while other part "A" is free from this. Here "A" is not given any instruction from the top to protect itself. It means, if one part is damaged/affected the other part is free from mishap. The other parts seem unaware of the mishap.

In another incident, if our own blood relation or kins, like our Parents, brothers/sisters are sick, we all pray to God, to protect them. We take them immediately to the doctor and try our best, to get them well soon. We will feel very anxious about their medicines, meal, health etc; because we know that their sickness, unhealthiness will directly affect our financial, psychological, mental, social state.

Similarly, at any work place, it has been seen that there are many seniors, who do not give proper response or adequate attention to any problem raised by the juniors. If they will come and tell them that their salary is very low in comparison to the current market, or he has some financial problems, so he needs some money as a loan or he has some urgent work for his family and he wants to go home or he has some official problems. The seniors completely ignore them and their problems.

Most of the seniors or in-charge will not listen to their urgent plea. They will not bother what they are asking, whether something should be done on humanitarian grounds or not? They totally try to ignore their plea whether it is related to any genuine problem or not.

The seniors know very well that such problems raised by their juniors, will not affect their status, service, position, monthly emoluments, or their own family, then why should they bother about them. That is why; they may listen but would do nothing in favour of their workers. However, when any problem of his junior will affect his career, then immediately the same concerned senior will try to solve the problem. At this situation, he will not ignore any problem arising at the workplace due to any reason.

In several cases, the seniors are getting more money or remuneration than they actually deserve for their work and they have no financial problems or crisis. It is sure that when a person has no financial problem and is satisfied with his finances then the same person starts ignoring his work as well as his assigned duties at his workplace. Such people always want to give advice to their colleagues without being asked. However, if they are facing financial problems then the same seniors / persons will not do so.

2. Who will Bear the Losses? or who is Accountable ?

It is said that ignorance is bliss. However, being ignorant in company affairs business causes loss. It means, the person gives attention to any problem, only when he knows that the losses / profit of the company would directly involve him or affect him.

For example, when a person drives a car and if he knows that if any accident / break down will happen / occur and, he will not have to bear the expenses, then suddenly, his attitude / behaviour towards driving the car will change and he will start driving roughly. On the other side, if the same person will have to bear the expenses then the person will drive the car very smoothly. He will try to drive very carefully. The person drives the car very carefully as he knows that he will have to bear the expenses if any kind of mishap occurs.

We also find similar circumstances, in our organisation. Some people of the company generally behave like the driver. If he knows that if he did any mistake in the company, he would have to bear the loss / profit, then he would do each job very carefully, otherwise he would try to ignore or overlook it.

If a person, comes to know that if he will ignore the duty /responsibilities assigned to him, his seniors or the concerned Management may punish him severely. He would automatically be very serious towards his job and he shall never try to ignore his duties, responsibilities or any complaint raised in Company's interest by even his colleagues or juniors. Therefore, a person will be responsible if the company holds him accountable.

3. Who has Raised the Problems/Question?

In our organisation or workplace, we generally find that, if a junior raises or points out a question in the interest of the Company , nobody would like to listen to his voice and most of them would ignore the raised voice or question and deviate, so that they could skip the issue. If they will entertain any question then they will have to answer to the management, which they never want to do. Even they know that the raised problem / question is correct but inspite of having knowledge related to that raised question/problems, they want to suppress the matter.

The senior knows that if he will take up the raised matter, then, it may be possible that he may himself be caught and sent into custody, so first of all he would try to question / condemn the question-raiser, so that such juniors do not cause any further problems.

In the mean time, if the question is raised by any senior to his junior then the situation will be just the reverse. Here his junior will not try to ignore the matter or try to suppress his voice. All the concerned people/workers whether senior or junior managers suddenly would, stand in support of the concerned person, and start appreciating his question and would say that it is very good for the organisation.

They will make a committee to solve the problems immediately without making any delay. If the senior asks his junior manager that this particular system should be changed because, it creates obstacles in the progress of the organisation. Suddenly, all will observe that it is true but when the junior raises a question, the concerned senior tries to ignore as well as suppress the question forever.

Such negative activities are very harmful for any organizational growth. The top management does not like such behaviour of the worker / staff. Whenever these type of activities come in front of them, the top management immediately takes action against all the concerned people.

The level of enthusiam seems very high when a senior person points out a problem in the organisational interest. Everyone will very attentively listen to the problems and try to solve it at the earliest, and give their best of efforts. In this situation, the worker will not ask for any help from others and will very enthusiastically look into the matter but when junior staff in the company's interest raises the same question, no one will support or come forward to support him. In spite of supporting the seniors, all of them will try to condemn him and would not support him.

This discrimination is only because of the authority. Everyone knows that a junior staff cannot harm his senior while a senior has an authority / power to take any action against the junior. They can impose any punishment on them. On failure to disobey their order / instruction, they can immediately suspend them or their salary could be stopped etc.

Because of fear of punishment, the junior worker obeys the orders of their seniors. One thing more, every junior worker wants to come in the good books of the senior, by hook or by crook, just to get a good remark or to get credit for the work done.

USELESS-GOSSIP

It is in nature, that every worker wants to express his views, opinion or feelings in front of others. No power in the world can stop them to express their feelings. The way of expression may be different. If anyone tries to stop them from expressing their views, their power to express themselves will be more. It is not necessary that the expression will be positive but it can be negative too. Whenever, a worker starts talking freely with his colleagues, he does not have sense, as to what he is talking about and what affect it will have on other people. He talks only to express his inner feelings, as he is frustrated.

Talking against the organisation or seniors or system gives them self-satisfaction because they are very frustrated. They think that during their service period, they did not achieve what they wanted to, or what they deserved. It is also true that everybody is useless in each other's eyes.

Most of the workers working at their workplace feel that the worker sitting in front of him or working in other department is useless. They have no work to do. They do not know anything and that they are the only people in this Organisation who really work. They think, if they will leave the organisation, the whole system of this Company will collapse.

There are some reasons of useless gossip in the workplace:

(1) Less work load
(2) Poor education/skill
(3) Less involvement/Immature behaviour
(4) Internal system failure for promotion/increment
(5) Work Evaluation
(6) Self Nature
(7) To impress others

1. Less Work Load:

Sometimes, it has been observed that if a worker completes his job regularly in a scientific and logical manner devotes his energy, time and efforts in a sincere way in the office, then he can save a lot of time in a week, which he can use for his development or improvement etc. He can review his work, which he has already completed on schedule. He can check the precious data, whether there is any wrong/mistake to be rectified. If he has some free time, he could discuss with his juniors about the difficulties being faced in the day-to-day routine work.

They could make a provision/planning on how they could do their work more effectively in the organisational interest. They should try to learn from the good qualities of others, but unfortunately, in most of the organisations, people do not like to do any beneficial work or to bind themselves with any rules and regulations, but they want to live without responsibilities.

They do not have interest in constructive discussion. They only want to engage themselves and their colleagues in useless gossip. They talk only to satisfy themselves or to kill time.

Through such activities, people are only wasting their energy and time. No senior or manager likes such kind of a person. Generally, people think that nobody is looking or watching them or their group, but it is wrong. They are constantly being watched and observed. Information is passed on to the concerned seniors about the ongoing activities at the workplace.

The Management gradually withdraws the power, assigned responsibilities, of the guilty workers, and gives it to others. People do this because they do not have sufficient workload and proper assignment, on which they have to work and produce results in front of the management.

At the workplace, most of the people come from some distant town or village and talk in a common language, which boosts them up to gossip and get friendly. They get friendly among their colleagues and if anything wrong happens in the company and if one of them is involved in that case, no one complains to the management about the truth.

Inspite of this if a new person raises any question to the management about any happening, no one will come to support that person. If by chance, any one comes and supports him, then the concerned superior or in charge of that new person, will ignore such workers in such a way that they do not know anything about the new happening in the Organisation.

2. Poor Education/Skill:

Education, knowledge and skill, gives an inner power to a person to think over a particular subject. It gives tremendous confidence, which accelerates their thinking power, working speed, qualitative performance etc. Due to good education, a person can easily differentiate between good and bad, they can easily guess / assume that on this particular action, what kind of reaction can take place. Such people can easily utilise their free time in constructive work in company's interest or their own benefit.

At the same time, if a worker is not skilled enough or educated then there is a dearth of thinking power, willpower or it may be very limited. They cannot exploit their mind in various directions. Their mind may not be fresh, careful or active. Generally, at the workplace some people are busy gossiping with their colleagues. The content of their gossip may be very cheap because of their poor education. They cannot discuss on National/ International topics or on company's future planning.

They cannot sit among the educated / skilled people. They hesitate to talk to them. They want only to talk with such people who are similar to them. In this way, they criticise people who are very advanced and have the latest knowledge and skill.

In the organisation, there are special types of workers, whose official (hidden) responsibility is to inform the senior about such things. The management never likes such people who waste their time in gossiping, thus lessening the Organisational output.

Thus, when the level of our knowledge increases, the level of our performance automatically increases. However, at the same time, if we talk or make discussions with similar people and colleague, whose level of knowledge is more or less similar, at such situation our knowledge will not increase but shall create confusion. We must try to maintain proper decorum in office or our workplace.

First, we should not gossip during the office hours, as the Management does not like such activities. They expect that the workers should not gossip during the office hours, they should abstain from it. On the contrary, they should discuss only with their seniors / other persons, or those who are in a higher position, so that their knowledge level could be enhanced.

Apart from the above, if we talk, we should talk about the organisation, its future planning, and rectification if any, the nature of job etc. All the gossip should be in a positive way because, when we talk positive, natural energy will automatically generate in our body, which helps us to perform our duty in a good and systematic way. We must represent ourselves in the right place at the right time in the organisational interest.

3. Immature / Less-involvement:

People mature with time. Some people join their job at the age of 18. This age is very tender for service point of view. At this age, they have no experience or working knowledge but they are just at their learning stage.

At this age, people do not have sufficient, proper, required or adequate confidence. They may qualify, as they may have adequate educational qualifications for that particular job/work but they may not have enough confidence because it comes from work experience and age.

For example, a person gets his driving licence from a Motor Training School, within a month but he has no confidence, so he cannot drive his own car smoothly or with confidence on the busy road, inspite of having the required driving licence. He has no confidence on his driving because; he is immature and lacks experience.

Gradually, when he gains experience then it is possible that his confidence level will increase. Similarly, if a person has less experience, his involvement in his work is also less, because the involvement of a person in his work depends upon his experience in that particular job.

Thus, when a worker is not fully involved in his work due to less experience, or lack of maturity, he will have enough time to talk uselessly with his colleagues. Such workers will have enough time to gossip. Thus, their performance level will be affected. They cannot concentrate their minds on their work and their output gradually decreases.

The management is aware of the gossiping workers. Management does not like such workers, who have no interest in their work and do not have competitive nature.

LACK OF SUITABLE POLICIES FOR BETTERMENT

It has been observed that many organisations do not have any suitable plans of promotion and increment for their employees, but their existing plans of the organisation depend upon circumstance. It means, it is not necessary to have a good performance of a person as criteria for their betterment or increment but it is necessary that the circumstance or situation or the existing system should also match with their performance.

In many organisations, the systems are so confusing that no one can guess / say that on what ground or basis a particular person got promotion or betterment. No one can say that inspite of having poor performance, lack of skill and a bad record, a particular person, got promotion or any betterment.

Such type of betterment, achievement, enhancement, in real sense, hurts a common person /workers, working in the same organisation in the same department/section. Sometimes, a junior employee gets better enhancement/ emoluments, while his senior, does not get the same benefit. A common person has many responsibilities due to which he has to work, otherwise no one will like to work in such an organisation where, a senior person is humiliated because promotion is given to his juniors and the management does not look into the integrity, dedication, honesty and performance of the real hardworking employees. These facts compel common employees to gossip or make useless talks in front of their colleagues.

They cannot concentrate on their assigned job / responsibilities but they try to engage themselves in gossip related to the office politics, back-biting their seniors, and to take out their inner frustration by gossiping with their colleagues.

From the employees' point of view, it is okay that they are releasing their frustration through office gossip but in the company's point of view, it is a very dirty thing for an organisational growth. These types of office politics is never liked by the higher Management.

Management desires from their employees that if anyone wants to be a good and loyal worker, they should not encourage this or any type of office gossip at the workplace. If their colleague is in a mood to start gossiping against the organisation, they should walk away or leave that place.

They can also avoid them by changing the topic and once the topic is changed, it should not be repeated. It is possible, that if the topic is very serious then, to avoid the gossip, one should start very funny/humorous topic by interrupting them. Inspite of all this if the other party is still talking then one should tell them directly that they are not interested to discuss that subject.

It is my personal view and since I am working in a private organisation, I never like to discuss on any anti organisational topic, discussion on age, personal life (sex) etc. My colleagues are very much familiar with my nature that is why no one discusses any useless topic with me. Inspite of the above, if any one starts, asking useless questions I prefer to leave the place silently and the people automatically change the topic or change their place. They understand that they are not supposed to talk to me on such topics.

BLUNT KNIFE

Each household keeps more then one knife in their kitchen and without its availability, it will be very difficult for anyone to cut vegetables. Good food cannot be possibly made without vegetables and we cannot make vegetables without cutting them in small pieces or as per the requirement. This knife helps the cook in cutting the vegetables in similar shape or as per the requirement of the particular cuisine.

If anybody is appreciating anyone's cooked vegetable or food then we can say that in this appreciation, the contribution of this small knife is also very important. The cook always takes the help of this valuable knife in the kitchen but no one appreciates this small useful knife in front of any one. In the absence of this small knife, it may very difficult for anyone to cut, the vegetables in a proper shape and prepare the vegetables according to the requirement or according to the liking of the house owner. The cook takes advantage of this knife and always desires that his knife should not be very sharp in cutting or its edge should not be very sharp because, if its edge is very sharp, then it is possible that it will harm or hurt his/her fingers.

This is why, inspite of having multiple advantages of this small knife, the cook, wants to use such knife, which is obviously sharp in cutting, but, if it harms the cook then it will be very difficult to keep such knife in the kitchen. The cook definitely will throw such knife from the kitchen without consulting anybody.

Similarly, in the Organisation, a senior never likes to appoint or keep such staff, like the sharp knife, who is very intelligent and has sharp mind to discharge any assigned responsibility within the stipulated period. As the cook, never likes to keep sharp edged knife in his / her kitchen to work fast but he keeps such knife whose edge is not so sharp, which may not harm anyone working in the kitchen.

This is my personal opinion and it is relative.

The manager, seniors like such type of juniors, subordinates, whose mind is not so sharp, and who are not so intelligent like their seniors, or managers. No one wants to keep subordinates, who are smarter looking or more knowledgeable, otherwise, the concerned seniors may be challenged in some situations. As a result, such subordinates or juniors will definitely give less output than sharp and intelligent workers.

Thus at the time of appraisal of any worker, the same manager or in charge will boldly report to the higher management that the workers working under him, are not good and have no adequate knowledge of work, take very long time to complete their assigned duties. Sometimes they are not in a position to provide the output, as they cannot understand even their assignment. They do not know what and how to discharge their duty. Therefore, we are very sorry not to give them good remark for their promotion or increment or for other benefits.

It means, the management likes only such workers or they want to promote such workers who are not very sharp but are labourious. They should not have their own mind but should do only what they have been told. His personal output is not welcome.

WEAK PEOPLE ARE LIKED BY ALL

It is a human attitude that people love those who are comparatively weaker from them, whether financially, physically or mentally. Even the Govt. gives reservation to the weaker sections of the society, those who are not very strong financially, physically, or belong to lower caste and are living under the poverty line. On the other hand, the Govt. never gives any reservation to people belonging to the upper caste of the society who are economically very weak and need financial help for their upliftment.

We give alms to beggars sitting near the temple, roads or at any public place. We feel satisfied by giving them cash/kind. We do not want to see them get stronger than us. We give them alms for their survival and not let them live happily and peacefully. We feel very proud by giving them anything but at the same time feel very bad when the same people demand anything from us or they refuse to take from us. We never tolerate such activities or behaviour.

In the similar way, in any organisation seniors or managers love all those subordinates who are in low cadre like the fourth grade workers. The seniors always like to do something for all the weak people (by cadre) or they want to support them not only because they are getting low payment or their salary is very low, because the seniors clearly know that such workers will never harm them. They cannot be their competitors, they can never be the contender of their chair. They know that if the seniors will tell them anything, the concerned people will never answer back in front of them.

Generally, people keep cats, dogs or parrots as their pets because these animals always have regard for their masters and they are very faithful to them. They do what their masters desire. They know that these animals will not harm them. On the other hand, the same master never likes to keep tiger or lion as their pets because they know that inspite of their care, this animal can kill them any time and they are not faithful to their master because they are savage.

Similarly, in the organisation or at the workplace, where, we are working, the nature or behaviour of our seniors / in -charge is more or less the same. The seniors also do not want to appoint a person who is not faithful to them and is stronger and more knowledgeable than the concerned seniors. The seniors only want that their subordinates working at any level should behave like cats, dogs, parrots or cows and not like a lion or a tiger. As these pets are very harmless and behave as per the desire of the master. The seniors also like that their subordinates should do their duties as per the desire of the concerned seniors and they should stand in front of their seniors by wagging their tail like dogs and speak the mugged words just like the parrot.

If the subordinates are strong, more intelligent, qualified, skilled then the subordinates will do their job in a very systematic way with time management to get correct result and the concerned seniors will not get a chance to say anything against them. They feel that after some days such subordinates may be eligible for their chair or position or they may be their competitor. This is why they do not like them. In general, the seniors or even in some case, the management also does not like such extraordinary educated, honest, workers because they will do their assigned duties as per their liking or they will not initiate any work assigned to them, if they think that it is not favourable for the organisation but at the same time, if the subordinates are not very educated or faithful, then such subordinates will work as their seniors want. If the result hurts or harms the organisation image, they are not bothered.

In some cases, the educated persons may make some arguments on any subject in company's interest, which cannot be digested by the concerned seniors. This is why such type of seniors always hesitate to work with the educated persons and hesitate to give any rewards or do any favour for them. They never want to promote them in a higher position, even, if they are deserving candidates. They clearly know that if they will promote them, the same workers will one day raise questions upon the seniors on any subject and the concerned seniors will not be able to give them a proper answer, as they are prone to making several mistakes in the work. Therefore, the seniors or management thinks that it will be better to leave such intelligent or educated workers as they are.

CHARACTERISTICS OF THE BOSS: IRON ROD, BUILDING & THE BUILDERS

Iron rod plays the most important part for the structure of a building and without it, a building cannot stand vertically. Any building or any type of structure is not possible without iron rods and if it is possible, then such structure may be made for a temporary period. The Iron rod used in that particular structure carries the whole weight of the building or bears the whole weight. Everyone knows that Iron rods of any building or structure is the basis or plays the most important role for that structure but the builder covers them with cement, so that no one can see them. Builders do not want to disclose the real amount of iron rods upon which the whole structure is standing because they want to take credit only themselves.

The Builder says that he is the builder, who has made such a strong building. The stronger part of the building is the contribution of the builder but the builder forgets the contribution of iron rods, cement, stone chips, concrete, on which the whole structure is standing. If the iron rods are pulled out from any building or structure, the building will cave in like a pack of cards.

The relationship between iron rods and the builder is very similar with that of the employee and their employers. Here we can assume, the iron rods as employees and the builder as the employer.

The few members or workers in every organisation are genuine and are the pillars of the organisation. The may be the founder members of that organisation. They work only for the organisational development and have emotional attachment with the company. The relationship is that of a mother and her child.

They do not bother about the boss and their position, where they are working etc. They devote their valuable time only for the organisational benefits. They think that the company where they are working is their own company and if the company grows fast, they will benefit or if the company suffers a loss, they will be the loser and not the others.

Such workers silently do their job with full enthusiasm without blaming any one for any grievance. They do their work just like a father does for his children with full responsibility and fulfils their grievances without making any noise or without showing his presence. The reason is that they are bound emotionally. Similarly, in any organisation, the pioneer members are also bound with a strong emotional bond. They cannot leave the organisation just like a mother who cannot leave her sick child suffering.

Through this example, I would like to say that in every organisation, the company does not give proper importance to the devoted worker, who works only for the company. If the management or seniors come to know that such workers are labourious and faithful to the company, then the management gives responsibility to such faithful employees, who are dedicated in discharging their duties. As the builder clearly knows that the whole structure is based upon the iron rods used in that building but employer like builders cover the iron rod, like faithful workers, with hard cement, so that they cannot claim credit and the credit only goes to the builder.

DISCRIMINATION

Discrimination plays an important role in nature. Discrimination among anything is very essential for its development. In the absence of the concept of discrimination, it will be very difficult for anyone to say that this particular thing is longer or shorter than the other. It will be very difficult to measure anything in any specification. If everyone is similar in length or weight then how can one say that such a particular thing or object is comparatively better than the other one. It means nothing can be differentiated or discriminated.

Nature has gifted us with five fingers on both hands with different lengths. Suppose for a while, if all our fingers had similar length then, we would have to face problems because it would be very difficult to close the fingers and make a closed fist. This is why God / nature has created them in different size in length or in other words, God has discriminated in the interest of human beings. It shows that, if anywhere we find that there is discrimination then, it means that there is going to be development and competition.

In nature, we find different atmosphere, climate, languages, and lifestyles, which is unique and beautiful. Due to this different climate, we can feel the pleasure of cold, hot, summer, winter, rainy season or other types of climate. We can feel or differentiate between summer and winter. In the atmosphere, discrimination itself in the air is the main factor which gives motion in the air or by which any type of movement in the universe is possible. In summer season, we feel heat while in the winter season we feel cold. In other words, Nature has created discrimination on the earth to make life more beautiful and diversified.

If, Nature stops discrimination for a while, then we will get the same kind of climate everywhere or the movement in the air will suddenly stop. The filtration system or the Ozone layer in the atmosphere will automatically collapse and it will be very difficult to survive on the earth for human beings or other living things.

If we take discrimination in a positive way then we will find the following factors, which automatically generates due to the discrimination made by the Almighty or by the concerned seniors or Management at the workplace in any organisation.

(1) Competitive mind
(2) Continuous Growth
(3) Learning Attitude
(4) Alertness
(5) Positive Energy
(6) Increase in Labour Turnover.

1. Competitive Mind:

Discrimination generates among us a competitive mind. When we see in our organisation or at our workplace where, we are all working together, giving the best of our efforts to the organisation. Our colleagues are getting promotion and increment from time to time or other benefits against their good work, dedication, honesty for which they had sacrificed a lot presently or in the past. We also start performing our best as per the desire of the seniors. We also try to achieve our goal without harming others. We start performing our best, utilising all our time sincerely and obeying the instructions of the seniors. Such factors will help a person to lead towards progress and such people will genuinely complete their assigned job within the limited time frame or finish the target on time. People without commenting should try to beat others in work, achievement, ideas, methods of work, in cost cutting, efficiency in working procedure etc. This will definitely give them more edge or enhancement in progress, both mentally and monetarily.

2. Continuous Growth

Generally, it has been observed in various organisations that if there is discrimination in salary, promotion, increment, responsibilities, department, seniors or juniors, work profile among the workers in the Organisation, then it is sure that such Organisation will get progress definitely in their financial and all-around development.

An unsatisfied person starts working more efficiently than a satisfied person does. A satisfied worker, salary wise or cadre wise is less sincere, while the unsatisfied worker tries to prove himself by giving more dedication, efficiency, honesty to the company only because he has to prove himself at any cost.

A person during his service period finds himself fit and healthy, as he has to struggle against the office politics and hard work. He always wishes to achieve the desired goal, meet several office or routine problems at his workplace etc, so he works continuously. As a result, the concerned person gets improvement in his career positively but as soon as the same person retires from his service, he gets complacent. He suddenly thinks that there is no charm in his life.

If he feels that, he has no responsibilities left; his own family responsibilities are almost complete. If his routine time is engaged in positive work, or if he wants to do something else or if he has to work for his survival then it is okay, otherwise his health starts deteriorating. As soon as he thinks that, he is satisfied with whatever he has achieved or whatever God has given him, he may start feeling sick and weak and his health will start deteriorating.

Thus, we see that discrimination in an organisation is very essential to get adequate growth for the organisation as well as for the employees. If we have not faced any problem, then we cannot enjoy happiness of life, so to enjoy the happiness, there should have been some bad or rough circumstances in our life so that we start valuing happiness. For example, God has gifted us a big discrimination in the seasonal pattern. We enjoy winter because; we had badly suffered heat in the summer season.

If a person is hungry and has no means of eating while others have many options of eating, then such person will try to get food at any cost or by any means to satisfy his hunger. Similarly, in any organisation when some workers do not get any promotion or increment and other colleagues get, then such workers begin to work more efficiently, meaningfully, objectively as assigned by the seniors or H.O.D... They begin to listen to all the instructions coming from their concerned seniors, H.O.D. or any supervisor. As a result, his dedication and labour comes in the eyes of the head or concerned management, who later on forwards his name for the next promotion or increment or any other benefit. I mean to say that discrimination is very essential for development. We should not take it negatively or otherwise.

3. Learning Attitude:

If we take discrimination in a positive way then we will find, that it has many merits, such as, it gives its worker a learning attitude or we can say in another way that due to discrimination, learning attitude, automatically develops among the workforce / employees.

I have personally observed that some workers, working in an old department where there is no scope of regular development promotion or increment, there is stagnation. At the same time their colleagues working in some other department in the same workplace, are getting promotion or increment, we should think that there are definitely some good factors on the basis of which our colleagues had been given promotion or increment by their seniors. We should take it in a positive way and inspite of pulling the legs of others; we should think or analyse our own weak points and try to overcome it.

This is the reason; some workers take discrimination in a positive way and start taking some sort of professional personality development course, as per the situation or requirement. They should not blame others but try to develop themselves as per the market demand. They should begin to work with more enthusiasm, dedication and to the best of their efforts and try to complete their assigned work within the stipulated period.

Thus, we should always be alert and think about our future. If anytime we feel that our profile does not give us adequate return, we should change our profile, department and get professional help according to the situational requirement.

4. Alertness:

Most of the time in an Organisation, Management gives promotion, increment on a pick and choose basis. It means, in a single department or under specific seniors, some people get promotion, while the others do not get while both have the same qualification, quality, experience and ability. In a private organisation, if people are not getting proper response from the Management, such workers think that they have done some wrong or they have done some sort of anti-organisation activity, and this is the reason they did not get any promotion, increment or other benefit. They start analysing on what ground or basis their senior had not selected their names for promotion or betterment. They think there is certainly some problem or obstacle, which are hurdles for them and their progress.

On analysing such factors, they begin to work more aggressively than before. They try to know what is going on around them and the reasons behind it, the side effect upon them and on the Company. They try to conquer the heart of their seniors. Their attachment with the Organisation and with their seniors gradually increases and they always make themselves alert about their future within or outside the Organisation.

5. Positive Energy:

It all depends upon a person how they take things in life or how they tackle or react on a situation. It varies from person to person. For example, in one department, when we see that a particular worker gets promotion, increment, or other benefits in the Organisation, it is seen that few of the workers of the same department are not happy with the development or the progress of their colleagues but some of them are very happy and come forward to congratulate the concerned person with good intention.. Their congratulations may be half hearted but at least they had the courtesy to congratulate them. Here, we see that discrimination is also going on, even in the thinking of human beings, which varies from person-to-person or how one takes things.

First of all, we should think about the positive factors of discrimination on which ground our colleagues had been promoted or had been given higher responsibilities, and secondly we should think about the positive energy which we generally receive from thinking positive and try to implement it i.e. by being positive. According to the adage, charity begins from home. Here good work should start from us, so that others emulate us or learn from our example.

Such people take inspiration from their seniors and start working with more vigour, dedication and devotion with an enthusiastic approach to achieve the target assigned by the seniors. They never react or pass any unwanted comments on their colleagues who have been promoted or have benefited. They always think about achieving their goal in a limited period. They begin to work accordingly to the assignment given to them by their seniors and try to complete it in a stipulated period.

6. Worker Turn Over:

The word discrimination, gives a qualitative meaning to workforce in an Organisation. In the Organisation, not every action against the discrimination can be similar for everyone. There shall be different reactions on different people. Discrimination gives a positive point to the

Organisation. For example: - Running water is found more pure or fresh than stagnant water. We enjoy running in the open while we feel very uncomfortable or claustrophobic in the closed space. A person can die in a closed room, if the air is blocked but the same person can enjoy fresh air. These are possible where there will be discrimination on the concerned situation.

The Air blows when there is a difference in the atmospheric pressure in the atmosphere at that particular place. The air blows from higher density zone to lower density zone to balance the atmospheric pressure.

In a river, water flows from higher level to lower level and we get fresh water, but if the water does not move and stagnates at a place then the same water may become poisonous. Thus, it is true that to get fresh air or water, there should be a continuous movement in the environment. These are all possible because of discrimination in the air or in the water level and in this case, the discrimination plays a vital role.

Similarly, discrimination plays a vital role in the Organisation as well. Sometimes, due to the discrimination, the Organisation makes more profit and because of this factor the stagnated work force is filtered and starts giving more productivity to the Organisation.

NEGATIVE ASPECTS OF DISCRIMINATION

There are two sides of a coin. Different aspect of any particular thing has positive as well as negative points. It all depends upon ourselves how we perceive things or how we take a particular situation in our life. It is not necessary that if we forgive anyone for his silly mistake, then others will also be forgiven. In an organisation, when a person gets promotion, increment or other benefits from the management, and at the same time other colleagues in the same department do not get such reward, then in this situation, such people may react in a negative manner or take things differently.

The following negative aspects of discrimination may automatically arise in the mind of the workers working at the same workplace.

(1) Increase in Labour Turnover

(2) Work without interest

(3) Decrease in Organisation Faith

(4) Dissatisfaction among the workers

(5) Low respect for the Seniors

(6) Demotivation

1. Labour Turnover:

Everyone knows that a person works at his workplace for earning money, to learn work or to fulfil his responsibilities. It is clear that without expectation from others, no one will work. If a person works and says that he does not want anything from the concerned person for whom he is working, or against the labour or dedication, then it means that such a person is getting some sort of satisfaction in some other way for his/her efforts. Sometimes people work for emotional bond. Such persons get emotional satisfaction to complete the assigned work.

A mother works selflessly for her child. Here she works only for her self-satisfaction or emotional bond, which is very essential for a healthy person. It has been observed in any Organisation that at one time all the workers cannot get promotion, increment, or other benefits, but only some of the workers get such opportunity. It is as per the Management discretion.

Often, at one workplace, if there are 50 workers working with the same responsibility, having same skill, experience. Inspite of having same qualities the management does not want to give promotion or increment to all of them but they give it only to 20 workers out of 50 and deliberately give birth to dissatisfaction among the employees.

At this situation, when people compare themselves from the market, they plan to leave the Organisation or plan for some other alternative. Nobody would like any type of discrimination done by any of their seniors. For Example, if we have one litre of water out of which, if we place half a litre of water in the fridge and half a litre of water under an extreme hot condition. Then in this situation also there is discrimination done by the head of the family or organisational head or the Management, because they had created an odd situation for water. Here water kept in hot place, gradually starts to evaporate according to the created situational environment while the water kept in a cold place or favourable place will remain fresh and there will be a positive change in the water and it will turn into ice in the fridge, which in a way is preserved.

Here, if we assume water as the workers, employees and one who had segregated water as the employer or the Management, it will be easier to understand the situation. In any organisation, the Management deliberately creates some sort of discrimination, so that those employees, who are not being able to adjust themselves in the organisation, may go out or leave the Organisation. Those who are more suitable for the Organisation or in other words, who can understand the Management and their requirement, can stay with the Organisation and are welcome to work in higher capacity.

If the workers will be harassed by the Management akin to subjecting high degree of temperature, then the degree of labour turnover will be on the higher side, akin to keeping water in a hot and unfavourable place where, the speed of evaporation will increase. Thus, we can say that the discrimination is a factor created by the Management in their Organisation to meet some specific goals in Company's interest. As and when the Management creates discrimination by any means, the degree of labour turnover increases rapidly.

2. Work without Interest:

Every human being first works for himself then for anybody else. In an Organisation every employee works for himself first and then for the Company. They can only give efficient output to the Organisation when they are satisfied with their financial side, workplace or assignment. If due to any circumstance, they are not satisfied, they will not be in a position to deliver their assigned responsibilities in effective, efficient way in the Company's interest. There are several factors in the Organisation, which directly or indirectly affect the productivity of the employees. Discrimination is one of them. It has been seen that in several circumstances, the productivity of workers detoriate gradually without harming any one. This is because they feel demotivated among their colleagues. They do not say anything to anyone but due to the discrimination, their productivity level is affected directly. Such circumstances arise when the Management makes discrimination owing to the betterment, promotion, increment or other benefits to only one section of the workers. When the Management makes such discrimination among the workers then automatically workers show less interest, less integrity towards their job, assigned duty. A sense of negativity generates in the workers working at the workplace of any Organisation in such circumstances. They work without interest or just for formality.

They work just for the sake of completing their work. They think that they have to complete their work quantitatively and not qualitatively. Their faith towards the Organisation as well as towards their seniors, Management gradually deteriorates. Their degree of morale, dedication towards work decreases or takes a downward trend and ultimately it is the Company, which has to suffer due to such created situation or discrimination.

3. Deterioration in organisational Faith:

It is necessary to have great faith in our work, in ourselves, working systems as well as in the workplace where we are working, to get a desired result. It will be very difficult to get a good result without having faith in the work for which we are working under any circumstance. In other words, a person can expect anything from any particular person in whom he has faith. When a person feels that the Management itself creates a vast discrimination among their workers then their faith in the concerned Management or in the Organisation begins to decrease or starts eroding. As soon as their faith level decreases, their confidence level also takes a downward trend, which directly or indirectly affects the dedication or integration of the workers and simultaneously affects the growth of the Organisation. Here growth takes a back seat.

Any type of business cannot get a desired goal or result, if their workers have no faith on their employers. For example, in our daily life, an emotional relationship between wife and husband totally depends upon the faith in each other. Whenever the faith level comes down, the relationship gets into unwanted trouble or problems. The Government also depends upon the faith of their members of Parliament(M.Ps). Whenever, due to any discrimination or circumstance,faith level comes down among the members of the assembly, or parliament, it becomes very difficult to run the Government. Therefore, it is very necessary to have faith of the concerned workers in their Management, to get continuous and consistent progress.

4. Dissatisfaction among the Workers:

It is not easy to give satisfaction to everyone. If one-person will be happy then the other person will be unhappy on the same proposal or work done. If the satisfaction level or balance, harmony level is 100% and if 60 % people are happy with any work done or with any proposal, then definitely the rest 40 % people will be unhappy or disagree with the same proposal or work done.

In a general situation, the Management does not give benefits to all their employees even if they are involved in the same goal or assignment. They usually do not give benefit to all of their employees but to a certain number, inspite of having full knowledge about the rest of the employees and their qualities, dedication and involvement as well as their achievement.

It means that the Management, knowingly or wilfully makes discrimination among its workers or employees, so that they can fight among themselves over their betterment. They wilfully generate dissatisfaction among the workers, working at a workplace in the same cadre or in the same Organisation. By doing this, the efficiency as well as the involvement level of the workers towards their assigned work, gradually decreases and ultimately, it is the Company, which has to lose their Brand Image along with their credentials in the market. At this situation, the workers working in such Organisation try to leave the Organisation and begin to look for another job elsewhere or start looking for greener pastures.

5. Less Respect for Seniors and Management:

Every person works or gives his best output to the Organisation as per his ability or capability, skill, knowledge, experience, interest and does the assigned work accordingly. If the work assigned to the person is favourable then the person will try to complete the target as soon as possible but if the assigned work is difficult or against his interest then the person will take more time to complete the same work. By finishing the assigned work, the person feels very much satisfied and when he is satisfied then he gets respect from his colleagues, seniors or the concerned Management.

Every worker working at any workplace in any Organisation wants or expects some degree of respect from his / her senior or Management. They work for the Organisation with their best of efforts. The Company should recognise their work, efforts or their contribution but when they do not get recognition from the concerned Management, department, then they start skipping their work or assigned responsibilities or they do not try to take any initiative in any new work of the Organisation. They start overlooking new responsibilities.

In many cases, it is observed that when the Management gives promotion, increment or any type of benefit to the selected workers or to their favourable candidates working under their supervision, gives birth to discrimination or creates a wedge between the common colleagues of a particular department or workplace. The workers are compelled to think about this discrimination, because it is the workers who knew clearly about their own contribution. Due to the concerned Management, overlooking their contribution the workers working at any workplace begin to give less respect to their discriminators.

The workers begin to give less importance to the senior. Giving less respect, does not mean that the workers start using obscene language but they start paying less attention on their instructions or they start delaying their work. They take more time to complete their assigned work or they try to ignore their presence. In this way, they begin to give less respect to their seniors or the concerned Management.

It is the Management, which has to face the loss. The workers are not at all affected, as the workers leave the Organisation and join other companies with better pay scale and perks. Therefore, the main loser will be the Organisation. Discrimination harms the Company in the long run.

6. Demotivation:

On one side positive discrimination among the employees gives several positives things to the workers as well as to the Organisation. It also gives some negative things. If the workers are given some special perks during their service rendering period the concerned employees will automatically be motivated and their efficient working will directly be affected with this motivation but on the other hand when the same workers inspite of having good skill, education, experience, seniority good behaviour with the colleagues and seniors, are not getting promotion and their colleagues, having less qualities comparatively get promotion or increment or some perks then such situation gives rise to great dissatisfaction and demotivation to the efficient workers.

Sometimes, the Management knowingly wants to demotivate their employees by not giving them the deserving credit. At this situation they give promotion to such workers who are undeserving for that particular position, just to teach a lesson to other workers who have good qualities but could not perform well or they did not show their seriousness to the assigned work. Thus, if we have some good inbuilt qualities, we should definitely use them for the Organisational growth or its benefits, otherwise the same Management will give credit to such workers who do not deserve the Promotion or the perks.

SENIORS / MANAGEMENT ONLY GIVE INSTRCTIONS AND DO NOT WANT TO LISTEN TO ANYTHING

A very peculiar thing is observed in the workplace of any Organisation. People generally get satisfaction when they give instructions, whether in the Office or at their workplace. We have seen that the guardian also gives instruction to his children to do a particular work, but people do not want to listen to anything concerning the assigned work and the procedure, methods to complete the same. They do not want to listen to the problems faced by the workers to achieve success whether in the Company's interest or not. They only want to see the result of their instructions and nothing else.

If the poor workers fail to manage, fulfil, or complete the assigned work within the scheduled period, the concerned seniors or H.O.D. wants to punish them, they do not listen to the problems or the reasons, why they could not complete that particular work. The seniors generally tell the concerned workers that the problems shall have to be solved by them by any means. They want to see only the result. Instead they should have tried to see the genuineness of the problems being faced by his workers.

EGO SATISFACTION AT THE COST OF THE COMPANY

Love is very necessary for human beings as it gives energy to our body to live a better life. It mostly gives positive energy or may be sometimes it gives negative energy to our body. Accordingly, our brain gives instructions to our body parts to act. If, for a while, we pull out the love factor and the positive energy from our life then it is sure that our life will seem aimless, dull and unhealthy. We cannot give proper concentration on any assigned work at the office or we may sit uselessly at home and our life will become hell, dull and drab.

Apart from the above, "EGO" is an important factor in our life, which is very necessary for a human being to survive in this world and without it, it will be very difficult for a man to live or survive because it gives several types of energy to our body to act. This can be divided into two parts.

(1) Positive Ego

(2) Negative Ego

1. Positive Ego:

Positive Ego is very rarely found in a human being or in another way, it can be said that there is a very low percentage of people having positive ego. If the person is fully satisfied with his/her education, assigned work, family life etc then he may have A positive ego. Positive Ego is found only in the top Management or the owner of any Organisation or the Company or highly evolved people.

It cannot be seen among the middle Management working in any Company. The people working in any Organisation themselves depend on the top Management and do not have the authority to take any direct decision without consulting the top Management who are answerable for their decisions and policies, never have a positive ego. This is not possible for the middle management as they are working for someone or for the Organisation on some fixed remuneration. If GOD forbid there is some financial loss to the company, its first victim would be the owner of the Organisation or the Company than any other person. So, positive ego can only be found in the owner of the company or the people who are highly enlightened and evolved.

2. Negative Ego:

The second rung of Management which is responsible for several assignments to be done for the Organisation under the owner of the Company for some remuneration fixed by them, are full of Negative Ego. Such people are sometimes very much biased during any decision making process that it becomes very difficult to explain their attitude. At that time, they get so blind that they cannot distinguish between good or bad workers, who work in the interest of the Organisation or against it. They only want to give weightage to particular selected persons and not to their performance. They only see how a particular worker has been appointed and to which group he belongs. If the person belongs to their similar or own group then they will have no objection but if he is from a rival group then it is sure that the particular worker will have to face a very adverse or difficult situation at his workplace and he will have to face many problems to survive there.

Most of the senior Management of any Organisation think only for their own benefit. They do not bother about the progress of the concerned place in which they are working or they do not bother for such Company on which they depend which is their main source of earning. They are working only to protect their job and for their ego satisfaction. One day, there was news of a person/worker, working in a private Organisation being suspended with immediate effect. The news was very shocking and everyone was shocked to know this as the concerned person was innocent, who had never done any wrong. After two or three days people came to know that the senior Management had taken such a drastic step because, they wanted to show their power to someone else in the same Organisation. This incident totally indicates their false ego satisfaction. They can go to any length to satisfy their ego.

It means, Mr. S. did not bother about the reputation or brand name of the Organisation. He works only to fulfil his ego and self-satisfaction by giving punishment to an innocent person without any valid reason. They do not want to see anyone living in peace even to a person belonging to the lower cadre.

Such Management or seniors sometimes take so many decisions in the Organisation, which costs the Company dearly, only due to false ego satisfaction. They do not want to see the impact of their order on the brand or image of the Company. In a nutshell, such Management or seniors are very dangerous for the Organisation or for the growth of the Organisation.

The behaviour of such seniors indicates that they have no respect for any one working in the Organisation. They love only themselves. They might be unsatisfied with their own family relationship and living in frustration.

DO NOT WANT TO LISTEN "NO"

In general, people are very egoistic and suffer from some complex. They always want to command other people but never give the opportunity to be commanded themselves. They never like anyone having demanding nature, in the office or in any division of the Organisation. The Management/seniors expect from their subordinates that whatever instruction they give to their subordinates, the subordinates should immediately accept the instruction, without blinking an eyelid whether it is practical or possible or not, whether it will benefit the Organisation or not. If they will say NO, the seniors will not like the concerned workers and gradually, the seniors will derail such persons from the mainstream of the Organisation. However, the seniors/ Management who do not like to listen, NO from any of their subordinates sometimes seem very dangerous for the Organisation. This shows their pettiness and such behaviour leads to their doom.

SADISTIC NATURE OF SENIORS

In most of the cases, it has been seen that the person sitting on the Management Chair/ Managerial Chair/Unit Heads have very sadistic nature or a very peculiar character. They themselves are frustrated by their nature. The family life of most of the people is very unhappy and disharmonious. They may have enough money to spend but are very narrow-minded and mean.

There are some causes, which compel the concerned seniors to be sadistic by nature. The following factors may be one of them:

(1) Un-skilled/ un-educated
(2) Not fit in the society
(3) Un-satisfied- family life
(4) Mismatched married life
(5) Aimless life
(6) Low remuneration
(7) No Promotion
(8) Destructive Mind
(9) Heavy work pressure
(10) Un-planned working systems
(11) Lack of proper Authority
(12) Selfishness
(13) Alcoholic / Drug addict or other addiction

Un-educated & Un-Skilled Person:

A Hindi phrase is very popular, " Adhjal Gagri Chhalkat Jaye", which means empty vessels makes the most noise. Having half baked knowledge is very dangerous (for himself as well as for the Organisation, subordinates or even for the society). Such people cannot achieve their goal like other normal people because they do not have sufficient knowledge of their work/assigned work. Due to their poor educational/un -skilled background their mental power is not very sound. They feel insecurity from their own colleagues. Such type of people generally become sadist and are dangerous for any Organisation / society. They cannot think about the growth of the Organisation and the subordinates working under their guidance. They lack positivity and are pessimistic by nature. They hate skilled and educated people.

Un-matched Position:

Sometimes people become sadist due to their age or the generation gap. If a person joined the Organisation 20, yrs ago when there were no facility or provision of computer. There was lack of general awareness, so they could not update themselves but presently people join the Organisation with a lot of computer knowledge and general awareness. They can finish their assigned work more quickly and systematically than their seniors. At this situation, the seniors of such subordinates do not like their own subordinates. They always plan, to harass or demoralise their juniors. It is only due to their age or generation gap. However, if they want to update themselves with the new gadgets / computer etc, they can do so, provided they want to learn.

Un-satisfied with their Family Life:

It is also seen in many cases that people working in an Organisation at the managerial cadre are very unhappy. It might be due to their earlier or present family life. There may be so many reasons like disharmonious family life disobedient children, unfaithful wife or extra marital affairs. They may not be able to give proper time to their family members or they may not be able to fulfil their other demands. They may not have time to fulfil their emotional demands etc, which is very important for a person having a family. Money is not so important to live a peaceful life but harmony among the family members is very important. The manager working in any Organisation is so busy in his job/responsibility that he cannot get time for his family members, which gradually makes him irritating, sadistic and makes his life messy or a living hell.

Mismatched Married Life:

If a person has a good official position but was married at a very young age and his wife is not so educated or is not at par with the present day society, then also such persons become very irritating / sadistic / pessimistic. If the concerned person has a second wife or if it's the wife's second marriage /husband the person sitting on the top position probably does not have a healthy married life or may be mismatched owing to other reasons.

Aimless Life/Saturated Life:

When a person is needy, then he might be very active in solving his problems, at any cost but as soon as his problem is solved, the same person becomes very lethargic and complacent. Before examination, a student studies hard for a long period continuously but as soon as his exam gets over he starts moving here and there in a relaxed mood. Similarly, when a person joins an Organisation, he works hard, until his confirmation, promotion, enhancement of his salary. He works hard during the time of appraisal form submission but as soon as he comes to know that his appraisal form is submitted to the concerned department, he changes his behaviour. People should be consistent in their behaviour and working.

Destructive Mind:

Sometimes, it is seen in any Organisation that there are several workers working in the Organisation whose mind is very destructive. They cannot think positively. Such people are always criticising their colleagues/seniors or try to sabotage the company related plans and strategies. They always try to escape from any official responsibility or do not want to be answerable. They do not want to give answer to their seniors related to any official work. The Organisation does not like such people as their mind is destructive and who waste their precious time mindlessly.

Low Remuneration:

The low remuneration of any employee, who is unable to fulfil the minimum essential / requirement of his family, makes a person frustrated and irritating. Sometimes, people are not getting promotion, increment due to their poor performance against their assigned responsibilities. Due to non-performance, people do not get promotion or increment at their workplace, but their personal expenses increase rapidly and gradually make them frustrated and irritating.

Not Getting Adequate Promotion:

Sometimes it is seen that some employees are very sincere towards discharging their assigned duties in a good and scientific manner in company's interest, within the limited time frame but unfortunately the concerned employees working on any senior position are not promoted. Due to non-promotion or any betterment, their enthusiastic approach gradually tends to decrease. The manager has many good qualities, which is required for a senior or departmental head but due to unavoidable circumstances, such persons are not able to boost up the morale of any weak workers, or of the subordinates. The top Management, after some times, thinks of absolving them from their responsibility. Their negative approach damages directly or indirectly the image of the Company and dents its reputation.

Heavy Work Load / Pressure:

Despite having negative nature in human beings, heavy workload also, encourages the tendency towards negative approach and attitude. When an office in charge, H.O.D, seniors are over loaded with their official work which should be completed in a scheduled time or when such people do not get adequate reward against their work in terms of promotion or recognition or in other terms, such involved people gradually start escaping from their responsibilities. As they are not getting time for their recreation, their mind does not think in a positive way and starts thinking negatively.

Such people are totally disliked by the top Management. The concerned manager should lessen the workload of such people or should divide it among other workers. This reduces the output of the company and leads it towards loss, which is bad for the image of the company.

No Worker wants to get any kind of punishment. They always wish and pray for rewards. Punishment decreases the energy, creates demotivation and destructiveness while on the other hand reward of any kind gives positive energy, strength, motivation and constructive energy to a worker in the Company's interest. In other words, rewarding them boosts their morale.

If a worker takes punishment in a positive way and learns from it then it will be very fruitful for the Organisation and for the persons involved. On the other hand, if the worker takes his punishment in a negative way and he does not take a lesson from his punishment then it will be very bad for the Organisation as well as for the person. In such situation people, plan to take revenge or leave the Organisation. Both ways the Organisation as well as the worker will lose. We should not take punishment in a negative way, on the contrary; we should try to re-evaluate ourselves to find out our faults and try to correct the same. Such exercise will be beneficial for both the worker and the Organisation.

Sometimes, the Management gives the instruction for any reward, increment, enhancement, appraisal, big responsibilities etc to be given immediately. Unfortunately, it has been seen that the immediate responsible person for such instruction to be implemented, does not take it seriously and takes the instruction very casually. However, it is seen that the instruction to punish/penalise somebody is taken very seriously and immediately. The same people became very lazy and lethargic in giving promotion, increment or appreciation related to the workers. The same person shows too much interest in penalising or punishing others.

In Organisational interest, it will be beneficial if the concerned worker takes both punishment and reward in the same manner or spirit, whether it is a punishment or a reward. The Management also expects from their workers or subordinates to have same spirit for accepting both reward and punishment. If one takes it in his stride, then he becomes an evolved being.

PROPER IMPORTANCE

In a family, each child requires proper attention from his or her parents. If the parents give attention to their children related to their activities, the growth of such children will be very sound. At the same time when the children are not getting proper attention from their parents, then their growth level will be directly affected, and their development will be very slow. They will be very irritated even by a very small opposition made my any one. Their tolerance power will also be very less.

It is very important to give proper importance to each and every one in the society or in our day-to-day life "e.g.". We plant small saplings and if we do not water them or take care of them, they will die but when we give them importance, take care, and water them on time, the same small saplings will give us satisfaction and the desired result. It is only possible, when we give them proper importance. In the same way, if we do not give proper importance or attention to our subordinates or juniors working under our guidance, they cannot give adequate output on time. They will never respect us. They are like small saplings to a gardener who nurtures them.

For example, there are two brothers, Ram and Shyam. Mr. Ram is very rich. He has all the Hi-tech comforts for his children. He provides and fulfils all the requirements of his family. His children make useless expenses, go to discothèques and party endlessly. He never went to see what his children were actually doing with the facilities provided. Mr. Ram had provided every possible physical comfort to his children but as Mr. Ram was very busy with his work, he could not give his time to his children for their care or attention. Due to lack of time, he was not able to provide love and emotional support to his children. This means Mr. Ram did not give importance to his children but only gave importance to his business or work.

On the other hand, Mr. Shyam who had four sons but was financially weak, was very God fearing & gentle. Mr. Shyam had great faith in his children. He respected all his children and their views, opinions as well as their comments. He never tried to hurt them in front of others. All his children also had great respect for their parents. It has been observed in several families that the children, who are getting proper attention and importance by their parents, are successful in their personal as well as professional life and are good human beings.

Mr. Ram was busy chasing his dreams i.e. succeeding in business. He only provided physical comforts to his children instead of emotional support, so his children grew up to be unsuccessful in their career and were very insecure human beings. So giving proper importance is very important whether it is a family or an Organisation.

As Mr. Ram's children were not treated properly or their parents had not given them proper importance, so their growth was not so healthy and they grew up to be insecure and unsuccessful in their professional and family life.

The same logic applies to any Organisation. While the Management or concerned seniors have faith on their subordinates or if the seniors give proper importance to their subordinates, then the output of the assigned work will be very high in such circumstances. The subordinates may give their assigned output before the expected time. That will save the expenses of the Company. If they also give respect to their subordinates like their own children and give them promotion/ increments and other benefits then the subordinates/juniors will be very dedicated, honest and answerable to their Management. So they should be treated humanely with love and respect.

The worker/staff of any Organisation also have it in their minds that their Management should have work strategy in place. Management also expects from their staff that they should have great faith in their Management and the day-to-day working of the organisation. In other words, the Management does not like such persons or workers who have no faith on their seniors, Management or the system of the Organisation.

TENSION

It has been observed in various Organisations that the seniors do not want to face any sort of tension due to their subordinates. The seniors expect that any problem related to any responsibility should not reach their table and it should be sorted out by the juniors themselves. They want their juniors to do each and every thing on their behalf but any type of complaint against the subordinates should not reach them. The seniors expect from their subordinates that no one in the Organisation should point out any problem or weak points of their working systems. If there is any shortfall in their working procedure, then that should come first to their subordinates. They want to live free of tension, thus shrug off their responsibility.

SYCOPHANCY

It is the nature of human beings that they like to be flattered. They may not work well but they like to be complemented or praised about their good activities and never want to listen about their demerits. They never like to listen to the truth about their true nature, behaviour or wrong decision through which they had hurt others or had harmed the company. Sycophancy is very harmful not only for any Organisation but also for the entire segment of the society. It is very much rampant in politics as well as in the Organisation where we work.

Sometimes, people are so much addicted to sycophancy that they cannot distinguish between good and evil, which later on proves harmful for the Organisation. We have observed that the Management expects from their subordinates that they should always praise them, whether it is true or not, whether they have any merit or not but their juniors should always praise them just to safe guard themselves from any unseen problems.

By such behaviour, the juniors may benefit for a short while but in the long run, the Organisation as well as such workers definitely have to lose many things. It may be their prestige or self-respect or eventually their job.

WORK PRESENTATION

For some people, the kind of education, Qualification or experience does not matter but their work presentation matters a lot. The main thing is how they are presenting their views in front of others. In an interview, a mediocre student can get higher marks than he might have scored in his written test but if he has a good knowledge of presentation, then his way of speaking, etiquette and good manners may charm the interview board thereby giving him very good marks.

In any Organisation, it does not matter whether one works honestly or with dedication but it is important that one should know how the work should be presented in front of the concerned bosses. If they have these qualities then definitely such people will get promotion, increment, or other benefits from their concerned seniors.

I mean to say that Management also expects from their workers that they should present their work in a scientific and logical way so that the concerned Management could understand it easily. In some cases, it is seen that there are some typical personalities among the workers whose main motto is to distort the main facts before the presentation to the Management. They do not want to give them in writing the actual facts and figures. It is because if they present the facts to the Management, then their position may get awkward. They conceal the facts so that they never fall into trouble.

Today the scenario is totally changed in the present circumstances, it has been observed that bookish knowledge is not required so much as talking fluently in English. The concerned Management is not bothered about the knowledge of a particular subject, whether the freshers have it or not. The freshers only want to impress, by their smooth talk than what they talk. They know only to dress smartly and talk non-stop English may be with an American accent to impress the female staff. What counts is their superficial smartness and not their in depth knowledge.

We should emphasise only on our presentation. The Management gets impressed with superficial knowledge of an employee. Based on such superficial knowledge and high technical presentation the concerned employees get promotion, increment or other benefits. However, when such workers/employees have to face a practical problem then such people will not survive for a long time. The concerned workers will then get demoralised and demotivated. Sometimes the situation becomes so bad that they are compelled to leave the Organisation. I mean that the Management always likes such people, who have original knowledge, clear concept and good presentation skill.

For example, a beggar when begging on the road or at the traffic signal, dresses up very shabbily. Then only he will be able to get alms from the public. If he dresses up like a gentle man, he would not get even a paisa in the whole day from the same public. The same beggar, when presenting himself properly will get more money. We meet certain smartly clad smooth talkers who ask for money on the pretext that they have lost their wallet, or have missed their trains, flight, or one of his close friends has met with an accident, or he has lost his A.T.M. card and he needs money urgently. He is also a kind of beggar albeit a smart one.

I mean that the presentation is the most important criteria to get anything from any one. Similarly, if we wish to get a promotion, more responsibilities, more salary, power than others do, in an Organisation then we have to present ourselves in a high profile manner in front of the concerned seniors, Management and then only it is possible to get these facilities.

STERN ORDER TO FOLLOW ME

Parents want their children to follow their principles, footsteps and in some cases profession. They expect from their children that they should follow their parent's philosophy and guidelines as well as business acumen. Following some noble traits and adopting them is very good and fruitful.

A businessperson, a carpenter, or a Doctor/Lawyer/C.A. always expect from their children that they should follow the business/ occupation of their parents. If a person belongs to a particular caste/religion/family, he also desires that his children should also follow his father/ parents religion/family and they should not deviate from their father's/parents religions/family values or profession.

Similarly, the same logic is also applicable to any Organisation. After a long and continuous labour, an Entrepreneur comes in a position to establish an Organisation under which few people work for a specific mission. The Management expects from their employees/workers just like their children to follow the rules and regulations of the Company like their own family, which were laid down by the Organisation / head of the family.

The concerned Manager of any department expects from his subordinates that they should blindly follow his rules and regulations made by him or by the Organisation in Company's interest. They can never tolerate any of their juniors or subordinates, who disobey overlook, or ignore their instructions or orders. They desire that they should follow the instructions of their seniors.

FEAR OF PUNISHMENT

A student obeys his teacher because he knows that the teacher is fully authorised to give him punishment, which can harm his full academic year. A beggar sits on the roadside asking people for alms. Generally, people do not give them anything but in the same case, when the same beggar asks the same people to give money and the beggar holds a knife in his hands, people give him everything, which they have at that time without blinking an eyelid. This time people gave their possession to the beggar because they were afraid that the beggar could harm them.

In any Organisation, we all come across several examples in our daily /routine life at our workplace/Organisation. If junior staff wishes to give any suggestion to his seniors, the seniors ignore him. They do not bother whether the suggestions were in favour of the Company or not. They do not even want to listen to his problems related to work, colleagues etc. because the seniors know very well that this junior will not be able to harm them or create any problem for them. They do not even bother to answer his small queries.

There are several hierarchies within the workplace. People at all levels are answerable to their seniors or the high positioned boss. When a person talks to his juniors, subordinates, he behaves very roughly with them but when he talks to his seniors to whom he is answerable, he talks very politely in a very low tone or volume of voice. He gives all answers to his seniors. If the seniors calls him at an odd hour, the same person goes to meet him immediately, even, if he is busy with his work, and will wait for his senior till, he is free. This behaviour is totally different with their seniors and juniors. Their behaviour fluctuates according to the people they have to tackle with.

The question is why people have dual behaviour ? This is because they know that his junior/subordinate cannot harm them or their health but the seniors can do so. At the time of promotion / increment / appraisal, people became very loyal to their seniors but the same people became cruel to their subordinates. When the seniors/H.O.D. gets into a problem officially or personally, all concerned subordinates stand in a row to help them without thinking anything. On the contrary, when junior staff gets into a problem, not a single senior will come forward to help him, even if he is in serious trouble.

The reason is very clear that any person is ready to help his seniors because he knows that his boss is very powerful and is capable of punishing or harming his juniors who had not come forward at the time of his need. In this way, I conclude that people are very self-centred. They have no time to think about other people's needs. Secondly, it can be said that people help their senior due to fear of punishment and not due to affection or emotion or respect.

In several Organisations, the seniors' staff/Management does not even want to talk or meet their subordinates or junior staff. They do not want to listen to their demands or problems because they know that their juniors' are not in a position to harm them in any way. But on the other hand , the same person will be very loyal even to his boss's dog e.g., if the pet dog of his boss falls sick then such people will go specially to see their boss's dog. Such dual behaviour in people is very dangerous for the Organisation and its growth.

BAKO DHYANAM (KINGFISHER'S CONCENTRATION)

In some circumstances, the Management does not want to give a clear instruction to their subordinates. In most of cases, they give the instruction "**do the needful**" which in itself is very vague. The seniors always create communication gap with their juniors but expect right output from them as per their desire or as per their requirement. Without giving the right instruction, they expect right result from their juniors.

For Example: - We all have seen, Crane/ kingfisher at the bank of any river/ pond, watching a moving fish in the water. When they see the fish they, immediately catch the fish and eat it. The Bird never gives any instruction to the fish, just like the boss sitting in the office; only waits for the subordinates to commit some mistake. The boss never wants to give any right instruction to his subordinates so that they can discharge their duty in a systematic way. The boss waits for his subordinates to do wrong or commit mistake, so that he could get the chance to reprimand them. They never want to educate their subordinates with their experience or with the Company's rules and regulations, but they always expect the right result from them.

Similarly, a Traffic Police always stands in a hidden place of the busy road to get the chance to catch the public breaking traffic rules, so they can extract money from them as a fine.

MISTAKE DONE BY ANY SENIORS

In some cases, it is seen that when a subordinate worker, catches his seniors/Management red handed doing any anti-Organisation activity. Then in this situation, the Management/seniors expects from their juniors or subordinates that he should shut his mouth and should not disclose it to anybody. Some times, such seniors transfer the concerned subordinates' workers to some other place, so that nobody comes to know of their misdeed.

COMMUNICATION GAP

In most of the cases, it is seen or observed that there is a big / huge communication gap between the Management / Bosses /Instructions and the responsibility dischargers / subordinates. The Management / seniors think that the subordinates should know all the information without giving them any instruction verbally or written or through other medium. They expect a high degree of work level from their subordinates/ juniors/staff/ workers. They never try to give instruction properly or in an easy way, so that a common person can understand. Due to several reasons, the communication gap arises between the Management and the concerned workers to give unwanted obstacles to the subordinates, so that they cannot perform well in Company's interest. If the juniors will do, their duty well then there will be no chance for any senior to condemn their juniors. Seniors always try to find fault with their junior's work or knowledge.

DEVELOPMENT

It is in nature that a big tree like the Banyan, does not allow another tree to grow under it. The main tree gives protection to everyone but does not like even a small tree/plant to grow near it. Similarly, the Management does not like from their subordinates / juniors that they start another / similar business or enterprise apart from their main assignment. In another way, we can say that, the senior/superior or H.O.D. of any department/section does not like that, his juniors or subordinates overtake them ever.

It is in nature that any Boss, never wants to share his knowledge, i.e. (if they have any) with their employees or subordinates, so that the employees gain some knowledge. They always condemn them in such a way that the workers, inspite of having good education, skill or knowledge, cannot get a proper place or position in that organisation. The Head of the Department likes to talk to another departmental head and share his knowledge and work experience with him but not with his own subordinates. That is why it is very difficult for anyone to take their place or replace them. They do not want others to grow under them just like a big banyan tree does not allow another small tree to grow under it.

LOUDSPEAKER

I wish to present a very simple example, which every person observes in his daily life. The Management does not want to listen to anything from the workers side. They believe in only one-sided flow of information / messages. Every human being wants to suppress the voice of the weak and dominate them.

If we take the example of a loudspeaker as a senior or Management and the listeners as the workers of any workplace, then it is very clear that the voice of the loudspeaker tries to suppress the voice of the public in any gathering. Similarly, the seniors/Management also tries to suppress the voice of their juniors or subordinates. They like one-sided communication, i.e. from their side. They like to gag their juniors.

This type of behaviour also shows the weak points of the seniors, which they want to suppress because of their power/position or seniority. They always want to dominate their subordinates or juniors. Some seniors do not know anything about their assigned work or department or how to tackle the situational problem at the workplace. They are always in fear of their juniors asking questions, from them, which they have to answer. In this condition, I have used the logic of the loudspeaker being the management and suppressing the voice of the juniors by using their loud voice of power/position/money etc so that the junior's voice cannot be heard.

DIVIDE AND RULE

Most of the living things, plants; animals or human beings want to rule or want to dominate others by any means. No one wants to see the progress of others but every time they think how to rule or dominate others, their juniors, and colleagues etc. In the Organisation or at the workplace, one colleague does not want to see the progress or any type of beneficial things happening to his own colleagues, on any condition. One senior does not want to see the progress of either his colleagues or of his juniors. Most of them make hay while the sun shines.

If we analyse the qualities of Divide and Rules Policy in general, we will see that it has a lot of merits and demerits.

WHEN WE TAKE "Divide & Rule" IN A POSITIVE WAY

We have 24 hours in a day. We generally, divide 24 hours into different segments and then try to work accordingly to achieve the target assignment. For a smooth working schedule, we have fixed the time for breakfast, lunch, studies, walking, sleeping and other routine works, otherwise it will be very difficult for anyone to live and get any desired result or output.

In schools & Colleges, we find that there are different classes for different subjects at different time schedule. The Management has divided the whole schedule into different classes, so that it will be very easy and convenient for all the students to study properly. If we study all subjects in one class at one time, taught, by one teacher then it will be very difficult for the teacher to lecture and for the students to study the lesson carefully. Therefore, a segmented timetable is required for the different subjects at different times to be taken up by different teachers.

In another example, if we have to pull a long and heavy log of wood, it will be very difficult to pick it up in one piece but when we cut it in several small pieces then it will be very easy to pull or pick it up. Therefore, to do a very difficult work, we should divide the whole work equally.

In the Organisation and at the workplace, for a smooth working system, people usually maintain different files having different contents or work for different departments. Then only one can produce a good report to the higher Management in a specific period, thereby finishing the target.

There are several Managers working in any Organisation to deliver different types of responsibilities. One-person cannot give full productivity to any Organisation but the whole work has to be decentralised in Company's interest to more than one Manager or person. Then only it is possible to get the desired result. Here we have taken the meaning of divide and rule, in a positive sense, to get the smooth working environment at any workplace of the Organisation.

When one person works, keeping in his mind a positive sense of divide and rule, then it is sure that the concerned Manager or person will get recognition at his workplace by his seniors or Management. The person will get different types of benefits both in cash and kind by the Management, because in this situation the person will work in Company interest and not in his own interest. Here the worker will think first about his Organisation then about himself. He will get positive energy to complete the assigned work and will have full satisfaction by the completion of his work. Here the senior or Management, will, praise the efforts and dedication of the workers/juniors, in front of the higher Management. They feel proud by doing so. The seniors must always encourage their subordinates to do well.

WHEN WE TAKE Divide & Rule IN A NEGATIVE WAY

In general, people take divide & rule in a negative way owing to the Britisher's policy of dividing India. Divide & Rule Policy is famous for its negative character. No one wants to see others being powerful and strong. Even our own kin do not want to see our progress i.e. of their own brother or any of their family members. They shall always think about putting an obstacle in the progress of their own brother or their own family members. In a family, in certain circumstance, parents give more affection or sympathy to a particular son or a family member. The other members of their family shall start creating obstacles in their way, so that they cannot get their desired result or achievement.

In several cases, it has also been observed that local Politics is also responsible to give the Divide & Rule policy a different light.

The following factors are directly & indirectly responsible for the divide and rule policy.

(1) Self Ego & High Handedness

(2) Lack of Security

(3) Unsatisfied family life

(4) Sometimes in Company's Interest

1. Self Ego & High Handedness:

Self-ego and high handedness is the most important factor, which generates the divide and rule policy at the workplace of any Organisation. There are different types of managers or seniors in any Organisation who are very temperamental and who bloat with false ego and high handedness. Their tolerance power is very low. This is why they never want to see other colleagues or even juniors, getting progress. If they feel that a particular person has been selected for any betterment without their consultation, then they begin to make plans to pull their legs by backbiting and gossiping about their previous work done or mistakes to the higher Management or seniors or to the concerned persons who have selected their names for the benefit. Such seniors never do anything for anyone, they only think about themselves that they are the top boss of the Organisation and any important decision should be taken with their permission and consultation.

Whenever, such seniors get some good news about their juniors/ colleagues, they try to discredit the contribution of such persons in such a way that they do not get recognition or betterment by the higher Management.

2. Lack of Security:

Most of the persons whether seniors or juniors are insecure at their workplace due to several reasons. Some of the reasons can be expressed and some cannot but it is for sure that all the seniors and juniors feel insecure by their own lack of knowledge or by other's skill, hard work and dedication.

They always make themselves alert to the hard working colleagues. They sometimes depute some spy in the Organisation or at their workplace to know about the dedicated and honest people, which may some times pose problems or threaten their own freedom. Whenever they come across honest people or dedicated workers at their workplace, the concerned seniors, start finding out the secret behind them. They want to reason on what basis they are working in Company's interest. They then gradually try to decentralise their power, so that they cannot do their job properly, and nobody can raise a finger on their work or dedication.

3. Unsatisfied Family Life:

Sometimes, it has been seen that, work performance of any senior or junior is very much related with his family life. If their family life is very sound and secure then their performance as well as subordinates are very progressive. They get timely promotion, increment and different types of benefit in their Organisation by their seniors but in the same case if the family life of the seniors, incharge, is not very sound then it is sure that such seniors or incharge will never like to see their junior's progress.

Such seniors, when they find out or come to know about the good work of their subordinates or colleagues, try to decentralise their strength on which they are working, so that the concerned unsatisfied seniors could always boss them and point out their faults.

4. Sometimes in Company's Interest:

Management never likes any type of group or union to flourish in their Organisation or at their workplace. The Management will immediately like to decentralise the power or crush the power on which such a group or union is growing in their Organisation to destroy the harmony and the growth of the Company.

It has been seen that some workers or employees, who have not been transferred for a long time or who work at one place of posting for more than five to ten years, are very dangerous for the organisational growth as well as for the subordinates working under their guidance or supervision. They make a lobby out of the workforce or subordinates and give benefits to them, only to support and follow their instructions whether in favour of the Organisation or in favour of their supervisors. The person involved in such a group gradually starts ignoring the instructions of the Management and works according to his boss. At this critical situation, Management does not have any option except to decentralise the local authority and the persons involved for a smooth running environment in the Company's interest.

For example, we have seen in our school, that if some students were making noise in the class room and creating disturbance and chaos in maintaining the harmony and decorum, the class teacher, immediately splits the group of notorious students into several groups, So that, calm and harmony among the students could be maintained and restored.

Similarly, at any work place, or Organisation, the Management follows some strategy in Company's interest but in general cases, it does not happen in the Organisation. Here the seniors follow some strategy not for the interest of the Company but for their own interest. If any subordinate, juniors, or colleagues are not properly obeying their instructions or doing the job according to their liking or without informing or taking prior approval or consent from their concerned seniors, the concerned seniors immediately throw such subordinates out or dump such persons to an unknown place of posting, so that they do not create disturbance in the implementation of their strategy or working system. They are totally shunned.

In practical cases, the honest, dedicated, labourious, emotional workers and those who follow company's norms are the main target of the corrupt and dishonest managers working in any Organisation. In Present days, most of the managers, seniors working in the higher position in any Organisation are found to be corrupt. They use their clout, power and the amenities in their own interest. They try to misuse the Company's funds in different ways. At this situation, if there are some innocent and honest workers working in their department, the seniors feel very uncomfortable with such workers, so they immediately try to transfer them to other departments or to a far off place so that they do not create any problems in misusing their powers and position.

TOPI TRANSFER / TRANSFERRING RESPONSIBILITY

Topi transfer system is very popular for any Organisational working system. Most of the people want to do liaison work in the Organisation, to escape from any responsibilities. Here no one is directly involved in any work because there is less writing job and less accountability for the job. If the higher Management gives an order to its subordinates related to an assignment, the concerned person or seniors just pass on the same order to their subordinates or the person next in the hierarchy and get themselves free from the said responsibility. The next person follows the same practice as his senior and ultimately the workload comes to the lower personnel. If the work is done well, the credit goes to the higher Management but if the result of that work is adverse, then the workers at the lower rung get punishment by the higher Management either for negligence or for lack of accountability.

This type of activity does not work for any Organisation. Firstly, in the real sense, the Management does not like such persons, who generally transfer their responsibility to others. Sometimes such people prove very dangerous for the Organisation because such workers live only for themselves. Such people are very dishonest, selfish and ruthiess.

I AM THE SENIOR; YOU ARE NOT:

It is an irony that nobody leads a complete life. There is something lacking in every ones life, no matter how rich and educated one may be.

God is great; HE never gives everything to any one person.

If one has a good pay package, position and prestige, in the organisation or at the workplace then he might be unsatisfied with his own family life. He may be alcoholic or have disobedient children or other serious problems in his life. Sometimes, some people get a good position in their organisation based on their experience, good luck or personal relationship with the employer. He may be working in a very good department but it is also possible that his subordinates are not happy with his behaviour or he might be a failure in his administration.

It has been observed that the concerned seniors/head of the department have a high or bloated ego which may be due to frustration / unsatisfaction or other things. Such seniors do not like to hear anything from their subordinates on any topic or official problems. They think that they are right and whatever they have said is final. Nobody has the right to challenge or create any obstacle in their decision. Such seniors believe that they are the main authority or the management of the organisation and take the decisions on an impulse without thinking, planning or thinking about its affects. Such seniors commit a lot of mistakes but nobody raises their voice against them because the fate of subordinates or juniors is attached with their whims. Therefore, no one wants to take the risk to annoy them. So the seniors take advantage of their weakness or vulnerability.

TO HARASS THE SUBORDINATES

At the workplace, the workers are working together, so everyone knows the merits and demerits of each other. But it is human nature that after seeing the mistakes of others, one may or may not keep his mouth shut or do not take advantage of other's mistake. Most of the workers are very happy to see others' mistakes and they want to take advantage of their mistake without fail. It depends upon the nature of the workers. It varies from person to person.

In general, the seniors or the management always try to know the weaknesses of their subordinates, so that they could impose their authority upon them. Most of the seniors fall in the same category who feel happy to harass their subordinates. They get sadistic pleasure.

❖❖❖

CHAPTER 7

WORKERS AND THEIR BEHAVIOUR

In this chapter I have tried to explain the behaviour of workers or employees working in any Organisation. The behaviour of workers change according to the situation of the workplace. How and why their behaviour changes on any situation at the workplace, how a worker reacts, how they perceive and take the assigned responsibility or how they adjust themselves with the seniors on different situations and also how a worker adjusts himself/herself on adverse situations.

I have tried to explain about the behaviour of the workers very simply with the help of various examples which everyone comes across in their day to day life, so that it could be easy to understand the real happening at the workplace.

Here I would like to explain some points related to the behaviour of the workers

DIVERSION OF ATTENTION

In every Organisation, there are some people who neither have confidence on their assigned work nor do they have any skill or education for such work, which they have to complete. In the initial period, such people are not interested to complete the work, as well as they do not want other's work to be completed. If they come to know that their assigned work is incomplete and the other people work is complete then there may be problem for them because the concerned seniors may question them and, it will also affect their progress, position and credibility.

At this situation, such people try to deviate the mind or attention of their concerned seniors/ H.O.D, so that the concerned seniors are unable to point out any fault from their assigned work, by gossiping or complaining about other colleagues. They try to break the unity of seniors/

juniors / colleagues, so that they do not gossip at a common place on a particular topic about such people. They try to project their best image, efforts to prove only in front of their concerned seniors, by misleading them that most of the persons of the Organisation are misusing the assets, power, and money in their own favour and they are the only persons who can look after the Company's interest or welfare.

Thus, the attention of the concerned senior deviates towards such persons and their faith gradually increases for the time being in comparison to their other colleagues.

Once the person conquers the faith of his seniors, then he starts misusing the name of the seniors, funds and assets of the Company because he knows very well that any complaint against him would not be registered by the seniors because all of the seniors are hypnotised by his sweet talk for the time being. However, this is short lived as one day the seniors would know his reality.

EVERYONE WANTS TO DO SUPERVISORY / LIAISON WORK

In general, it has been observed that most of the people work jointly at the workplace for a common goal. They do not want to involve themselves fully in all the work. They do not want to take any responsibility in writing. They generally try to avoid giving any information in writing, which they try to substitute, by giving oral instruction because they may be caught. They want to involve themselves in such work or take up such responsibility in which there is no need of written presentation or written instruction.

These people are always found around the boss. If the boss stays in the office for late hours, then such people also stay late in the office, whether they are required in the office for late working hours or not. They always keep all the information about the movement of their boss, when their boss is supposed to leave the office, etc. Such people would always be present near the senior even very late in the night.

At such situation, their seniors think that these people are very labourious and dedicated workers of the Organisation. They always try to gather the right and accurate information of most of the departmental work along with the latest development if any in the concerned department or division of the Organisation.

This type of person wants to become the yes-man of his senior. He may take the responsibility from the higher Management directly and immediately forward the same instruction to the junior workers. As he has no knowledge about the assigned work, he cannot distinguish between right and wrong. It is possible that such a supervisor would also pass on the information to the higher Management without verifying it. Such workers do not have self-confidence. They are always afraid of other workers. They think that their colleagues are jealous of them. Their own junior workers will never like such seniors. The subordinates do not have any faith in them.

In other words, it can be said that the seniors / Management just for a short while and not for a long time like such kind of people. These people are very dangerous for the Organisation. The Management should always keep themselves away from such kind of people in the Company's interest.

TO TAKE CREDIT HIMSELF & DISCREDIT THE JUNIORS

It is human nature that we love to hear our own praise. We usually like such people who appreciate us. People never like harsh words, statements given by any one, which is against their liking. People do not like to be discredited by anyone.

In any Organisation, there are some workers, who are very popular in the Organisation due their hard labour, dedication, knowledge, skill, quality of work. Inspite of having all good qualities they do not get promotion, increment or other benefits or they do not get the credit for their efforts, which they have done, in the Company's interest. They are the real workers of the Organisation on which the growth of the Company depends. Every worker of the Organisation is fully aware with the real facts but during the time of assessment towards the individual contribution towards the Company's interest, these dedicated workers are totally ignored. Truth or true workers are very rarely rewarded.

If the higher Management desires a report from the department and seeks the name of the workers or the concerned persons who had contributed towards the assigned work due to which it could be completed successfully, the concerned Head of the department, without thinking anything, forwards the name of the workers who are his sycophants and takes whole credit himself. Even the seniors hesitate to take the names of their own subordinates who are true and sincere workers in front of the higher Management. However, they never hesitate in taking credit thereby ignoring the true workers and crushing their morale.

It can be explained in another way. In a department, the head of the department usually gives instruction to his subordinates or juniors to complete a particular job in a particular way and in a specific period. The concerned workers work with their best of efforts, energy to complete the work on time to give good result to their head of the department. The concerned head or in charge, forwards the report to the higher Management putting his name and signature as if he had prepared that report. He never writes the names of his juniors or subordinates.

He does not like to disclose their names or to say that the subordinates had done a fantastic job and because of their sincere efforts this tough task could be completed and they be given promotion or incentives. (However, if they do some wrong then the H.O.D. would discredit his subordinates immediately without hesitation.)

When we get credit, we get positive energy in our body while discredit gives us negative energy. Everybody wants positive energy to boost up his or her morale. It means whenever we appreciate anyone for their good work, behaviour, efforts, thinking, achievements etc, a positive energy automatically generates in their body as well as in their mind. By appreciating others, we can easily get a good result on any assigned project before the scheduled time.

For example, when an artist plays his/her instruments/ or gives his/her performance on the stage. He/She expects from the audience good cheers and positive response, which gives positive energy to the artist. If the audience will not clap after his/her performance, it will be very difficult for him/her to perform well. He/She cannot enjoy playing and cannot entertain the audience. I mean to say that appreciation and credit is very much required for any human being to give a good result. It is a part and parcel of positivity, productivity and performance.

In any Organisation, a person involved in any assigned work also expects from his respective seniors that they should give credit to his job done well. If any senior can give discredit to the workers for their work done then it is their responsibility to give credit to the workers for their good work. No one else would give them credit except the person responsible under whom they are working.

Credit gives recognition to the workers and this helps them at the time of their promotion and increment. At the same time discredit gives, a bad name and this would create a problem at the time of their promotion, increment or other benefits. However, practically it has been observed that no one in the Organisation wants to give credit to other persons. They always try to get all the credit themselves on behalf of the subordinates but would discredit their juniors, subordinates, workers without sharing it.

That is why most of the seniors give vague instructions to their juniors/subordinates. They do not want to give a clear-cut instruction to them, so that they cannot do their job in a good manner.

The Management /H.O.D. very well know that if they would give clear instructions to their subordinates/juniors for any assigned work, they think their subordinates would do the job correctly, which somehow they do not want. Mostly the seniors, Management /H.O.D. do not want to give the right information or right instruction to workers for the assigned job. They very well know the calibre of their subordinates/juniors/colleagues/ staff. They know that if they would give the right instruction/information, then their juniors would do their assigned job easily and they would not be able to discredit or disqualify them for being un-skilled and illiterate. They would not be able to harass them due to their non-performance and would not get the chance to abuse them for their unproductivity.

Inspite of the hurdles, if their staff, subordinate do their job in a good way in the interest of the Organisation then the seniors/Management/instructor, change their views and pass on the message immediately to the higher Management that they have done the job in a good manner, only due the right instruction of the concerned, seniors towards the particular job.

It means both ways they want to take credit for their junior's achievement. As per my views, it will give a wrong impression on the innocent mind of the junior staff and their family members regarding the seniors and the management.

They should never do such activities and they should always give due respect and credit to their junior staff. This would boost their morale and would give them high level of enthusiasm, confidence etc.

If we would give credit to the right persons for their job, they would never raise their voice against the Organisation or the Management or any senior or their policies. Such gesture would boost up the Company financially as well as the brand name and image.

WHO WANTS TO WORK ?

It is human nature that nobody wants to work, if the work is not compulsory. People work only to earn money, so that they can survive in this society. If they will not work, and will not get money, then it will be very difficult for them to survive. It means need compels them to work and earn money. A beggar stands whole day in the Sun because his needs compel him to stand in the Sun to get money, so, that his daily needs can be taken care of.

A student has to study, at home and in school because he has the fear in his mind that if he does not study properly or does not complete the assigned task, then the teacher would punish him. That is why his feeling of fear compels him to study hard and complete his homework otherwise he would not take his studies seriously.

If a person knows that he can live without eating or drinking anything then he would never eat or drink. However it is not possible, to stay alive without eating and drinking. It means, there is fear in our mind, which compels us to do work according to our needs. There is a fear in our mind that if we do not worship God or anger him somehow, He would punish us and we would get into unwanted trouble.

We mostly respect those persons, whom we know are more powerful than we are and if we do not respect them, probably they can punish or harass us. At the same time, if we know that, a particular person cannot give us any trouble or is harmless; we would not respect him or would not take him seriously.

In any Organisation, whenever we come across a senior, we immediately wish him or extend him our due courtesy because we know that showing disrespect to him would invite his anger and he may harass us. Similarly, in most of the cases, workers do not want to work or finish their assigned job within the scheduled time frame and if they are working, it is only because they have hidden fear that if they do not work, they may get punishment or face harassment. Their names would not be forwarded for promotion, increment or other benefits. Their names may be deleted from the good books of the seniors. Therefore, there are so many factors owing to which a person has to work harder.

Apart from the above, the Management expects from their employees that they should do their job very carefully and sincerely. They should devote all their efforts to the assigned job and perform their duty with the best of their efforts. There should not be a single mistake in their work. As several important decisions, depend upon the output of their workers. Therefore, if their workers perform poorly, the higher Management would not be able to forward a favourable and qualitative result to their top Management and the growth of the Company would automatically be affected.

It means, if we depend upon the Organisation then the Management also depends upon the workers and their work performance. If they perform poorly, the ultimate result of the Company would be affected. However, most of the workers do not want to work but due to unavoidable circumstance, they have to do their duty.

At this situation, the Management and the workers, both of them should think over this issue together, jointly. They should make joint efforts and should work hard and help each other, so that the growth of the Company should not be affected at any cost. The workers should place their grievances, problems in Company's interest (if any) in front of the Management. The Management should express their limitations and problems in front of the employees clearly, so that both of them should understand each other's problems, and there would be no misunderstanding.

If they solve their problems or grievances mutually, then it is sure that the growth of the Company would be manifold and no one can stop them from achieving the highest position in the market.

If a worker says that he does not want to work then the Management should take it positively and try to understand his feelings and problems, which should be solved at the earliest by the Management.

PYRAMID (UPWARD & DOWNWARD GROWTH)

Being human beings we know that the head of the family frames the rules and regulations of the family along with the do's and don'ts, teaches discipline, co-operation, how to respect and treat the elders in the interest of the family. The growth or development of such a family totally depends upon the strategy made by the head of the family. If the head of the family makes strategy for the family development but if the members do not respect or take it seriously and do not implement them in their life, then the development will be hampered. It means that the development of a family totally depends upon the co-operation, sincerity, dedication, decision-making capacity and honesty of the members.

For example, a car can run smoothly, only when all its four wheels and engine are in good co-ordination and aligned. If the engine is smooth but they do not co-ordinate with the wheels, then it is possible that the car will not move at all. It means the whole load / weight of the car is not divided on the four wheels but it is co-related with the engine as well. At this situation, if the car moves, then the engine will consume more fuel and the carburettor as well as the engine may be damaged.

Similarly, when we co-relate this car with the Organisational Head and its four wheels with their employees, we find that both are very much similar. Here the car is the Organisation, which depends upon its four wheels which are the employees. When the engine of the car, like the head of the Organisation pulls the load of the whole vehicle, it will run very smoothly subject to the conditions of its four wheels. It means for the continuous growth and smooth running of the Organisation hand the employees like the four wheels of the car should be tuned and lubricated properly, to attain the Organisational goal. Then only the growth of the Organisation will increase and the load upon the head or the management can be automatically lessened.

All the employees should utilise their total energy to co-operate with the head of the Organisation to get the desired result. No one should think that a single employee has no strength in the Organisation because each worker is very important for the Organisation. For Example, an ocean or a sea is a combination of drops of water accumulated together over a long period of time. The river grows bit by bit by drops of water and flows into the sea. Therefore, each single drop of water has the strength to make the river overflow to meet the sea. Similarly, each employee should give his full contribution to the Organisation to make the Company prosperous and successful. They should obey the rules and regulations laid down by the Management in Company's interest. They should all work hard and help each other to protect the Company from any mishap, so that the Company does not have to face loss. When all the employees will contribute sincerely, then the head of the Organisation will definitely be proud of his employees and the company will grow day by day.

In these circumstances, the burden of the Organisation will be distributed evenly among all the employees and the head of the Organisation will experience renewed strength and the Organisation will be able to touch the sky both financially and reputation wise. In such Organisation all the staff are free to take decisions on behalf of the Company. They are authorised to use their common sense in Company's interest. They do not depend upon any instruction, which comes from the top Management. However, the power is delegated to all the capable authorities, so that the load of decision-making process is very less on the head of the Organisation and the Organisation runs very smoothly, (where decision-making process is de-centralised)

However, it has been observed in most of the Organisations that the decision making power is centralised. No one is allowed to take any decision except on the day-to-day routine work related decision. As a result the inner strength or morale of the concerned worker/ staff becomes very less. They gradually lose their self-confidence. They are always in fear of some mishap or losing their goal. If they have to take any decision, they have to first forward their letter to the top Management and ask them what they should do. Thus, the load of the Organisation, which is centralised on one person, may decrease or increase. At such a situation, people do not take their job seriously, as they are not directly responsible for any assigned job or its result.

In this way when each worker begins to transfer his job responsibility to other person and the other person delegates it to other person, then at last all the burden of the Organisation comes upon the head of the Organisation. The top Management would be responsible for any mishap and one day would come when the Organisation would start getting loss. It is possible that a prestigious Company would shut down owing to its faulty system and wrong rules and regulations.

CARELESSNESS / OVER LOOKED

Need generates killer instinct in human beings to do some extraordinary work. If we do not eat or drink anything, we may die very shortly. If we do not feel hungry, thirsty, we definitely will not try to work or solve our basic needs or problems and our energy level will gradually stagnate and start decreasing. In an Organisation, when a person is appointed on a temporary basis, he will start working, before the office hours. He will never ask for any leave, will be eager to work even on holidays and will stay in the office without complaining to anyone. Even if the senior asks him to do a personal favour, he will never give any lame excuse. He will attend to the assigned job willingly and will successfully complete them. He will wish his seniors, no matter how many times he meets them.

He will stand on one leg to listen to the order and instructions of his seniors. However as soon as the same person would get confirmation of his job, his attitude, behaviour, sincerity would suddenly change. This is because his job is now permanent. It means, the Management cannot terminate his job without any valid reason. No one can harass him knowingly or un-knowingly with or without reason.

The same worker starts coming late to the office and if any one objects, he will create a scene and argue with his seniors. It means as soon as the basic need of any person is fully or partially fulfilled, the person becomes lazy and lethargic. Based on this observation, it has been seen that the following factors are responsible for this type of attitude to develop in human beings.

(1) Un-skilled workers

(2) Un-healthy Family background/Unsound Family background

(3) Lack of Education

(4) Limited Aim in life

1. Un-Skilled Workers:

Being un- skilled is the main reason of carelessness. If a worker is not properly educated or trained, he may feel that he knows everything and become careless. He will ignore the assigned work and will not take it seriously. Since such workers are not properly educated, therefore, they cannot be emotionally attached with their work. He will work just to give service or just to protect his job. Such a type of worker is very dangerous for the Organisation. Sometimes, a minor mistake or a minor ignorance may incur a huge loss to the Organisation worth crores. Unfortunately, if such a worker becomes the head of any department, then he may take abrupt or arbitrary decisions on any serious or important situation without thinking of its pros and cons or of the brand image of the company.

He would hardly give any promotion or increment to his subordinates. In general, it has been observed that a common worker tries to escape from the clutch of such a careless Manager because everyone knows that such a manager can give one-sided decisions whether it is suitable or not. No one tries to talk to such people because they know that such a manager, can embarrass his colleagues or subordinates any time, so everyone tries to ignore such people. Such a Manager probably has less ego problems and he does not take it otherwise. He listens to every query but will take revenge whenever he will get the opportunity.

Limited Aim:

When a person is not very educated or not trained properly as per the job requirement, then he may suffer from inferiority complex. He always worries about his survival and how his job can be saved. How can he protect himself etc. He probably knows very well about his market value. He knows that if he will leave the present job, then there may be problem for his family and their survival. He may have a joint or a nuclear family, but may be very backward or uneducated. He may not be able to equip his family with all the modern gadgets, due to the lack of funds or due to poor financial position. He may know his limitation as up to what extent he can spend. He may think God will solve all his financial problems. In a way, such workers gradually start deviating from their main objective or their assigned work.

They live only for the present and not for the future. Thus, the health of such people gradually starts deteriorating. They became so careless about their work at the work place that they do not think even about their own life as well as of their own family members. Due to their carelessness, they cannot perform well at their work place, so their manager/office in charge, also do not like them. They think that it would be better if such a manager takes a transfer to another department or leaves the present Organisation.

The level of enthusiasm, attention to the assigned work, co-ordination with the colleagues becomes very poor, so the Management does not like them. Such workers, if working in a Managerial position would never promote their juniors or subordinates. They would always try to convince their juniors that the company they are working in is not in a good shape and unproductive. Their future is not bright in this Organisation. All the seniors are useless (according to him), and he is the only person who was punished by the seniors without any proper reason. They can never take any positive decision in favour of the Company.

2. Unsound Family Background:

Apart from the other reasons, "Family Background" is one of the main reasons, which plays a role in driving the worker towards carelessness or vice versa. Most of the people, who come from poor family backgrounds, are generally good in work and are very sincere in their job, because they need money to survive, so they do their work very carefully to avoid any mistake. At the same time, when a person comes from a privileged background or family, or from a good financial background, they may not be very sincere towards their assigned job because they know very well that they are doing this job just to engage themselves or just to pass time.

If they leave the present job, they would not have any survival problem. Thus, their attitude is different. They do not take interest in their work inspite of having good knowledge of the work assigned because they do not take their job very seriously. They think that their family members are financially sound and well off, so such persons generally are found to be moody or careless at their work or workplace.

However, such people are mostly big hearted and have no objection in giving promotion or increment to their subordinates/workers, working under them. Such people sometimes take very small things or trivial matters seriously. They may order punishment to their juniors on minor mistakes. Such persons are very careless but they discharge their duties very promptly and as they are financially sound, they do not hesitate to give promotion, increment to their subordinates or workers working under their supervision.

As they have a good family background and their public relationship is very good, they have good contacts and may contact prominent personalities of the society. So the Organisation as well as the people are very much obliged by them. One thing more as per the observation, it has been seen that such persons, have no fear of their job, and are very moody. They can leave the job on a very small matter or issue, if hurt. They cannot tolerate humiliation, torture or negligence. They do not work to support their family. This type of people do not take their work seriously. They know their market value and they would get a better paying job whenever they wish.

The organisation has to face several hidden problems with the Govt.. norms, rules and regulations, so they need people with good Govt. contacts, so at this situation, they generally appoint people who have recently retired from the Govt. Organisation and whose personal rapport could be utilised in the Company. Sometimes, they also oblige some Govt. officials by appointing them or their relatives in junior or higher positions. The persons who are appointed on higher position after their retirement generally do not take much interest in the Organisation dealings because they are at such a stage in their family life when their responsibilities are over. They have enough money for their future. However, sometimes the persons appointed to oblige some of the Govt. Officials on not a very high position, are generally found to work very seriously, as they need to take care of their family. They are very hard working and sincere.

The attitude varies from person to person. It does not apply to all the people. Apart from the Organisation, there are several examples in our general life. A student whose father is very rich and avails of all the luxuries provided by his parents is found to be very poor in studies most of the time. Such students do not study seriously. They are also very careless and they do not respect anyone. As a result, such students never complete their education because they have got everything in life and they know that they would never get into financial problems. They are more or less aimless. They know that they have enough money and property to take care of their expenses.

Do not get Happy to see other's Happiness:

People are not sad with their own problems but are so by seeing others happy. At the workplace, it is not possible, that all the workers will get promotion or incentives / increments equally at the same time. God has given us five fingers in our hands but their size is different from each other. God has created human beings, but all look different and have different size, colours, qualities, looks and characteristics etc. They are all different in each respect both physically and mentally.

In a classroom, there are many students studying together but only one student stands first. All the students should learn from him. We should develop ourselves in such a way that our dream and requirements are realised. At the workplace, it has been seen that if one person is promoted or gets some increment, the other colleagues working in the same department get jealous of him. They do not try to understand that on what ground the Company has given him promotion or increment. What type of quality they have found in him or what type of work or attitude is needed for getting promotion/increments.

For Example, if a worker gets a reward for some extraordinary contribution, we as well as other people / workers should also learn from him and should take inspiration from his innovative method and fresh approach.

We start getting negative thoughts to see other's achievement, success and we start reasoning that we are better from him or we are more capable and energetic but could not achieve anything great. At this situation when we start getting jealous of him, our inner force, self confidence, dedication, loyalty and devotion towards the Organisation starts decreasing rapidly till we stop our negative thoughts. Apart from the other drawbacks, our health and morale also starts decreasing and ultimately it is, we who have to suffer due to jealous or negative feelings. There are several factors, which affect the individual to be envious of his colleagues.

(1) Immaturity or lack of experience
(2) Lack of Education
(3) Frustration
(4) Being Un-skilled
(5) High -Expectations.

Sometimes, when a person is not mature as per his age, has no length of service, or experience, cannot bear to see the achievement of other people. When a worker gets achievement his colleagues get jealous of him and plan to embarrass or demoralise him in front of other colleagues. They try to create obstacle in his progress. Sometimes, they hide the important files, so that he has to face his boss's ire. They also give false reports about such workers to their respective seniors, only to pull him down. They want to see him down somehow. However sooner or later they have to repent for their action.

3. Lack of Education:

Education plays a very important role in shaping a human being's life. The behaviour of an educated person is different from un-educated/semi educated person. An educated person has more knowledge, and sense of propriety. They know how to present a particular thing to the management and when. They never disrespect others. They always try to boost up the morale of weak people. They are comparatively less jealous. If anyone is promoted or gets enhancement, in the same department, such people get happy to see their progress. As they know that, no one can beat them and their knowledge. They understand that the company had given enhancement to some of its workers due to some of their extra work or exemplary qualities and after sometime or in due course; they would also get enhancement along with the rest of their colleagues and there is no need to worry about the same.

At the same time, if the people are not qualified, skilled or are uneducated and not familiar with the Organisation systems, they cannot tolerate the progress of other people. They cannot see any one bypass them or get higher position than them. Management expects from their workers/ employees that all the employees of their Organisation should live like a family. They should not pull each other's legs or else they will not be able to come out from the problems or mess. Let the people, working in the higher position; learn from the example of successful people. Everyone should adopt their strategy, which can take people to higher positions. They should learn something extra than the routine job. They should update themselves with current knowledge and should also develop their skill as per the present requirement of the Organisation.

Frustration:

Everybody aspires to sit on the revolving chair, give dictation to his steno in his air-conditioned office chamber. They also want to be a class -I officer or a popular personality in the Country. One cannot get the desired position without working hard. Because all of these need hard labour and lots of perseverance. Every person has his own destiny and all actions and reactions are predestined. Along with all the required efforts, the fate of the concerned worker is also responsible for his success or failure but believing in destiny is quite relative. Some people rely only on their work or labour which we call Karma.

Therefore, in any Organisation, there are several workers, working at different levels with different responsibilities, who had worked hard in the past but they did not get their due success or their desired goal. If the workers, who were inferior to them, were promoted or highlighted by the Management, then they get frustrated or go into depression. Many times, both are found working in the same department/section but one was promoted but another was not though both are labourious, dedicated and honest. Destiny plays a role in shaping ones life.

At this situation, knowingly or unknowingly workers are found to be jealous of other workers, who got promotion. Their willpower, confidence and dedication as well as faith towards the Organisation gradually tends to decrease. This situation will not last for a long time, as it is a passing phase. This is natural truth and no one can stop one from thinking, although we all are human beings.

Inspite of several causes, which lead to frustration, the Management does not like their workers being differentiated or discriminated. The management does not tolerate this attitude of the seniors. They try to sort out these problems by transferring such people to some other place or department. At this situation, it is most likely that seniors might leave the job to avoid giving an explanation. In some cases workers get frustrated because, inspite of having all the qualities they never because, get a proper platform or an opportunity to show case their talent or prove their worth.

Lack of Opportunity:

Not everybody is lucky to get the right opportunity and avail of it to be successful. In our daily life, many people buy lottery tickets but only one-person gets the first and the highest prize. In the Organisation, all the workers give their best of efforts to complete their assigned work. In several cases, some staff are found to be working in the same post for many years without getting any promotion or recognition. When a person does not get promotion / increment or appreciation against their work done, while their colleagues get it then the workers get frustrated by the lack of opportunity. They never got to work independently, so they could not prove themselves to the concerned Officers. This is why such workers, become sad and jealous. When they see others getting promotion and other benefits, while they sit on the fence waiting for the day when they would reap the benefit.

In the Entertainment field, there are a lot of talented people who never get an opportunity to prove themselves. There are several people, who struggle for several years to become an Actor, Singer, Music Director, Writer but due to lack of proper platform or an opportunity, they get frustrated. It is not that they lack talent. At such a situation, one cannot tolerate other's recognition name and fame. In this field, people are so jealous of each other that everyone tries to pull the legs of each other. This is why it is very difficult to get success in this field. Everyday lots of artists/ talented people come to Mumbai with stars in their eyes to become famous but a minuscule few get name, fame and recognition.

It is very rare for strugglers to get the opportunity to meet the right person at the right time, who give them an opportunity to showcase their talent in their field. In our Country, there are several talented singers who can sing better than the famous or established singers can, but they did not get the right opportunity to sing. In the film line, famous actors and singers are so jealous that they never support or boost any fresher and they do not even want to take their names in front of others. First of all the Producers/Directors utilise the new comer's voice to sing as a dummy singer before the final take of the Original singers. The newcomer knows very well that his/her voice will not be used but in some cases, dummy singers too have become famous when the famous singer failed to turn up or his/her voice was liked by the producer or suited the actor/ actress.

There are many examples of the highhandedness of the seniors at the workplace. In a reputed Organisation, there were many heads in the Organisation. In a particular department, the Head did not want to leave the position or did not want to give opportunity to the subordinates, so that he could explore their capabilities. The subordinates possessed all the qualities, which are required for a H.O.D. to run the department smoothly. One day suddenly, due to some unavoidable circumstance, the Head was called by the higher Management and asked to leave the Organisation. No one was aware of the reason why the Management asked him to leave the Organisation but it was an Order, which had to be honoured at any cost.

Organisation is a sacred place, which cannot wait for any one or for any work. The working of the Organisation should not be hampered due to a single person's impropriety. The Management will give chance or opportunity to the next person of the same department to run the department. The second man gets the God given opportunity and he starts working more diligently than the previous head. The higher management recognises his talent, likes his working and his approach thereby appreciating him.

WORK PRESENTATION

A good work presentation can make or mar a product. It can make it a hit or a flop in the market. Without proper presentation, it is very difficult to sell a product in the market. When a person comes for an interview, the interviewer asks several questions to the candidate, which she/he has to answer. The candidate, apart from giving the required answer to the raised questions, presents his knowledge, skill, work experiences, ability and his/her expertise in such a way that the interview board gets highly impressed and selects him/her for the job.

In the vegetable market, we see that a vendor advertises his product i.e. the vegetables to the customers in such a way that they can get the best bargain and product from him. No one can beat the quality of his or her vegetables. They are the only ones who provide fresh vegetables to the customers. If anyone will purchase vegetables from any other stall, it may not be as good and fresh as his vegetables.

When a person goes to attend a party, the concerned person, dresses up immaculately, so that he gets maximum attention or he may dress up in such a unique way that people would remember him for his dressing sense or his personal style or for making his own style statement.

A beggar begs on the roadside/temple/ where people come and go frequently. The beggar sells his /her poor status by making his voice pathetic or sings a sad song, which easily touches the heart of the common people. If his voice is sentimental, and melodious to the ear, the beggar will definitely get more money and alms from the public. It means his work presentation (begging) is correct as per the situation and demand. If the beggar starts begging in an irritating voice, then no one will give him money or anything else against his efforts. It means he is not able to present his feelings to the public or advertise himself properly.

AT THE TIME OF CONVERSATION

At the time of conversation with a friend, family members, office colleagues, seniors or any unknown person, we should always be careful about the topics on which we are going to discuss. We should listen very carefully to the questions raised by the opposite side. We should answer them clearly or if we do not know a particular answer, we should clearly say that we do not know the right answer, immediately. Apart from this, we should not talk on politics or a vulgar topic at the time of talking and we should sit straight in the right posture.

At the time of conversation, we should not speak in a loud voice and our pronunciation should be clear. We should not eat or chew anything during the conversation so that our voice would be clear and audible to the listener. When a worker will adopt the above factors during the conversation his personality will improve and will be noted by the management as well as other colleagues. All the co-workers, colleagues, seniors and H.O.D., will start appreciating him. This is also one of the important factors of presentation.

BEING RESPONSIBLE / FEELING OF RESPONSIBILITIES

The feeling of being responsible plays a very crucial role in a human being. In general, life, when a person seems to deviate from his motto or goal, does not care for his parents or family members, the parents want to marry off their son, so that they could fulfil their responsibility. When a person sits in the back seat of a vehicle, he becomes very carefree. He does not want to know about the road/traffic rules and the ongoing problem on the road but on the other hand, when the same person sits on the driver's seat, the situation becomes different and the person becomes very alert, serious and responsible. He obeys traffic rules and drives the vehicle very carefully. He does not waste his time talking uselessly. He tries to reach the destination in a fixed time safely.

In schools, we see that mostly the teachers give chance to the naughty students to become the class Monitors. As soon as such students take the charge of being the Monitor, the same student becomes very serious in minding the class and maintaining discipline. This feeling comes due to being responsible, to maintain peace in the class. The feeling of responsibility gives the right direction and meaning in life, of being disciplined which can benefit all.

Similarly, at the workplace, the feeling of responsibility is necessary for both the concerned persons/workers as well as for the Organisation where we work. Without having the feelings of responsibility, a worker cannot discharge his duties properly. Management also expects from their employees that they should love their work as well as their Organisation. They expect that the workers should do their work/ discharge their duties/ responsibilities with a feeling that they are doing their own work and discharging their responsibilities for their own sake. Then only it is possible that they can conquer the faith of the Organisation or the Management. Those workers who are very labourious but they lack being responsible are not liked by the management because at the end of the day we are responsible for all the deeds or misdeeds whether personal or professional.

Worker Stagnation:

God has created each and everything and to maintain its freshness it should be in motion. Water of a running river is fresher than the water of a pond, due to its movement. If we keep water in a bucket for a long time without using it, the water may turn turbid and get infested with small insects or bacteria, due to its non-movement or stagnation. At such situation, it would be better to remove the water from the bucket because such water would be harmful for the health of all the living beings. This is the reason, people clean the water tanks of their house from time to time to rid it of the bacteria or dirt which would be harmful for the persons living in that house.

The condition of water in a pond, bucket or tank is very much similar with the workers working at the workplace of any organisation. If a worker is working in the company for a long time without having any promotion or increment or any kind of betterment, his dedication or the level of discharging the assigned work, will deteriorate. The person becomes very irritating. His tolerance power decreases and he begins to feel frustrated and stagnated in that company where he has spent the valuable period of his life. His behaviour changes and he tries gradually to skip his responsibilities.

At such situation the workers should update themselves with the required knowledge in such a way that they can work along with the newcomers /newly appointed workers. They should upgrade their knowledge by taking further additional courses as per the market requirement.

If their upgradation is not possible due to any reason then they should leave the organisation for better options or for greener pastures. The frustrated and stagnated workers are very dangerous for the organisation or for their own family. The workers should change themselves if they have to survive in the market.

Whispering/Back Biting

When a person feels that, he and his service are not secure or he is not getting adequate response from the local Management. His work is not recognised or appreciated by the seniors and the immediate seniors give more importance to other colleague's work in the workplace or department. The workers think that they might be transferred somewhere else or their service might not be required by the Management in the coming future. These circumstances, give birth to the backbiters in the Organisation.

The following factors are responsible for backbiting at the workplace:

(1) Low Confidence of Management on the workforce.

(2) Job insecurity

(3) Open Mind of the Management.

(4) Listen to the problems of each person.

(5) Too many meetings with some selected persons.

TYPE OF WORKERS

There are different types of workers, working at the workplace of any organisation. I have tried to categorise them as:

(1) Hard working Workers and who are willing to work

(2) Workers who do not want to work / Lazy workers

(3) Workers who do not let others work / Jealous workers

(4) One who watches silently

(5) One who just advices

(6) One who is always busy in finding the weak points or faults of others

(7) Backbiting Workers

1. Hard Working Workers and who are Willing to Work:

Such workers are very dedicated, honest and live for the organisation. They always think about the organisation, its working procedures and the strategies made by the company to achieve the target. They have full capability and learning attitude. They are the assets for the organisation.

As per my personal observation these workers are very hard working and willing to work because of the following factors.

- Joined the service at an early age
- Low Education/Unskilled

- Lack of option
- Willing to establish themselves.
- Very far from home town
- Unmarried/Single
- Less family responsibilities
- Not enough knowledge about the market in the similar field

Some people join the service at an early age owing to some compulsion. If a person did not get the proper opportunity to study and had to share family responsibility at an early age due to the death of his father, poverty, big family or simply did not feel like studying further. In such situation he may not be able to get proper schooling or he did not have enough options and had to start working to maintain the family.

If a person has joined his work at a far off place or distant place which is new for him. So lack of friends, and his single status would give more time, dedication, efforts to his assigned work. If he has less family responsibility and not got enough knowledge about the market of the similar field, the worker may think that he has to prove himself as a hardworking and dedicated employee. He would work with the best of his efforts.

The management likes such dedicated and hardworking workers. If, unfortunately or unknowingly such a worker does any wrong, the management does not like to take a harsh decision/action against him but gives him a chance to improve or rectify his mistakes.

2. Workers who do not want to work/ Lazy workers:

As we know that, a tree has a number of branches and all the branches do not bear fruits. If one branch is full of fruits then another branch may be without fruits but the branch is a part of the tree. Inspite of knowing that a particular branch does not bear fruits and it is useless, we still nurture it. If the same branch does not give fruits, again in the next season then we get alert and try to know the reason. If the reason is curable then it is alright otherwise we generally cut the particular branch from that tree in the interest of all.

More or less the same logic applies at the workplace also where not every worker/employee gives the required output to the Organisation. In the same department, one gives his full efforts for the best while the other tries to escape from the responsibility. He does not want to work and gives different types of excuses for his incapability. In the initial period, the Management does not say anything to him but after some time, if again the same worker is escaping from the responsibility then the concerned authority takes an appropriate action against him. Such a worker does not like to work but never tries to disturb or misguide others. They don't like to upset the apple cart.

3. Worker who does not let others work/jealous workers:

Some children are so naughty that they cannot sit at one place silently but they like to engage themselves in doing something or the other. They do not bother about the impact of their work on others. By nature, such children are very naughty but are good in studies. They are very jealous by nature. They do their work very carefully but do not like others to do the same or similar work.

The jealous nature of such children does not change even when they grow up and start working. They behave exactly the way they were behaving in their childhood. Here they also do their work or the assigned job very carefully but do not like others do the same as they are very insecure. Inspite of having several inherent qualities they have lack of confidence. This is why they behave in such a way. They don't want others to get good remarks.

At the workplace, this type of workers try to deviate the attention of others or try to engage them in other activities so that they cannot complete their assigned job. They try to engage other workers in useless gossip to divert their mind from their assignment to secure themselves from any forthcoming problem. Such workers basically are very jealous and are never happy with the progress of others/colleagues.

4. Worker who Watches Silently:

Most of the people are familiar with an eagle, the bird of prey. She can see from a long distance and can easily target her food. She flies in high speed and within no time, she grabs her desired food. She does not give the chance to alert her prey.

In school days, we have seen the teacher invigilating in the examination hall like an eagle and grabbing the answer sheets of the students who were found cheating/ copying the answers.

Similarly, at the workplace, there are some people who resemble the eagle in their characteristics. Here the person or seniors do not want to do anything constructive but they make themselves busy in watching others who are gossiping or sitting idle. If a person is found working then they would try to find out errors from their work performance or if they are sitting, idle, then they would reprimand them. Their main work is to find out such workers or subordinates from all the departments and pass on the information to the management or concerned seniors to give them suitable punishment. They get satisfaction if they succeed in others getting punishment.

They survive at the workplace only by passing on the information to the seniors about the happenings and get promotion and increment from time to time, without giving their output to the organisation. The seniors do not give any specific work/assignment to such workers so that they could get enough time for this job of spying.

5. One who just Advices:

I belong to a small village and am very much familiar with the behaviour of most of the people living there. During marriage or other ceremonies/ functions, some people like to give their advice or expert opinion regarding the menu, rituals and the guest list without being asked. They cite the example of all the important people of the village or families who had spent lakhs of rupees for their functions.

They show off their knowledge about the culture of the village as if they are the custodians of the culture and the rituals, but if they are requested to extend their help, they excuse themselves by citing health or family problems. The fact is they are elder or senior only in age but not in experience. They are good for nothing.

The same situation is seen more or less in the organisation / workplace where people give lip-service willingly. The seniors or others who are not directly responsible for an assigned job, give only advice to the juniors whether the subordinates are directly concerned with them or not and would definitely give unwanted advice to prove their importance.

Such workers are very fearful /scared of the official documentation. They shall think twice before signing any official documents because they have less confidence on their talent/calibre.

6. One who is always busy in finding the weak points of others:

In every organisation there are some workers who never like to work in favour of the company. Such people suffer from ego. They think that they know everything. They are the only workers in the organisation who know each and everything. In fact they have an inferiority complex and a low confidence level. They do not have confidence on their work performance. They do not know whether their work is correct or as per the desire of the seniors or not. They are very jealous in nature and do not want to see the progress of others. The work which they are assigned to complete, may not match with their capability or the interest or their profile. They always think that they may fall in problems at the workplace due to their nonperformance. This is the reason they always plan how they would make themselves safe from the problems and how they should divert the mind of others so that the general workers do not pay attention to them and only see the weak points of other workers.

Due to the above reasons such workers are always busy finding out the faults and weak points of others. But they don't know that they are being constantly monitored by the Management and one day they would have to wash their hands off from their assigned responsibility. The management does not tolerate such workers for a long period.

7. Backbiting Workers:

At the workplace there are different types of workers having different temperament, level of confidence, knowledge, skill, personal nature. Some suffer from job insecurity. Some of them may have many qualities or can handle any type of responsibility assigned to them while others may have problems in handling even their own responsibility. They may always live in fear. They do not know how to save their job. Their satisfaction levels are different. Some are satisfied by giving good performance of work, while others may escape from their responsibilities by talking rubbish about their colleagues.

In most of the organisations, some people are found busy updating their knowledge by the information and happenings at the workplace to the seniors or other concerned persons who had deputed them their official assignment. The workers officially assigned directly or indirectly to this job usually give the entire report to their concerned seniors. They do not do anything except this job. The other workers generally try to escape from such workers due to their behaviour, because no one wants to fall into any unwanted problems. During my survey I met a worker and by mistake I had questioned him and wanted to know about his assignment as I was authorised to ask him. He very casually told me that he has been assigned a special job by the management. After that I never tried to ask anything about his assignment.

In general, this type of workers have no common sense. They cannot differentiate as to which information they should forward or which not to forward to their so called seniors. They think that the more information they would forward to their seniors, the better, and they would be rewarded all the more.

This type of worker is very useful for others as a messenger. Anyone can use his reach as per their requirement. If anyone has to give particular information to the seniors where it is difficult for a general worker to reach or if anyone has to give his information about anything to the seniors, he can simply leave the message in such a way that this specific worker could listen and pass it on to the seniors. In a very short period the concerned message would reach the concerned seniors and the desired action would be taken (if it is required.) The main work of such a worker is to collect the information from the workplace and forward it to the concerned seniors. At the workplace they do not like to discharge their assigned duty. If anyone would ask about their responsibility, they would immediately reply that they are very busy on a special job assigned by the senior. They do not have time to give clarification to anyone. If anyone has any confusion they are free or welcome to consult the seniors.

If we take this attitude to be positive, then it can be said that the management takes help from such workers in knowing about the actual problems and happenings going on at the workplace, otherwise it would be very difficult to know about the same. It helps the management to control the workforce and their integrity. The management comes to know about the dedication, involvement, level of performance of the general workers, unwanted expenses at the workplace, misuse of company's funds, anti organisational activities if any, good efforts of the workers or forthcoming problems etc through this system.

On the whole, I can say that backbiting gives a wrong impression about the concerned workers among others but it creates alertness at the workplace. People are afraid and sometimes give more dedication to prove themselves as good workers which helps in the growth of the organisation and the workers concerned.

In a nutshell, I would like to say that all the above demerits are harmful for any organisation or for a workplace but it is the workplace where human beings work for a common goal and the human beings are a combination of different qualities. We cannot avoid them at the workplace. We have to work with them in co-operation and co-ordination and gradually try to rectify their bad habits.

❖❖❖

CHAPTER 8

RESPONSIBILITY & BEHAVIOUR OF THE MIDDLE MANAGEMENT

According to Mr. J. Beatty, the Management can be divided into the following levels.

The Four levels of Management are:

(1) Top Management:

- President (Board of Directors)
- Managing Director

(2) Top Middle Management (Departmental Heads, e.g.)

- Sales Department, Purchase Department,
- Materials Department, Production Department,
- Finance Department (Designated as Controllers...)

(3) Middle Order Management

- Regional Managers
- Departmental Superintendents
- General Accountant
- Cost Accountant

(4) Supervisory Management

- Foremen
- First Supervisor
- Second Supervisor

In general, the Management levels are divided in this manner:

(1) Shareholders
(2) Board of Directors
(3) Chief Executive
(4) Specialised staff

In a nutshell, I can say that the levels of the management is not fixed for every Organisation but it varies from one management to another or from one organisation to an other depending upon the nature and size of the enterprises for which levels are being decided upon.

Top Management:

In any organisation, the top management is usually made responsible for the following functions:

(1) To define the purpose of the management, organisation and the enterprise. In fact, it is the purpose which defines the management and organisation and which these two different wings of the enterprise strive to attain.

(2) To frame different policies for the enterprise within the framework of which the whole of the enterprise works.

(3) To set out schedules and programmes.

(4) To give general direction.

Middle-Order Management:

Middle-Order management occupies a central place in the hierarchy and is generally responsible for implementing the policies enunciated by the top management under its direction and supervision. Middle-order management is answerable to top management. Its main functions are:

- To provide plan
- To guide
- To supervise
- To co-ordinate and
- To exercise control over the lowest level of management

Middle-order management sometimes functions in an advisory capacity also. It advises the top management and guides the lowest. It often functions as a link between the two.

Supervisory Management:

This is known as the lowest level of management. It functions under the control and direction of the middle-order management. The supervisory management is asked to render advice to the middle order. This level of management takes orders from the middle order and explains them to the workers at operating level. In fact this level of management is accredited with the responsibility of getting the work done and is made accountable to those who occupy the middle-order management.

Operating Management:

This level though strictly does not come under the management hierarchy, but ultimately it is this level, which is responsible to accomplish the given task by carrying out the instructions. This level is the actual performer. It is this level, which is engaged in production and carries out all the policies and programmes to their logical ends. The level is directed, supervised, controlled and led at different stages by different levels of management either directly or indirectly.

Functions of Middle-Level Management:

This level of management takes over the functions of both the top level and that of supervisory level. The functions of middle level management differ from one organisation to another. It usually comprises department and sectional heads and top supervisors of which are as enumerated below:

- To direct all activities of the enterprise so that the top management is made free from direction and supervision. They are free to plan for any level and administer the whole enterprise in the best interest of all who are related directly or indirectly with the enterprise.
- To see, the enterprise goes on moving without hindrance of any kind.
- To establish co-ordination between the activities of different wings of the enterprise.
- To elicit co-ordination from the entire workforce.
- To create a duty loving, responsible, satisfied, honest, sincere, efficient and skilled team of workers.
- To prepare the workers for future work and progress.
- To develop a team spirit among workers.
- To establish harmonious human relation based on human psychology within the framework of the policies and prepare for the purpose by the top management.
- To see that self- interest gets the second rank and common goal goes on the top.

It is an irony of fate that middle-level management is required to function under pressure. It is always under pressure from three sides- top management, supervisory, managerial staff and the operational staff. It also functions under the constant threat of dissatisfaction from any of the sides and that too even on very flimsy grounds. The middle-level, therefore, has to handle different situations with perfection without leaving room for those who in every type of organisation are always prepared to fish in troubled water.

The middle management always tries to run the undertaking according to plan, policies and programmes and direction without ifs and buts. Certainly, the top management is interested in getting its plans executed to its utmost satisfaction.

Middle Management in general Practice:

The roles of middle management at workplace towards the top management or towards the subordinates or towards the image of the company are different from the theoretical functions. It varies from person to person depending on the various factors of the organisation and the relationship with the top management of the concerned organisation. This is the reason some organisations grow very fast while others do not.

- Responsibilities
- Responsibility towards the Management
- Responsibility towards the Subordinates
- Responsibility towards the Image of the Company
- In Practice, the Behaviour of Middle Management:
- Towards the Company
- Towards the Subordinates
- Role of Middle Management towards growth or downfall of the Organisation

Responsibility towards the top Management:

In general, as per the norms of the company, the middle management works according to the desired policies and the instruction of the top management. It makes smooth co-ordination between the top and middle management representatives in the company's interest. Its main motto is to work as a bonafide military chief to protect the organisation from any mishap or any hidden problems and make the organisation profitable and secure.

No doubt, middle management of some organisations work accordingly but in most of the organisations, the middle management works as per their own whims and wish. They do not bother about the sentiment and the instructions of the top management but they follow their own strategy and instruct the subordinates accordingly, whether it is in favour of the organisation or against it.

In general, everyone wants that his subordinates or juniors should work according to his instruction, desire or direction. A father desires that his son should follow the family custom. A doctor also expects that his patient should follow his instructions and advice, and then only they can have good health. I mean, whosoever spends money for a particular thing or for a common motto / goal / interest, thinks that the rules and regulations of the concerned project should be made according to his will and the workers working in that project should follow it.

Similarly, in any organisation, whether private or government, the patron or the top management of the concerned company, desires that the middle management or the person answerable should follow all the rules and the regulations laid down by the top management without any hesitation.

The middle management works as per the desire of the top management, on the following grounds.

- Short Tenure of the middle management
- Clear instruction
- Non interference in the day-to-day working procedure
- Clear & Fixed Business target
- Selection of Team members as per the middle management
- One person is answerable
- Full faith on middle management and their capability
- The person should have interest in the concerned field
- The middle management should not be a close relative of the top management.

As per my observation, the tenure of the middle management should not be long because if a person works in a company or organisation for a long tenure then he may become lethargic and dull and shall try to flout the rules and regulations of the top management. He would start taking the top management for granted in various decision making process. He does not bother to follow the rules and regulations and moulds it according to his convenience. This attitude works like a sweet poison or a fatal disease like cancer for the organisation.

Secondly, it has been observed that the instructions coming from the top management usually do not indicate clear vision or clarity to the middle management and they get a chance to change or mould the rules and regulations according to their convenience. For example, a driver drives his car very smoothly on the road in clear weather but the same driver faces too much difficulty in driving his car in foggy weather. I mean a clear vision is required to drive smoothly, whether a vehicle or an organisation.

It is human nature that people do not want interference in their personal life or at the workplace. If anyone interferes frequently in their work, then their performance would be affected and they would not be able to utilize the best of their calibre. The middle management would be able to do their best provided the top management does not interfere in their decision.

The middle management always desires that the instruction coming from the top management should be clear in every respect. The decision making power at the middle management level should also be clear. Those organisations where business is target oriented, generally grow rapidly in comparison to the other organisations. It means, if the top management gives full charge to the middle management to run the organisation independently with the guidance of the top management, on a fixed business target, (which they have to achieve), the organisation would definitely grow very fast.

It is common nature of human beings that people want to make their own group to achieve their common goal. They never want that any member of their team be against their opinion. This is the reason, they always prefer to select such people, whose behaviour, attitude and interest are common and match with the middle management. Otherwise, it would be very difficult to manage them and get the desired goal in the company interest. Thus, if the team members of the middle management are selected only by the middle management, then the company would grow or the organisation would run smoothly. If the team members of the middle management are selected by the top management, headed by the representatives of the middle management then I doubt that the company would run smoothly.

A very important thing is the responsibility or the accountability at the middle management level. In our life, at every stage, one person should take responsibility and be answerable for the progress or decline of the business. It is not possible to control the entire unit by the top management. Every one being responsible or accountable means no one is responsible or accountable. Therefore, the middle management could work with more enthusiasm and interest when the top management would give them full authority for a particular unit and make them fully responsible and answerable for the progress or the deterioration of growth of the unit. If we make a survey on this, we would find that behind the progress of any organisation is the responsibility and accountability rendered by the top management to the middle management.

Along with the other factors, having faith or trust is very important as, without faith it would be very difficult for anyone to work at the workplace where everyone is unknown to each other, except the system made by the top management for the middle management and the organisation. We spend our whole life waiting for the day when God would listen to our prayers and remove all the hurdles from our life because we believe that God is the supreme power and only HE can solve our problems. This is also because we have great faith in God. This does not apply to the atheists.

I mean that faith along with emotion is required between the top management and the middle management to get the desired result or output of the organisation. The middle management does most of the work on behalf of the top management, because they think that the top management has faith on them and they trust and respect their honesty and integrity. In any case, if there is any doubt under any circumstance, on the middle management by the top management, then it is not possible that the top management could supervise or run the organisation without the help of the middle management.

Along with the other qualities, interest in a particular field is one of the most important factors. The top management gets the desired job done from the middle management, smoothly because the middle management takes interest in their job or responsibilities. If under any circumstance, the middle management does not have interest in a particular field of work and has been given the responsibility by the top management forcefully, then it is not possible that the top management would get the desired result from them. Therefore, having interest in the concerned field is necessary for growth and progress.

Sometimes, if the middle management is a close relative of the top management then the position of the top management becomes very awkward in front of others. The middle management would not be able to work properly and would not be able to justify their position in front of top management. The middle management should never be a relative of the top management in company's interest. If it is so, then the company would not grow properly. It means for a smooth co-ordination between the top and middle management, there should be no family relations between them. (It would be akin to incestuous relationships.)

RESPONSIBILITY TOWARDS THE SUBORDINATES

Everyone has seen and is aware of the electric meter, installed at our home, office or workplace. If we minutely observe it, we will discover that this small meter-reading unit plays a vital role in our life. It works for the consumers on behalf of the Electricity Board or the main supplier of electricity. This meter is neutral and important for everyone. It works as per the direction, rules and regulations laid down by the Board of Directors or the top management of the electricity board.

There are several electric points at home or in the office. Some are for normal light while the others maybe for heavy wattage consumption. There are different kinds of electrical appliances whose level of electric consumption is different. If we use our television and air conditioner for one hour each, the electric consumption for both the items, would be different. If we do not consume electricity then the same meter reader would not show any electric consumption. The electric meter is installed at our home or office, but it reports to its top management i.e. the electricity board and gives the proper report about the individual's electric consumption. Accordingly we get our electric bills. In normal cases, the electric meter never gives wrong or false electric consumption to its top management unless it is tampered with.

As the electric meter shows the actual consumption report to its top management and based on its report, the Board/ top management makes annual report related to the finance of the whole organisation. The top management makes future planning and strategy for the whole organisation accordingly.

Similarly, at the workplace, the middle management also gives the right and actual information about the development of all individuals or departments/units to the top management on fortnightly, monthly, quarterly, half yearly or yearly basis, (which should be impartial) for the evaluation of financial growth or otherwise.

I mean that the middle management gives the feedback on a regular basis to the top management, so that they could take proper action as per the submitted report. As the top management sees the organisation through the eyes of the middle management. Therefore, the middle management should show the actual picture of the organizational status.

After analysing, the different routine responsibilities of the middle management to be taken for their subordinates to be submitted to the top management may be categorised as:

- Presentation of transparent report to the top management.
- Actual financial presentation of the individual divisions.
- Actual and hidden problems being faced at the workplace due to any reason.
- Proposal of future planning and strategy.
- Strategy: how to get a break-even point or how to make a profitable unit with the help of existing manpower and resources.
- Actual feedback report of the implemented rules and regulations made by the top management.
- The middle management should speak the truth about themselves and their subordinates without having any hesitation, in the organisation's interest.
- If the organisation is not doing well due to any circumstance, the middle management should present the actual reason along with the proposed remedies to the top management.

RESPONSIBILITY TOWARDS THE IMAGE OR BRAND OF THE ORGANISATION

The middle management is also responsible for the image or the brand of the organisation. They should keep a keen eye on its reputation. They should conduct a survey through a reputed agency from time to time to know where their company stands in the current market. If its image or branding is deteriorating owing to any reason, they should take immediate action to rectify the shortcomings and simultaneously inform the top management with a proper and genuine report, so that the message would be passed on to the board of directors accordingly, as the total inflow, financial position of any organisation depends on its branding or the image of the company in the market. If the image of any company would decrease, most of the financers, shareholders or the agencies would not advertise or would not like to invest in such an organisation or company.

All the existing well-wishers of the organisation would gradually try to excuse themselves. Therefore, it is the most important role of the middle management to evaluate the branding and the image of the company.

THE BEHAVIOUR OF THE MIDDLE MANAGEMENT IN PRACTICE

When we evaluate our life, we find that there are two parts, one is dark or grey (which only we know and try to hide) and the other is bright (which others know). It is not necessary what we see or observe is correct or the statements coming from any person is correct. It might be wrong. Nobody looks or evaluates anybody internally but evaluates on the external beauty, glamour or how we look or present ourselves.

For example, we get attracted by the shiny peel of a fruit but do not know it from within. The peel may seem very smooth but the internal part may be rotten. When we co-relate it with the organisation and its middle management, we would find that there is a lot of similarity between the two. The attitude or behaviour and the role of middle management towards the subordinate is not so easy to understand for common workers, because it is very complex and different with the top management. What they are observing at the workplace, is not necessarily being conveyed to the top management. It is possible that the information they deliver about the subordinates working in the organisation, might be different from the actual fact or they might deliver only those matters in which there is no problem or they would be answerable for the damage or loss.

As per my opinion, the behaviour of the middle management varies from person to person and it depends upon their upbringing, personal attitude, nature and the surrounding of the workplace.

On the basis of the present scenario related to the work and responsibilities of the middle management, can be divided into the following two parts.

(1) Behaviour towards the Company

(2) Behaviour towards the subordinates

BEHAVIOUR TOWARDS THE COMPANY

At present times, most of the companies are not doing well as per the top management and the board of directors of the company. Everyone is troubled because the financers who invested funds in the company for good returns, are not in a position to back the same. It may be owing to the global recession or other reasons. The companies are not doing well and its business is suffering. The top management changes the middle management from time to time in the hope of getting good business, but unfortunately the behaviour and the attitude of the middle management is almost the same. Everyone is misusing the workplace for making money. They do not bother for the company as well as for the top management and its respected investors.

In general, the behaviour of the middle management towards their company can be categorised as under:

- They do not bother about the rules and the regulations laid down by the top management in the company's interest.
- The middle management always tries to present a fantasy filled presentation, which is far away from the reality of business.

- They never want to give the right figure and the situation about the happenings of the company to the top management, so that the right message could be passed on to the board of directors.
- They always convey half baked information, so that the top management would be dependent on the middle management.
- As the expenditure is not going out from their own pocket, the middle management always tries to present future planning where huge investment is required.
- They always try to divert the mind of the top management from the crisis and weak points of the company.
- They always try to transfer the cause of crisis or loss to the top management.
- The middle management tries to make an exclusive upper level group, so that no one would dare to complain against them to the top management.
- Most of the middle managements are ungrateful to the company or the top management. They always hold grudge against them.
- Most of the time the Middle Management gives distorted information to the top Management to hide their mistakes or defects. They never show their accountability.

BEHAVIOUR TOWARDS THE SUBORDINATES

If we talk about the behaviour of the middle management towards the subordinates, working in the concerned organisation, we would find the following:

- The middle management seems very arrogant and full of false, inflated and bloated ego.
- They make their own rules and regulations.
- They make their own group of workers/H.O.Ds, (coterie) who prepare the report according to them.
- They depute workers for gathering the gossip going on in the organisation and pass on the confidential report of the individuals, so that they could disrupt their strategy.
- Frequent meetings with the heads of department, to engage them so that they could not think about anything except the routine work.
- To keep distance with the relatives of the top management or do not involve those workers, who have personal relationship with the top management.
- To provide some additional benefits to selected workers, so that they do not open their mouth or reveal their true colour.
- Always try to create hurdles for the workers to divert their minds from the weak points of the middle management.
- The Middle management never likes anyone to meet the top management or try to contact them or show respect or extend their courtesies to their contemporaries or rivals who work in different departments.

In short, they change their colour and attitude much faster than the chameleon.

❖❖❖

CHAPTER 9

EXPECTATIONS OF MANAGEMENT FROM THEIR WORKFORCE

INTRODUCTION

There are two big Es. One is the fragile Ego while the other is Expectation. Every human being has some expectation from the fellow human beings. It is all the more between the Management, seniors and the subordinates.

Everyone works with an expectation and every senior/management gives responsibility to his subordinates with some expectation. This expectation sometimes may be expressed or sometimes it may be very confidential but every senior expects good conduct from his juniors at the workplace. I have tried to explain the various expectations of the seniors, in an easy language so that a common worker/employee could easily understand that the desires of their seniors are related to their assigned work.

EXPECTATIONS OF THE SENIORS, IN-CHARGE, H.O.D. FROM THEIR CONCERNED SUBORDINATES & JUNIORS.

We all are human beings and to remain alive, it is necessary for us to take a proper balanced diet, water, and fresh air. If we will not get fresh air, food and water to survive then it would be very difficult to lead a healthy life or to remain alive. Everyone has to take care of their family along with their own physical, financial, mental, emotional, and social needs.

All the factors whether it is positive or negative are very closely associated with the expectations of the individuals. In the absence of expectation, the growth of the human being will totally be stopped. No one will work and the life of the human beings will become hell.

No one is happy in this world and everyone has different kinds of sorrow, difficulties, and problems, according to their social status. Satisfaction and happiness varies from person to person as per their state of mind. Not all the difficulties can be solved inspite of having knowledge and awareness. It cannot be solved immediately or as per our will but people, pray to the Almighty God, to solve their problems immediately. People pass their time, waiting for a miracle to happen. Parents pass their whole life, expecting that their own child will help them when they will grow old and God will solve all their problems.

A Culprit spends / passes his whole life in the Jail, with a ray of hope of being freed some day. A farmer works in his farm hoping in his mind that after a few months he will get a good yield thereby getting more money for his needs. Students study hard throughout the year hoping that at the end of the year they will get good marks and position in the class or school where they are studying. After the completion of their studies, they look for a good job in a good company, hoping that their life will be settled and they can lead a good life.

It means in every aspect / sphere of our life, we have some hope and expectations and we try to lead a better life, otherwise it may be very difficult for any one to live, prosper and succeed.

In other words, expectation in any aspect generally gives us the following factors in our life. It means whenever we expect or desire something, automatic energy generates or charges our body in the form of the following, which are explained as under:

- Energy, enforce, progressive,
- Pleasant, continue, control, thirst,
- Thinking power, awareness, innovation,
- Inter-dependence, object,
- Oblige, navigator, systems

If, we plan to get something immediately, a positive *energy* starts generating in our body. All the cells in our body and our blood circulation become more active and our ability to think increases. Our mind *enforces* us to get more work done and starts going forward towards *progressiveness.* We will feel happy and have the satisfaction that we are doing something for ourselves. We automatically try to get more information of the surroundings, with eagerness to do any *innovative* work to fulfil our mission. There will be a clear object on our life, which will navigate us forward towards the right direction *systematically* to achieve our pre-planned goal.

A blind person standing at the road crossing, waiting to seek help from the passersby also has the expectation from the pedestrians to help him in crossing the road. Beggars spend their whole day in the bright sun without any grievances hoping that their desires may be fulfilled at the end of the day by the alms he will get.

Similarly, in the organisation or at the workplace, the management as well as the workers, working under a supervisor, in charge, H.O.D., seniors have their desire, which they expect to be fulfilled in the company interest or their own interest. On the other hand, the management, and the organisation also has some expectations from its workers and subordinates, which they have to fulfil to get the common goal.

In the present day's working scenario or atmosphere, we feel that some sort of expectations which generally the Seniors, Incharge, H.O.D., Management have from their subordinates without saying anything or in other words have hidden expectations are as follows:

Do not Complete the Work Quickly but do it Phase by Phase, Slowly and Steadily

I met a person working at a high position in a very reputed private company. I was in regular touch with him for some official work because, I am a very enthusiastic person and I want to complete any assigned work without any interruption or hassles as soon as possible. I do not want to take rest until the assigned job is completed for self-satisfaction and in company's interest. It is my thinking that quick completion of assigned work would definitely impress our immediate seniors or the top management of the company. This is not only my thinking but also of the common people who think the same.

The manager, whom I had met, was very friendly with me. So, he advised me not to complete any work, so quickly because, when a person completes his assigned work before its scheduled time frame, the top management thinks that the concerned person, does not know anything. This is why; he comes to us frequently and disturbs us, so this person is not fit for this particular job.

The management expects from its junior staff that they should complete their assigned job, gradually or phase by phase. It means in the initial period, the person should start the assigned work but just after the start, the work should be stopped until the management gives him a reminder for the assigned work. In this way, the management will think that the work assigned to this person is very difficult and inspite of its difficulties, this person is trying to complete it or it is at a completion stage. In such a circumstance, the management or the seniors will think that this is the right person to complete the job. So, he definitely should get promotion, increment, or other benefits as soon as possible.

At the same time, when we complete the assigned job before the expected period of completion, the management thinks that it was completed because it was already in their working systems due to which the workers could complete the assigned work so quickly and the credit for job completion will not go to the workers but to the company's working systems or to the management and not to any individual's working style.

Therefore, if we want to take any credit for any of our assigned work, we should complete only 25% of the assigned work in the first phase, and it should not start again, until the management does not remind us for the same. When the management will give us a reminder to complete the pending work, we should tell them that it is very difficult and will take more time to complete or otherwise company will suffer.

TO WORK WITHOUT CARE OF CRITICISM

Criticism is very necessary because without criticism there will be no development. It is all up to us as to how we take criticism. If, we take criticism in a positive way, then it will be very useful for us to develop and balance ourselves. It gives us the chance to know our weak points, which can be rectified for our benefit. After that, our work efficiency will definitely increase and when our work efficiency will increase, we will automatically benefit from the management without any grievance.

We should always listen to the criticism patiently and should not get irritated but think over it peacefully. We should think what the other wants, or desires from us. Criticism indicates the weak points of our working procedure, which should be rectified immediately. For example, a cricketer, on a bad performance, is always criticised by the society. At this situation, if the player takes this criticism in a negative way then he may have to leave the team but if he takes criticism in a positive way then he may try to rectify his mistakes, improve his techniques and performance, to conquer the heart of the public.

Therefore, we should not pay attention to what the people are talking. Any person is free to speak anything against or in favour of anyone. Those persons may be our colleagues, working partner, seniors or any third party. We should react positively to criticism, but if we react negatively it will divert our mind and attention from the creative activity in the wrong direction thereby affecting our potential.

Management also desires from their subordinates that they should not bother about their criticism. If they are not getting proper attention of the respective management or seniors, they should not leave their assigned job or work but they should do their job in a positive way because one day the same management or the seniors will consider their good performance and the concerned workers will be appreciated by them openly in front of everyone.

If one person is doing a good thing for the organisation, he will definitely be criticised by the other colleagues because it is human nature to criticise any or other's work. Most of the workers working in any organisation desire for a good result, beyond expectation without making sufficient effort for the same.

IS THERE ANY FURTHER ASSIGNMENTS OR WORK FOR ME:

The nature of human beings is very peculiar. Without expressing their views, they have big expectations from others. In the organisation, the managers also expect something from their juniors, subordinates without asking or telling them anything. The Managers also expect from their juniors that they should tell them about their requirement or before leaving the office the subordinate should ask their senior whether any work is pending which needs to be completed from them or should they leave.? They expect from them that their juniors or subordinates should ask in a routine way about such things without hesitation.

Such activity definitely promotes a good relationship between the manager and his subordinates. A good relationship as well as mutual faith gradually develops between the manager and the concerned subordinates, which is very necessary for any sound working atmosphere of any organisation. It will also increase the all round development of both the sides. The manager as well as the subordinates will be benefited.

In another example, when we employ a servant for our own housework, we expect several things from him without instructing him anything. We never like our servant doing favours for another person without our permission. We expect from them that they should be very well versed in household chores as well as look after the dog, tend to the garden, wash the car, finish cooking in time as well as be courteous and take care of the family he is working for, along with the guests.

The Head of the family expects from his servant that he should do him special favours apart from his routine work, like giving him a massage etc. Similarly, the employer of a company also expects from his employees that they should always take care of the umpteen tasks of the company apart from their assigned duties. The management also expects from them that they should be fully aware of the market atmosphere along with the indoor development, happenings within the organisation and should inform them from time to time. The subordinates should not wait for any further assignment that will come from the seniors but the subordinates or juniors should ask their concerned seniors and enquire about the further assignment left to be done.

BE DIPLOMATIC

There is a very popular and ancient shlok in Sanskrit:

Satyam Bruyat Priyam Bruyat, Nabruyat Satyamapriyam:

It means, we must always speak the truth, which is sweet, and never speak the bitter truth.

Practically, it means, we should always speak favourably at home or at the workplace, where we work, where, we discharge our duties / responsibilities and where we have to complete our job in a specific time frame as well as under the supervision of the seniors. At the workplace, there are different types of people having different temperaments with different likes & dislikes. Nobody or no one can guess at what point our senior will react badly or be happy, what work they will like or dislike, even, if the work has been done in the company's interest, but it is not sure that the concerned seniors will agree with the work done. If we have done good work in the company's interest and if we want to share it in front of other colleagues, it might be possible that our seniors may react favourably or adversely at our enthusiastic approach. Sometimes, we may be correct but it may be wrong in the eyes of the concerned senior, boss or any H.O.D.

In the same cases, if we are working with a particular department where the freedom of expression is totally censored and we have to think before delivering any statement in public and the situation requires that we have to say something then we should express our opinion in vague terms, so that no one can point out in the department that secrecy was not maintained, which is a very essential factor in the company's interest or as per the organisational norms.

In general cases, people use vague words for their instructions; *Do the needful,* which in itself is very vague. If the junior has done his work well or he has competed the work with a good or fruitful result then, the concerned senior will give a good remark and if the result is bad, then the senior will remark that we are not capable of doing such work or given assignment because we do not understand the instruction of our seniors or in other words are lazy in discharging our duty.

Therefore, this vague instruction is very diplomatic in nature, which we generally use at our workplace. If we have to say something to a senior and we do not want to tell him the right thing then, we should choose an isolated place where we can talk freely but at a common place, we should talk about such matters, which are associated with the common people, not targeted to particular work or a person. Nobody wants to get humiliated at a public place due to their own or other's mistake, so they expect from their subordinates or juniors that they should give priority to the place where they want to express their views. Seniors should also remember not to humiliate or embarrass their subordinates in front of others. They should also choose an isolated place for this purpose.

TEAM WORK

Nothing can be moved without applying specific force or action in a particular direction. It means when a thing moves from one place to another place, then there are several hidden forces applied, contributing in the same direction, then only it is possible to move a particular thing from one place to another place.

If, the force is applied in more than one direction for a particular thing or object, then it is possible that the movement of the concerned object will be very slow or negligible. Sometimes, the action applied on a particular thing to get it into motion may not be visible but it is sure that the forces are being applied.

There are several examples in our daily life, which shows team work and its result. If we say anything on any subject, then our mind, body, memory, eyes, tongue etc are working together simultaneously. Then only it is possible to speak. When we drive our car or any vehicle, one can say that only the driver is driving the car but there are several factors like, fuel, engine, tyre, air, even the smallest part of that car is contributing together, then only it is possible to get the car in motion.

A single man cannot play and win a cricket or football match. It is only possible, when we play together as a team and apply force for a common goal of winning, then only it is possible for us to win the match. In any match or game, the team manager has some winning strategy for the concerned match or the game. As per the norms of the match, all players have to obey the instructions of their team leader without fail. If the team members do not obey the instruction of the team leader, then as per the norms the concerned player may go out from that team because of his or her misconduct or for breaking the rules or discipline.

More or less the same thing happens at any workplace or in any organisation. Every organisation has its own set of rules and regulations and they have given some sort of authority to each and every manager or seniors working in that organisation, which they apply for a common goal in the organisational interest. If any person or worker is not working according to the norms of the organisation or as per the direction or instruction of their concerned seniors, the work done by such workers may seem an anti-organisational activity. Such a team can never fulfil the growth target of the organisation. Therefore, we have to work together for a common goal as a team specified by the concerned management or the seniors.

In one department, there are several workers working together under a specific manager or senior and all of them are working in the organisation for a common goal. The seniors have given them different types of responsibilities to complete in a specific time frame. Continuous organisational growth is only possible, when the workers work together as per the direction or instruction of the seniors

The seniors or H.O.D of any concerned department expect from their subordinates or juniors working under their guidance, that they should obey their instructions and follow their directions carefully without fail. The management thinks that their concerned workers should do their duties first then only they should divert their mind anywhere else.

If, any one of our team member diverts his mind from the mainstream or targeted work, then he can fall into many types of problems. For example, when we drive our car, there are several factors working together or we make co-ordination with several things like, clutch, brake, horn, accelerator, front/ side/rear mirror and attention of driver's mind towards driving. During driving, if any one factor is missed, overlooked, or ignored, it is sure that we will meet with an accident and not reach our destination.

It means the seniors want from their subordinates that they should not ignore or skip any specified strategy of the company or they should not bypass the concerned seniors or H.O.D. They should not supersede their seniors but they should work together by making good co-ordination among all their colleagues. Then only they can expect increment or betterment from their seniors.

DUAL PERSONALITY

Human beings are very intelligent and have complicated personality. They have a great capability of thinking beyond imagination. They can easily differentiate between good and bad characters. Therefore, it is very difficult to know about a person, what sort of activities are going on in his mind whether it is positive or negative. Sometimes, we have seen that a visitor knocks at our door and asks for a glass of water or asks about the next-door neighbour. We people innocently open the door and provide them or fulfil their requirements but actually he may not be thirsty or not in a mood to know about any person living next door. He may actually be a robber and as soon as we open the door, he may enter our house and rob us of our valuables or may even stab us. He had his strategy preplanned before coming to our place.

In a train, we find several passengers who seem soft spoken, courteous and good-natured. Based on their personality or activities no one can guess or say that they have bad character or they are robbers and they are there to deceive or rob the passengers.

Generally, it is seen that persons who speak in front of others without thinking anything are very dangerous for the general public, as no one can guess about their mood/intention / likes, dislikes, what they mean, how they will react on any particular situation. They are very unpredictable. Such people behave in such a way because they are suffering from inferiority complex and they want to supersede their colleagues working in the Company or department and they also want to draw the attention of others in a negative way.

In our society, many people are very soft spoken and talk very sweetly and know how to hypnotise their listeners. They make a good relationship in a short time but on the other side, the same people are not exactly what they seem. In reality they are very crude and emotionless, because after some times the same person may kidnap one of our family members for a small or big ransom. Sometimes they also kill their victims, when they do not get the ransom. When we try to investigate their background, it is found in most of the cases that they were related to the victim. They could also be a disgruntled ex-servant or ex-employee or a close or distant relative.

Such, people usually spend their maximum time with our family but their behaviour is very different from what the people see. This category of people speak very politely; but very soon their attitude suddenly changes and they begin using abusive language and their behaviour changes. Just like Dr. Jekyll and Mr. Hyde, the story of dual identity, which we have read in school.

Similarly, we also find in our office or in our Organisation, the behaviour of some workers or seniors are very similar, which I have already discussed earlier. In any Company, there are some people, workers, who apprise the seniors and colleagues about their work in front of other people but in the absence of the same people, the same worker starts talking baselessly against them.

The junior who was apprising a particular senior about his contribution in the Company and different types of welfare work done for the juniors. His behaviour changes in the absence of the seniors. The same worker starts cursing the senior by using cuss or abusive language. The same case is also seen in the colleagues' lobby. One colleague does not want to see the progress or growth of any of his colleagues working at the same place but when they meet once in a while, no one can guess that they do not have a good rapport. One worker always tries to pull the leg of others secretly.

In my point of view, this is a very objectionable behaviour. The higher and top Management do not like such attitude in their workers / employees. The seniors usually trust the straightforward people because in the long run, these straightforward workers are assets for the Company / Organisational growth. They are very useful for any Company. They work just like the opposition party in front of the immediate seniors, because by their straight forwardness they want to alert the other workers/seniors/ colleagues. They want to prevent the Company from any casualty, which may occur in the near future.

PHOTOFINISH CHARACTER / PEOPLE EXHIBITING SUPERFICIALITY OR PEOPLE HAVING SUPERFICIAL CHARACTER

In the modern working culture, everybody wishes to give their own valuable contribution to the Management. All the workers want to convey their thoughts or views in front of the Management by different methods. They do not bother about the positive impact of their contribution on the Organisational growth and at what level their views will damage the brand of the Company. Apart from the above, even they do not bother about their colleagues and H.O.D's temperament, their likes and dislikes.

In this connection, there comes a character called Photofinish Character of workers working in the Organisation who are very superficial. Such people do not want to participate in any responsible work or they do not want to take any responsibility of a particular assignment. They do not want to be answerable for any assigned job. They only want to supervise the job being done by other people from the upper level. If the workers are having any problems in finishing their work, they cannot help them but if the worker is not doing or performing his job perfectly or as desired by the concerned seniors. Then at this stage, such people definitely convey their weak points to the higher Management, that the assigned workers are dull, lazy and would not be able to get the desired result.

They are not, suitable, or valuable for the Company. They always devise new methods of troubling their juniors and want to harass the people working under them because they enjoy themselves by giving problems to others. They try to impose their views and show them their own importance. Such people are very popular for a while in the Organisation. The seniors believe that they know each and everything related to work but as soon as the real fact becomes known, such photofinish/ superficial people automatically go out from the Company and are absolved from the assigned responsibility.

Such workers have no sympathy, emotional, attachment, loyalty with their Organisation as well as with the workplace where they are working and earning their livelihood. They never speak the truth to the concerned seniors but they always try to give value or half answer and try to confuse them. They never try to forward or give attention to any problem related to the Organisation. They never try to point out any genuine problems of the Company, which could be rectified for the Organisational growth. Due to their behaviour, the concerned seniors have to face an awkward position in front of the higher Management. They are least bothered about the organisational growth, progress, and think that let everybody go to hell and why should they bother?

In the real sense, the Management or the concerned H.O.D. does not like such workers in their Organisation. If, due to any unavoidable circumstance, such workers are given work in the Organisation, the seniors do not give any attention to them or do not assign any crucial work to them. They never want to give them any benefits. They think that their juniors or subordinates should not have a photofinish character but they should be labourious and hard working. The Management cannot have faith on such people and do not want to give higher responsibility to them.

DUTY FIRST AND SELF LAST

The saying "Duty First and Self Last "is very important and we should adhere to it in principle. The people, who follow this, cannot be unhappy. They will always be happy whether in their family or at their workplace where they are working for their livelihood. If they have problems, then it will be for a very short period. Their problems are very short lived and all their important works are finished without any hitch.

In the Holy Book: Geeta" Lord Krishna had said that, *"Do your Karma or Do your duty and do not bother about the result"*. One day will come when God will give us the result according to our deed. No one can stop it. Everything, takes its own time. According to the Geeta, getting result for a good deed may take time but one gets result for his misdeed very quickly.

If we are working in an Organisation/Company, we should have full faith in the Organisation and we should obey Lord Krishna's teachings which will be very fruitful for ourselves as well as for the Company. On the other hand, the Company also expects from their subordinates that they should do their work as per the given instructions. The Management will look into their future accordingly. It is only possible, when we perform our duty very efficiently in the Company's interest. If a person gives the importance to himself or herself in comparison to the Company's work, the Management or the concerned seniors would never like such workers.

Management cannot tolerate such workers who follow the principle of "Self First and Duty Last". Such workers might be beneficial for a while but suddenly they may have to lose everything. They may have to lose at least more than twice, of what they had gained by unfair means. By doing duty for other people selflessly will give us confidence and work satisfaction. This cannot be imagined, if we do the reverse. We must have a high degree of confidence integrity and high moral in our life to get or achieve a meaningful or successful life.

A Mother first wishes to feed her child then only she likes to do other work. She takes care of her children in all possible ways. She gives them food, cloths, education, love and entire financial assistance before she thinks about herself.

A bird also likes to feed her young one then only she eats. In other words, we can say that small birds also discharge their duty first by giving food and care to their kids then only they think about themselves. There are so many examples in the environment, which gives us lessons as to how we should perform our duty and upto what extent should we exert ourselves. Soldiers guard our country first then they think about themselves. During the festival season when we all are busy celebrating Holi, Desshera, Id, Christmas etc with our family, the soldiers are performing their duty at the border. They are also human beings like us. They can also enjoy the festivals with their family but they are unable to do so as they have to guard the country, which is their first priority than celebrating festivals with their family. In their opinion, all comforts are immaterial in comparison to the National Security and peaceful existence for the fellow beings.

If we link this logic with the Organisation/ Company where we are working, on which our family members and we depend, somehow it is very similar. I would like to explain by another example. We first want to safeguard our family members from problems. If any mishap happens in the society, we first rush to save our family then we think about saving other people. If any person falls sick, we generally take it very casually but if our own child falls sick, we absolve ourselves from all the responsibilities and rush to take care of our child. We try to get him checked by the best of Doctors available in the city and pray to God for his or her well being and quick recovery. We always worry and are in tension, until our child gets well.

In short, we can say that when we are facing any problem, which affects us or our family directly then we perform a high level of duty selflessly without caring for others. We try to do our best to complete the task so that we can get out from the immediate problems. At the same time, if the problem is concerned with the Organisation / Company or with some other person, the scenario will totally be different.

Whenever the Company or the Organisation where we are working, falls into any problem, we generally do not bother, and do not take it very seriously. We do not want to know the reason behind it or never try to think of any solution for the same. We are not at all bothered about the well-being of our company. We do not give a damn.

For example, whenever, the guardian or head of the family is facing a problem, the children do not bother about his problem. They play, sing and dance or go to school as usual. On the other hand, when we see that an accident takes place, people walking on the same road do not bother even to see who has met with the accident. They do not even want to know the reason behind it or what measure should we take to help the victims. They move from there ignoring everything without giving a second glance and seem to be unperturbed and indifferent.

Such human behaviour is very harmful for the society and the Organisation where we are working. The Organisation, the Management at different levels also desire and expect from their employees, workers that when the Company/Management, faces any problem, their employees, workers, staff directly or indirectly associated should also take care or should at least feel a part of the problem. They should also try to find out the procedures, measures how we should work, for the Company so that it comes out from the problem. We should give advice to the higher Management with a proposal that if we adopt such measures or take certain steps, the problem in our Company may be solved. They should show their faith and feeling in front of the Management that they are with them in the crisis period or at the time of need.

The Management expects from their workers, juniors or subordinates that their first duty should be to save the Organisation or put forward their help in the adverse situation. They should treat the Organisational problems just like their own problems and not shrug off their responsibility.

DO NOT WANT TO TAKE ANY PAIN

Sometimes, there are peculiar seniors/authorities /supervisors/ H.O.D. in an Organisation. They only pass on the responsibilities to their subordinates, juniors without knowing their capability or how will they complete their job or what strategy should be adopted to fulfil the assigned job. They do not bother about these things. They only pass on the responsibility to other juniors or subordinates and lead a hassle free life.

Before forwarding the responsibility, they do not even want to know about the nature of the work to be done and what would be the result. They give them the authority to solve them as per their knowledge and adopt their own strategy. They even do not like such people who want to take the initiative to do the assigned job. According to the middle Management, the work assignment should be taken from the seniors and should be done as per their view but no pain should be given to the assigner, as they do not want to take any pain about the work, which they had assigned, to their juniors. They believe their duty was only to give or assign a job to the subordinates but not to look after the assigned work. It is the duty of the workers, juniors, or subordinates who have been given to complete the assigned work, to solve the problems. The seniors have to work more so the juniors or subordinates should not disturb them. The Management expects from their juniors that they should work freely according to their own strategy within limitation and without harming any one or flouting the rules- and regulations or the systems of the Organisation.

The subordinates are not authorised to take any credit for any outstanding work done for the Organisation. The juniors should work hard but they are not authorised to let others know about the particular work but they should tell others that they could complete such difficult work, only under the guidance / supervision of their respected seniors, otherwise it would have been impossible for anyone of them to finish the job.

It is very much possible that the immediate senior does not have sufficient experience, knowledge etc, regarding the completion of the assigned work but inspite of having other weak points, they expect from their juniors that they should openly appreciate their work, planning & guidance. They also expect from them that they should always appreciate them or *flatter* them.

The seniors also want that their juniors should not appreciate any other senior except their concerned senior nor give credit to others.

DON'T INVOLVE OTHERS; MAINTAIN SECRECY

People should have the ability to maintain secrecy. From childhood, we learn in our family that we should not discuss our family matters with others /outsiders, even with our close relatives. The elder members of the family are only allowed to discuss about the sensitive matters in front of other people, or relatives because they have enough experience as to what and what not to be discussed with others.

Among our friends, we usually discuss on various topics or irrelevant subjects and want that it should not be discussed with anyone. Even our parents and other people should not know about these things. When we maintain secrecy, our friends have faith in us but as soon as we disclose the matter to others, our friends lose faith in us and in future they would not discuss any secret matter or any private topic with us. It means even our own close friends expect that we should maintain secrecy or we should not discuss the censored matters no matter how close we are to our other friends.

If, we are working in any Organisation, then it is our duty, not to involve any outsider in our official work as well as we should not discuss the official matter in front of the outsiders. If we work in the armed forces then it will be compulsory and in the country's interest, not to discuss any official secrecy or classified information in front of others. Even one is not allowed to discuss these sensitive matters with their own family members because nobody knows whether the family members or friends might disclose the country secrets to anti social elements thereby jeopardising national security.

It means the Management/Govt. expects from their employees that in Company's/ Country's/ Nation's interest, we should not discuss the official secrecy anywhere. If we are caught disclosing national secret, the Govt. will definitely penalise us or put us behind bars for this act. We may be terminated from our job and may be treated as a traitor. An Army personnel may be court martialled for his act.

In any Organisation, where we are working, the same logic is more or less applicable. Here also we are not authorised to leak out any official information anywhere. The Management cannot rely or have faith in such workers who try to leak out the secret information or who are not able to maintain secrecy on confidential matters. There are various positive and negative aspects associated with the office. If we are working with the HR Department, then it is our duty to keep mum on the confidential matters. The Management or seniors also expect from us that we should not discuss any official matter even with our colleagues. If we do such an activity, the Company will call us anti-organisational workers and the Management will kick us out from the company. The seniors desire that their subordinates having full knowledge of the departmental matters should be indifferent as if they do not know anything.

WORK ACCORDING TO YOUR VISION / JOB INTEREST

There are two major points in our behaviour, one is 'like' and the other is 'dislike'. Everyone wants to act according to his/her interest. If a person likes a particular subject / assigned job, then he/she will definitely try to finish the assigned job with full enthusiasm, interest, put in the best of efforts and try to get positive result. The worker will never mind, the duration, period of working hours, difficulties faced etc, if, he/she likes the project. He/she will work tooth and nail to finish it on time and on a positive note.

In this connection, there is an example from Sant. Tulsidasji's life. He loved his wife very much. One day, there was very heavy rain, which flooded the whole village and the surrounding villages. As Sri Tulsidasji had great love for his wife, he eagerly wanted to meet her. That day he didn't care for the flood water. He went to his-in-laws place to meet his wife and during his journey he held a snake, thinking it was a rope and entered the house of his wife.

An engineer loves his job/equipments/machines and does his work with interest. Since he loves his job, he will never say NO. in doing any work. He will never deny doing any assigned work related to engineering which gives him job satisfaction.

It means, one can easily face any problem/trouble during his working hour, if the assigned work is according to her/his choice. A musician never says NO, for any musical performance because he /she loves music. The musician never feels tired and inspite of being tired, he feels fresh and rejuvenated when he plays music for any number of hours.

The worker can give positive output with dedication and enthusiasm, which helps in the Organisational growth. On the other hand, the same person may not perform well, if the assigned job responsibilities are against his interest and knowledge.

However, in practical life, we generally find the truth of the working environment in any organisation, is very different from our belief. In some of the Organisations, there are few people whose motto is mainly to harass talented people and they play dirty politics, so that the deserving people do not get their due or the job.

They think that if the right people will get the right job according to their interest or knowledge or educational background, then they will be very happy and popular in a very short period. They may get more sympathy or attention of the concerned seniors and as a result, the concerned workers may get promotion/increment or other benefits from the Management without consulting the departmental head. At this situation, the concerned departmental head would never like that his subordinates or juniors get promotion or other benefits without taking him in confidence, If the Management gives more importance to the subordinates then in such cases, the concerned seniors do not want to see the progress of their juniors.

Sometimes, the Management makes the remark, "Do the needful" to the subordinates according to their view/ opinion. However, this kind of instruction is a very vague command for anyone to work further. The workers do not understand what they have to do, because here the concerned seniors do not have enough experience or educational qualification related to their work profile. Therefore, even if they have noble intention of helping their subordinates, they are unable to do so.

In the private Organisation, the maximum number of workers, initially get their department as per their appointment letters but as soon as they develop themselves in that particular department and the department seems to run smoothly, the immediate senior starts feeling jealous of such employees because such workers gradually get more popularity, promotion, increment and more attention of the higher Management. Everyone in the Organisation comes to know their working style and the contribution in the Organisational growth and public starts giving more importance to them.

The concerned seniors of such workers cannot tolerate their progress or, achievement, so they transfer them to such obscure departments where they have no knowledge or experience, so that they cannot discharge their duty properly and would be unable to finish the assigned job on time, and would get reprimanded which in turn would blemish their popularity.

In a new department / job, in which one has no experience, relevant education then it is sure the workers will not have enough interest to do the work in such department because they will have to learn the work from scratch then only they shall be able to work or carry on the assignment further.

In most of the cases, the top Management does not want to see such activities but the middle management of the same organisation who are themselves jealous of their own subordinates are always planning to create a situation to transfer them forcefully with bad remarks.

I can site many examples from the Govt. Departments. If a class- I, officer does a good job in his field and prevents other people to do any wrong practice already going on in the department from a long time. The Management sitting in the higher position does not like such an honest person and they take immediate action against the officer and try to transfer him in a remote area or undeveloped area where he would have to work from scratch. In short, we can say that some people from the higher Management do not like any energetic, enthusiastic worker or sensible person, who can work independently or can take decision on his own in any given circumstance in the company's interest. They do not like those people who in real sense work for the Organisation. They also do not like such people who do not leave any point for others to discuss about their error/mistake. Such so-called higher Management people like only those workers who make mistakes or cannot take any decision without the help of seniors. This is the reason an energetic, honest, enthusiastic, educated, and experienced worker is harassed in any Organisation.

The Management usually gives them such portfolios to handle in which they have no proper idea or experience, knowledge and a new place of posting; so that they cannot perform or reach the desired goal or they could get punishment from the concerned seniors. The example of Kiran Bedi – First woman I.P.S. officer was posted in the Tihar Jail in Delhi as a punishment posting which she reformed in such a drastic way that it has become a case study. Every cloud has a silver lining. Sincere, honest and dedicated workers should not be afraid of punishment.

It always happens that if a person is very hard working and the department is making profit, the Management wants to remove that person from that position and place its own crony or a close relative. Before removing that person, the Management starts condemning that worker by giving vague explanation/s and excuse.

On the other hand, if we take it in a positive way then we will find that there are many hidden factors, which the Management enforce to control the workers otherwise it will be very difficult to handle the workers at the workplace.

It has been observed that everybody wants to lead a confortable life. If the senior/incharge does not ask the workers to finish their work in a specific period or if it is not so important for the organisation then no one wants to complete his work at the workplace. When a worker does not work properly according to his job profile or when he misuses the liberty of the management or fails to give proper result to the Organisation. When he does not obey the instruction/order of the respective seniors or management or when he avails of continuous and frequent leave which hampers the work of the organisation, then the Management adopts strict measures and transfers such workers to relatively unknown place. Sometimes the Management gives them such a work profile, of which they have no knowledge or expreience. Sometimes the Management uses these factors to punish or teach a lesson to its non-performing workers. The Management wanth that such workers either learn to perform or perish from the organisation.

Sometimes, it also happens that if the seniors/immediate Management is not happy with their subordinates or on the other hand if the senior has some weak points and he is afraid of the intelligence, I.Q., spontaneity, good behaviour, contacts of his juniors with the higher Management then at this situation the immediate seniors, supervisor, head of the department get jealous, of such workers knowingly or unknowingly. Simultaneously, such seniors start false propaganda, so that such popular workers get transferred to any other department of which they have no experience. The jealous, incharge or superior wants the worker to get defamed by hook or by crook.

This circumstance can also occur if the seniors are not faithful with the Organisation. If the immediate boss, incharge, head of the department is corrupt or he has lost his senses. If he is involved in any financial irregularity, which defames the Organisation and his subordinates, know about it, then at this situation, also the Management adopts this strategy.

The Management knows very well that if its subordinates discharge their duties in such a manipulated way in their own interest then the higher Management may get into trouble and the genuine worker may never want that the Organisation face any trouble due to such tainted workers. So they try to transfer such workers and even the concerned seniors, if any, to some other place.

The seniors also adopt this strategy to transfer such people/ workers from whom they have fear or due to them, their service could get into trouble. They play as a villain and give wrong information about the sincere people in front of the higher Management only to condemn them or to damage their image in the Organisation. Here presentation is more important. All the corrupt people give their joint presentation to the higher Management in such a way as if they are the real well-wisher of the Organisation and present their proposal to them that if such workers will be transferred to a particular department, the Company will benefit more. They appreciate their activities to convince the Management for transferring them to a new department / field, in which they do not have any knowledge or experience. It means the immediate in charge or seniors want that such laborious, honest, dedicated persons should get away from their eyes, so that they could work according to their wishes, for or against the Organisation without fear of being caught.

Most of the people working in an Organisation do not want to work in favour of the Organisation. They do the job only due to fear of joblessness or unemployment. If the person is financially, stable then he usually misbehaves with his subordinates and harasses them because he does not have the fear of losing his job. He has sufficient bank balance to take care of, if any emergency arises.. However, on the other side when a worker is financially weak, then he cannot do anything except to make himself say yes to the whims and fancies of his concerned seniors or in charge. He never disobeys the rules and regulations of the Organisation because he knows that if he loses his job, he would be from hand to mouth. His family will get into a financial mess and will have to face problems. Such workers will never oppose anything. They never try to oppose any rules and regulations or even participate in any anti-organisational activities, going on in front of their eyes by their concerned seniors or middle Management, as they are helpless and need to secure their job.

As soon as their financial position improves and their job is secured, or the concerned Management cannot do anything towards their wrong practices, their behaviour immediately changes. They start anti-organisational activities at their workplace. They do not want to work. They have no interest in Organisational benefits; they are only interested to save themselves from the trouble, if anybody starts to think as to how they could make money from the Organisation, so soon or in such less time. They have a hidden strategy and manipulate the rules and regulations of the organisation for their own benefit.

JEALOUS NATURE

Having a little bit of jealousy is a good sign for the health and growth of an individual or an organisation. Jealous nature is an inbuilt character of human beings. If we do not have jealousy then it is possible that we cannot develop ourselves in various ways. During our childhood, we are very jealous of our own brothers, sisters, friends and neighbours. Our Mother always told us not to be jealous but try to have healthy and competitive rivalry, which would benefit us. Therefore, it is necessary to improve ourselves, so that we could get more marks than our friends and siblings in the examination. Due to the feeling of healthy rivalry, one starts studying hard and gets good marks in the examination.

Jealousy can be of two types: Positive and Negative jealousy. If we take jealousy in a positive way then it is sure that we will have a good, growth and a positive and healthy attitude in our life. On the other hand, if we take it in a negative way, then its result can be fatal and dangerous. Our progress will be hampered and we will not succeed in our life. We will deviate from the main objective of our life. The society, where we live, will never like us. We will have to face hidden problems in our practical life. At the workplace, we also face similar situation where all the colleagues are working, sitting and eating together; are very jealous of each other. They do not want to see their progress and development and they cannot see their colleagues or seniors getting promotion or other benefits.

Even a junior worker also does not want to see the growth of his boss and the boss in turn does not want to recommend the juniors for promotion, as he also feels very jealous of them. Sometimes the boss or seniors suffer from great inferiority complex. They think that if they will recommend them for promotion, then they will lead a good life and in future, they might supersede their seniors, will have great responsibility and reputation, and they in turn will be ignored by the seniors as well as the juniors.

Due to the jealous feeling, dirty games of politics develop in the Organisation. One person does not want to see the other person when both are equally responsible and important for the Organisation. Since the Management does not want to tolerate such jealous natured persons as their business may get hampered. The growth of the Company may also reduce. Management expects from their workers that they should be satisfied with whatever they are getting. They should not bother about the others.

They should only concentrate on their own business. So, that the result of their efforts should be proven good in the Company's interest.

It has been observed that if the Management feels that due to the jealous feeling of some workers, their business is decreasing or is getting affected then it is possible that the Management may transfer them to another place, or may compel them to leave the Organisation. In both ways, the workers will be the losers. Therefore, it is better that such attitude should not be adopted by any of the workers working in the Organisation. If anyone has the feeling of jealousy, then, it should be in positive way in the Organisation as well as in the general life. Jealousy is bad but healthy rivalry is good for both the individual and the Organisation.

Sometimes, the bosses feel that their juniors, who are working hard to achieve their goal or objective will not harm them in future and help them. They will work on behalf of them and credit will automatically go to the seniors, then it is quite possible that the bosses would recommend them for higher position and promotion and would not feel jealous of them.

FRIENDSHIP WITHIN THE ORGANISATION IS BAD & DANGEROUS.

A magnet attracts the opposite pole but when we correlate/compare it with human nature of the workers, working at any workplace in any Organisation, we find that like-minded or like pole or same pole attract each other and the different natured people or opposite pole repels each other.

It means in any Organisation, if there are two persons of negative character working and thinking negative things for the Organisation, are very good friends. They gradually come very close in a short period. As per the observation of the people, it is found that friendship first develops in the school and then gets less in the college but if it develops at the workplace then it is very bad and dangerous for the Organisation. If a person develops friendship with other colleagues working in the same, Organisation then the following situations may occur:

- Friendship between the opposite sexes.
- Friendship between the same sex.
- Friendship between the departments
- Friendship between the seniors and the juniors working in the same department.
- Friendship between the Management and the Employees.

It has been observed that in an Organisation there are some people who are still unmarried and are crazy to talk to female co-workers. They do not bother what the others will think, what impact it will have on their career and performance. They always have it in their mind to develop friendship with a particular female staff. Their meeting place is the office canteen, where they have enough time to exchange their views about each other. They share their food, lunch with each other and in some cases; dangerous liaisons or extra marital affairs begin. SMS and internet chatting is also very harmful.

Such people gradually shift their attention from their assigned job to the friendship towards female staff.

Every time they think / engage their mind on how will she get happy, what does she want, her likes and dislikes her problems, how they can be solved etc. They do not bother about their official assigned job/responsibilities. They do not think that their activities, attitude is hampering and damaging the company's financial growth or the brand name, thus tarnishing its reputation in the market. If they feel that they are not comfortable in that Organisation then they start planning to leave the job.

The new Company may prove better for them but in normal cases, people get into problems, if they develop friendship with the opposite sex in the same Organisation, as old habits die hard.

Sometimes, they pass on a confidential report to their partner who is not concerned with the matter and working in another department who may leak the information. This is very dangerous and we should be loyal to the mother Organisation. The Management never likes such workers whose better half is found working either in the same field or in the rival Organisation. As of today, we are facing a tough competitive market. The Management always remains cautious about their confidential report, planning, and strategy about the Organisation growth.

For example, two workers who are working in the visual media but in different channels. At such a situation the Management keeps their eyes on such staff whom they fear would leak out the channel's information regarding the upcoming programmes and new strategies to get good TRP to the rival channel. In short, it is clear that the Management does not want or like such staff who are faithless. In the Organisation such staff face a lot of problems, and do not get desired promotion and increment or other benefits even if they are hard working and devoted staff because of their misdeed or misconduct.

Sometimes, it is found that two male staff, working in the same Organisation and in the same department, have a good friendship. After getting friendly these staff members start skipping their work and responsibilities. Unfortunately even, if they are giving more time to their department/Organisation their work quality is bad. Then we should think that in the long run their activities would lead to heavy loss/damage to the Organisation. Such people gradually become very corrupt, start taking bribes, start unfair activities against the Organisational norms. There are so many Organisations, Private / as well public, where the workers are found working late hours.

A worker gives his eight-hours of duty at his workplace to meet the assigned job/ responsibilities but if the same worker starts giving more time in the office to complete the same assigned work and sits in the office for late hour just to chat and gossip. It means during daytime, they are not utilising their time in finishing their work but they engage themselves in useless gossip with other colleagues, official friends. Due to their friendship within the department or with other department, they become very popular among the staff. Gradually such workers become very familiar with all the demerits of others or the so-called official friends. However, each friend knows the weak points of each other, so all of them maintain secrecy of the misdeed/ anti-organisational activities. Working long hours in the office also means that they might be engaged in financial irregularity or indulging in immoral activities.

In the present days we read in the newspapers usually that a particular worker of a particular Organisation/ Company had stolen/cheated the Company, where they were working. Such an incident occurs due to the development of inter department or intra department friendship.

Without having friendship with other colleagues of the Organisation, it is very difficult or impossible to cheat a Company or commit any fraud in the Organisation. Overall, the Company loses its reputation as well as its financial growth. Hence the Management does not like such friendship among its workers. If the higher Management knows the fact, the Management gradually starts ignoring them and removes them from key positions. At such situation, the personal relationships of the workers start disbalancing the harmony of other workers at their workplace in any Organisation. Management expects from their loyal disciplined workforce that they should come to the office as per the office schedule and discharge their assigned duties, responsibilities accordingly without harming anyone.

In daily life, we come across the news that in some Bank, a group of employees pilfers the Bank Accounts by fraud and Bank loses in crores. This type of fraud is not possible for a single person working in the Bank but it is only possible when a group of staff conspire against the Bank with their colleagues. Without involvement of many colleagues, it cannot be possible, for a single employee to commit such a heinous act. These incidents occur due to the friendship between /among the workers of the Bank. The development of quick friendship is one of the main reasons of frauds or scams, which the like-minded staff conspire to get quick bucks and subsequently punishment.

Sometimes, we read in the newspapers that some people had taken loan from the Bank without depositing margin money or based on duplicate papers. These activities are possible when the staff within the loan department and the payment department are close friends or buddies. This is also possible due to the friendship, between the employees of the Bank. In this way, we can conclude that workers should not develop friendship at their workplace. They should worship the responsibilities, profession and should not cheat it come what may. We must pay respect to all the seniors, colleagues but we should not develop or encourage friendship at the workplace. If somehow friendship among the colleagues develop then one day will come when they would be caught red handed doing wrong against the Organisation. Wrongdoing cannot be hidden for a long time as the pot of evil breaks very soon.

Apart from the friendship, some persons in the Organisation always condemn their colleagues or other people. They never seem to be happy with the other people's work, performance and in their mind; most of the workers are corrupt and take bribes. They are not at all courteous or talk politely with their co-workers. They always try to create difference between two employees by giving false statements against each other. Though such persons may be in a high position, so a common man does not raise his voice against them, that they are speaking lies and the seniors are taking advantage of their position. However, God is great. He oversees all the happenings in the world. Therefore, one day the top / higher Management comes to know the reality or true colour of such seniors and the Management sacks them from the Organisation.

As the Management does not tolerate such seniors and their misdemeanour so at a suitable situation, the person involved in such activities are asked to leave the Organisation directly or if they are on obligatory post then the Management may change their department or transfer them where there will be no work for them. They cannot demote them but by providing no work, portfolio, they are punished which leads to frustration and depression thereby challenging their market value.

TAKE IT FOR GRANTED

Everything has its own importance. One should always respect others. Nothing is in our control. Everything has its own limitation and nothing can happen beyond limitation. One person can give respect up to a certain extent or limit to others. For example, if we have a pet cat. She may be familiar, innocent and obedient to her master. He may play with her, give her milk and food, and take her for an outing because the whole family loves and dotes on her. Inspite of her innocence, we should not take her for granted. We should not think that we are the master of her destiny and she cannot do anything wrong.

The character and behaviour of a cat, is very dangerous and by nature, she is violent. If we put her in a closed room and begin to irritate her then, for some time, she will play with us but as soon as she comes to know that, the person is going to harm her then she starts getting savage like a leopard. She can strangle the neck of the concerned person, or scratch him with her claws, which may result in his death.

Similarly, in practical life, we should respect other's views and opinions. If, it is required, we should also learn from our subordinates without any hesitation. It is upto us as to how we take it or how we react. Apart from the above, we read daily in the newspapers that the junior had insulted his seniors/superior and vice versa and sometimes killed him due to some unavoidable circumstance. Once, we had read in the newspaper that Namdev, a para military personnel had killed his senior in the daytime in front of many people at the Mumbai Airport as he was desperate to go home and he was not granted leave by his senior from a long time.

This crime took place because the senior had taken his subordinate staff for granted. A senior believes that he is the boss of his subordinates or he is the decision maker of his subordinates. He can do anything, according to his fancy. If the senior harasses his juniors then the juniors will not react but when the same seniors cross their limit, then the juniors too will not tolerate their seniors nonsense and will definitely react just like a pet-cat or leopard as they are provoked very badly. They will not bother about the punishment, which they are sure to get. The juniors too can take the law into their own hands when provoked or insulted. Nobody is invincible, so nobody should be taken for granted.

It means, nothing is under our control, so we should not take anything or any person for granted that they cannot harm us. We should always remember, that "Excess of anything is bad." In school, where children are studying and fortunately, if one of their parents is working there as a teacher and is teaching her/his child then he should not address him/her as dad/mom in the class. He has to call him/her either Sir or Madam, and not Mom or Dad, because, he should maintain a proper decorum in school. He cannot take them for granted. If we tease or **bully** our lean-thin or fat friend. For some times, he and all the other friends will enjoy it but one day will come when he will get irritated and begin retaliating. It means we should not take him or her for granted that they can never be angry at our behaviour.

We can get several examples from our general life on this subject. Our Boss may be our school/college friend but at the work place, he is the owner of the company and many workers/ employees are working under him. However, the boss can be our old friend and we might have made several unofficial talks on various subjects and enjoyed each other's Company. But when we are working in the Organisation, where the friend is our boss. We should never take him for granted. We should always respect him and his position. He may not say anything to us, whether he had felt bad or not at our behaviour but gradually the same boss may start avoiding us. He expects that even the junior person who was his friend should behave courteously at the workplace, as he is the boss. We are like general workers at the workplace, and office decorum should be maintained.

We should always remember that the employer is like GOD for us at the workplace. We all depend upon him and we must obey his decisions. If we have devoted so many years in one Organisation or if we are working in a single Company for the last 20 Years or so and the owner of the Company wants to introduce his second generation on the key position then no one should take it otherwise or in a negative way. We should welcome our new guardian/ boss/ employer. We should not take him for granted and that the supreme boss/ owner's son/children do not know anything or are very young and in-experienced. Even if we have seen them as small children from their childhood we should respect their decisions and take them seriously, guide them and take their order where needed.

Management expects from the old workers of their Company that they should always guide their children at the workplace and co-operate with them in making the working system smooth. If their children do any wrong or take wrong decision due to the influence of colleagues or lack of experience then it is the duty of old workers to inform about the happening to the higher Management in a very polite and diplomatic way in such a way that the snake dies without the stick getting broken.

Everybody knows that the Company is of supreme importance than any individual. Management expects from their employees that if their son/children are going in a wrong direction, due to any reason, which the higher Management does not know about and it will hamper the Company's image / reputation / financial status etc, the workers or so-called old workers should tell the truth to the top Management in Company's interest. If the children have done any commendable job, then this too should be conveyed to them.

If anyone or any old employee is not working in favour of the Company or does not care about the new boss then the top Management gradually starts maintaining distance from him and after some time he is transferred to any other place or department whether he likes it or not. Thus, it is clear that at the workplace, we should not take anything /any person/ any seniors/ Management for granted under any circumstance because excess of anything is bad. We should live within our limitation. It would be very fruitful for the Organisation as well as for the employees.

Sometimes, it has also been observed in many cases that an old staff /worker did not give due importance to the Management and took several decisions arbitrarily without the consultation of concerned seniors/authority and gave the order of termination to some employees, by giving the instruction of being fired from tomorrow onwards or dismissed or appointed someone without the consultation of the concerned authority. The Management will never tolerate such activities and take legal action in the Company's interest against the concerned people who misuse their authority and take the Management for granted towards planning and decision-making.

At this situation, we should keep ourselves in touch with the higher Management along with giving right information and advice in the company's interest.

ILL TREATMENT & BEHAVIOUR

The treatment and the behaviour of others have a great impact on our life and the development and achievements of workers depend upon the degree of treatment and behaviour of seniors with their subordinates. If the society, Management or /family treat and behave well with the members of the society, employees or family members, then the atmosphere of such society will be very sound and healthy. People of the society will try to be friendly with each other and they will be helpful to each other.

The development of people living in a harmonious atmosphere, will be sound and will be able to get their desired goal but if they will be treated badly or ill treated by their associates/ members, it is sure that the development of such members or the family, cannot be good, sound or healthy.

For example, if the parents always quarrel at home, fight for small things or petty issues and condemn their children for small faults and if the parents do not listen to the facts and always abuse and ill treat their children, then the children gradually become frustrated, and would not be able to concentrate on their studies. They will not be able to get good marks in their exams. It is also possible that they will run away from their home. All this depends upon the attitude and behaviour of the parents. As the parents are our natural guardians, our name, prestige and social status are all associated with the parents and without the guardian /father's name one will have to face many difficulties in the society to survive.

When we co-relate the above facts and the incidents with our employer/Management, we will find that both are very similar with the working environment. Sometimes, the Management, few Managers, incharge also behave very roughly and rudely with their subordinates. They condemn their subordinates for small negligence and faults. At this situation, the Management thinks that the subordinates should treat their seniors like a father or an elder brother and should not react on small things or issues. If today they are condemning their subordinates then tomorrow they will also love them. If they give any punishment to their subordinates then it is sure that tomorrow their senior/ Management/ incharge will also appreciate them for their work. They will definitely promote them or recommend them for a raise or incentive, so that the subordinates do not take it otherwise. They should always take their treatment in a positive way. If they will not react on their ill treatment/behaviour, then after a few months or days the attitude of the management or incharge will automatically change towards them.

Management expects from their subordinates that if the Management/Senior/ incharge are doing any wrong, the subordinates should mind their own business and they should not disclose the facts to others. However, in the same situation when the middle management expects from their subordinates that they should keep their mouth shut and should not highlight any wrongdoing, which is going on in the Organisation or in the concerned department. At the same time, the top Management expects from the same subordinates that they should not keep their mouth shut when they see anything wrong or any wrongdoing in the Organisation. They should immediately inform the top management with the facts and figures in the Company's interest. If they do not do so, then it will definitely be observed by the top Management regarding the concerned workers that they are not faithful/loyal employees of their Organisation.

For example, in a big/ large Organisation, there may be a person in a high position. Since he was not very much educated, so, he did not like to see any educated subordinates working under him. He was a sadist but due to some unavoidable circumstance, he was working in that Organisation from the first day of the beginning of the Organisation. Everybody was familiar with the ill behaviour of that senior. Most of his time was passed in harassing the juniors; He always used to treat his junior like a servant/slave. He was expecting from his subordinates that they should work under him just like an idiot, who cannot distinguish between good or bad, right or wrong, what is to be done and what not is to be done, which work is in the Company's interest or which is not etc. Such seniors expect from their juniors that they should talk to their colleagues about their harassment, because due to their sick attitude, they may command their subordinates.

The seniors want to create panic among the junior workers, so that they live in fear and the concerned seniors could easily impose their ill will on them. If anybody wants to expose them or speak up, they immediately transfer them to other departments or divisions or to some other establishment as a punishment.

At the same time, the top management's expectations from their subordinates are very different from the above. The top management had openly instructed each staff that the subordinates should not have fear in making any complaint about anybody to the top Management. The top Management expects from the workers working in any division/section/ unit, that they are very much free to report against anybody (positive or negative) in Company's interest. The complaint/ report made by any one may be very fruitful for the Organisation. His complaint and report sometime may rescue the Organisation from any future mishap or difficulty.

After hearing the voice of the common workers, the top Management takes immediate decision. They take proper action against the concerned person/s. The top Management always boosts up the morale of grassroots level workers / employees, who give the right information at the right time. Such staff gets appreciation and reward from time to time. They never try to harass them in any way.

No one is bigger than the Company or its interest. In this way, when a worker, working in a junior cadre makes out right complaint against the ill treatment and behaviour about the Middle Management. After listening to the whole matter face to face, the top management must issue a show cause notice to the middle Management for their fault or demerit, which could have defamed the Organisation. The top Management can also ask the middle management to work without any portfolio. The middle Management would be getting the salary but would have no work. It is like a minister without a ministry or without a portfolio. It is a big slap on their face.

The workers/employees are also human beings. They also have some problems and those problems may be associated with their personal life or their family. In real sense, the management at any level does not like to entertain the grievances of any person /worker because it may be an obstacle in the growth of the Organisation. If a person is greedy, then it is sure that he cannot discharge his duties / responsibilities within a specific period of time in the Company's interest. Due to his nature, the subordinates working under him would be unsatisfied and due to their dis-satisfaction, the development of the Organisation would be very slow. The workers / employees would not be in a position to give the desired result and gradually the reputation / the market value of the Organisation would become very low. Considering these factors the Management does not want their staff/ employees/worker to be greedy or unsatisfied.

TAKE THE INITIATIVE AT WORK

The word "initiate" is a very important factor for the human beings. From birth, the mother tries to teach her children, how to take initiative to walk, speak, and study as well as how to react. If a child does not take the initiative to speak or walk, then it might be possible that such child would not speak, walk or would be a late learner. We react due to the internal natural initiative taken automatically by us. This initiative depends upon the interest of the concerned person in the concerned work/action/reaction. If a person has his / her interest on a particular work then, he will do the job without getting any instruction from his boss. He will take decision either wrong or right according to the situation without consulting his concerned seniors.

If a person knows that after the completion of the assigned job, he will certainly get more incentive, salary hike, promotional benefits etc. Then such a person will complete his assigned job, even after the office hours. He will try to complete the work in a scientific manner, so that the result could be highlighted in the Company. Management expects from their juniors/ subordinates that they should take initiative at their workplace. No one will come all the time to guide or to give them instructions on how to compete the assigned work as well as what work is to be done in the Company's interest. It should be competed first on priority basis. For example, at the workplace, if a fire breaks out, the Management expects from their employees that they should take quick decision themselves on how to control the fire. They should neither ask the Management how to control the fire nor wait for instructions at the time of emergency.

If anything is going on at the workplace against the Organisational interest, the worker/staff should confidently take decision to apprise the real facts to the Management so that such happening can be stopped/ brought under control or it should not be repeated in future.

Management expects that the employees should work and take interest in their work in such a manner that they are doing their own job and not for the office but for their own sake and interest. They should treat the workplace as their own. Then only the workers will get attached with their assigned work and the work will automatically get accelerated. Company will increase their productivity and the concerned workers will be benefited accordingly.

When, we travel in a train, we have to take care of all our belongings. No other passenger will be responsible or answerable for it being lost. All the passengers have their belongings to be taken care of. No one will ask them or guide them in reaching the destination. Similarly, they will have to take interest/ initiative to confirm their tickets during the journey. If it is not confirmed then no other passenger will bother for the same. They will have to take their own initiative, to get reserved tickets by buying it on time so that they do not face inconvenience during the journey.

More or less the environment of any workplace is also very similar with the situation in the train or at the railway platform.

As all the passengers have to reach their own destination, they are responsible for their own safety. Similarly, in an office, all the workers have their own separate job responsibilities/ mission/ target. They will have to take self decision/initiative for any assigned work/job on how they would finish that assigned job in a good and result oriented manner in Company's interest. It is just like the passengers waiting at the railway platform for their desired trains. They are only responsible for which train to take and how they will accommodate their belongings. After reaching the destination, they will have to check whether all the belongings have reached safely or not.

In the same way, at the workplace a person is assigned to do a particular work at a definite schedule. It will be the sole responsibility of the concerned person to take initiative and do the homework concerning the assigned work. The concerned person will have to think how he will complete the assigned work/task in the stipulated period in company's interest. The management also expects from their employees, a good result. If a person is appointed in the Company as a driver then the Management expects from him that he should know every road, route and subway. They should know to drive the car very smoothly. The Management expects that if a road is found closed due to any reason, the driver should take the initiative to drive the car in another direction or alternate way, so that the officers sitting / travelling in the car reach their destination without wasting too much of time.

Sometimes, the Managers sitting in the car may not have the knowledge about the direction or address where they have to visit. At this stage, passengers expect from the driver that he should take interest to know the correct address of the destination with the help of local people, which should not cause inconvenience to the people sitting in the car. Similarly, the Management expects from their employees /workers that they should also take interest themselves in getting the desired result and if they are having difficulty then they can take the help of the experienced workers without any hesitation.

If a worker would take interest as well as the initiative in the right way feeling that he is working for his own office, then he should take decision assuming that he is the owner of that Organisation. If he would take the initiative then it is sure that the result will never be wrong. He should work, assuming that the Company belongs to him.

If any planning/norms/rules made by the Management are not followed by any of the workers or disobeyed by the workers, then the Management expects from their workers that they should inform them immediately, so that they can take proper action against such disobedient workers. Such activity would be highly appreciated by the top Management and such employees should be encouraged to do good work for the welfare of the organisation. The Organisation always comes first and foremost before anything else.

At the workplace, the workers are from different age groups. There may be a generation gap between them. In some cases, in the same department, there are two people; one is of the father's age, while the other is of the son's age. However, the experience expertise, enthusiasm of both the employees is necessary for the Organisation. The older one is one of the oldest employee as well as the most loyal staff. The older one may be very faithful but may have less knowledge of modern technology and may even have less information of the modern working systems compared to the younger staff. They may have less knowledge about the computer and may not be highly equipped with the electronic technology, which is necessary in today's competitive market while the younger employee must be very tech savvy and smart.

At such situation, the Management does not want to leave this loyal staff, who has devoted his most valuable time/ life in this Organisational development. The Management expects simply from him that he should take interest in learning about the modern gadget and its operation from his juniors, colleagues or may be from outside institute as well as develop his basic knowledge about the computer and the competitive market without harming any one. If he is finding it difficult to learn the modern technology then he should join the refresher course somewhere nearby, so that without harming the daily routine, he can develop himself by joining the technical training course. He should not feel shy in learning because there is no age limit in learning. People always learn something from the other since their birth to death. When the old employee had joined the Organisation, then at that time English might not be the official language of communication. Then at this juncture, he may have to brush up his English.

In the modern days, people may not have much knowledge but they are very fluent in English because of the modern Public Schools and environment/society. In few cases, the younger generation is found to be very dynamic towards making the presentation to the Organisation whereas the older employees are found somewhat weaker than the new ones. The

Management expects from such workers that they should try to develop themselves to learn the new trends of marketing/ presentation. They should always try to update themselves with the new happening/ news and technology, so that they should be able to make themselves equal to the junior or the new employees. This would only be possible, when the older employees would take initiative to try to learn as well as also try to understand the reason why they are not invited or their names are not included in the Company level presentation or image branding of the Organisation. Therefore, the catchword is to try to invent, innovate and update themselves.

Apart from the official work assignments, if the Management is going to organise a function anywhere, whether in the office premises or at a private place. After the finalisation of the venue and of the programmes, the people or staff who are finally responsible for the execution of that function, start expecting from their juniors staff/ workers that they should come forward themselves to help and organise the party/function, because only the finalisation of the date of any function is not enough for its success. There are many works to be done which have to be completed before the function starts.

The Management expects their juniors to come forward and ask them frankly that they would like to participate/ organise the function successfully and have already prepared a strategy, but need their guidelines.

Therefore, they must request the seniors for their guidance and they would manage everything. They should prepare a checklist, of what should be done, how things would be managed and that they need their wholehearted support.

If the function is going to be arranged at a private place of any senior/H.O.D. However, if the function is not official and it is totally a personal function of a senior then at this situation, the Manager cannot involve any official staff for their private function. However, they expect a lot from their juniors, without telling or instructing anything. They expect that their juniors / subordinates should come forward and be ready to help /cooperate and they should manage all these responsibilities without botheration. They should be ready to take all the responsibilities or burden. After all, they are helping their own seniors. That is their duty.

It may be quite possible that the payment of that party will have to be borne by the subordinates. The Management / seniors / in charge, expect from their subordinates that they should also cooperate with them financially without being asked. The employees should take interest or create their interest in each work of the Organisation whether it is official or personal. The employees should take interest in the work in such a way that their name could come in the good books of the Management/H.O.D./ In charge, because without coming in the good books,, they would not forward their names for any benefits or they would not recommend their names for promotion, increment or for other benefits.

The employees should always be careful as well as attentive towards responsibilities, as a common man takes too much interest in useless gossip at the workplace regarding the office and colleagues etc. They listen very carefully at the useless talks. In the same way, they should also take interest to complete their assigned responsibilities within the given schedule. If a woman has no interest in cooking, then it is sure that she cannot prepare a tasty meal in spite of having every facility available. She can prepare only those food items, which she likes. The food items prepared and liked by her, may be very tasty but on the other hand, when she has to prepare food for others in the family and she may have less interest in those particular food items then the prepared food will not be good or tasty.

I mean that each worker should take interest himself to learn new things so that his or her output should be very good. A new bride when she comes to her- in-laws place, may not know to prepare a good meal and she may have to bear the comments from her in-laws. Her mother-in- law may always compare her with other women who know cooking very well. By compulsion or situational demand, she has to take interest in the preparation of different varieties of food. She gradually learns to make good food. This could only be possible, because she had taken keen interest in learning and preparing tasty food.

Similarly, at the workplace, when new recruits join an Organisation, they may be a fresher for some time and they may not have knowledge of working as they had never done such work before. Such workers shall also have to listen to various comments and bear the brunt from the seniors, colleagues etc. Without learning, they may not be confirmed in a pre-determined period. As soon as, they develop themselves to learn and bear the workload for which, they were hired. Then the concerned seniors become satisfied with their work performance and the concerned Managers/ incharge recommend their names for confirmation of their job/service. I mean that a worker shall have to take interest, in his work without fail and without taking interest in his assigned work, he cannot survive and also none of the Organisation will tolerate such people, who do not take interest in their work. Such workers can never be promoted or given other benefits.

ANTI-ORGANISATIONAL ACTIVITIES

We may live in a big or a small family and each family has the head of the family who makes the rules and regulations, which all the members of that family have to follow for mutual satisfaction and peace. If a single person disobeys the rules and regulations of the family then, the harmony of the family is directly affected. If a member makes an unnecessary expense without taking permission by the head of the family then the peace and harmony of the family gets affected. If, a student does not obey the rules and regulations of the school or college, if he does not attend the classes regularly and he does not study seriously, then his result immediately gets affected. The image of the concerned family as well as the school/college will also be affected due to his misdemeanour. The parents and the teacher also do not like their wards/students being absent without any reason. They expect from their children/students that they should take their studies seriously and do their work very promptly, so that their result could improve and get more marks. They expect from them that they should not do any work, which harms the growth as well as the reputation of the family. They think that if there is any problem in the family, because of some members disobeying the rules and regulations, knowingly or un-knowingly, should consult the head of the family directly, so that some immediate steps could be taken to avoid the problem.

Similarly, in the Organisation, there are certain rules and regulations, which all the workers/ staff have to follow in the Organisational interest to achieve a common goal. No one is allowed to disobey the said rules and regulations of the Organisation, which is directly connected, with the reputation of the Organisation. For example, if a person, is taking bribes for doing any official work from any outsider or, if he is selling any Company's Asset without taking the permission of the concerned Management. This way the reputation of the Company will be affected due to the anti Organisational activity, which is highly objectionable for any Head or the Management.

Sometimes, it has been observed in many Organisations that workers gossip uselessly with their colleagues or with the outsiders, about the merits and demerits of the Organisation and the Seniors/H.O.D./incharge, which is very objectionable in the eyes of the Management. The Management does not like that their workers who are totally dependent upon the said Organisation, where they are working should not talk needlessly, which is against the organisation. No child likes to listen anything against his parents and the parents also do not want to listen anything against their own children. So, in the family interest, children do not like to discuss anything related to the parents and the parents also never like to know that their children uselessly talk about their merits and demerits.

If the parents find that, their own children are talking against them, they become very upset and angry and may punish them. They may stop giving them pocket allowances for the required and necessary items, which they may have asked before. They should learn to respect the parents first. If we do not respect our parents, then it is sure that we will never be good citizens. In the long run, such people cannot love the country as well as the Organisation where they would work, after the completion of their studies.

Therefore, it is very important to respect our elders and parents. In spite of having several demerits, children or the workers of any Organisation should not point the demerits about their parents or the Organisation. The workers are like children to the management. Therefore, they should not speak about the demerits of their H.O.D., seniors, incharge. If the seniors, H.O.D. or incharge comes to know that their subordinates are talking about them negatively, they may become very angry and may use their official power/authority immediately upon the concerned workers to punish them. The concerned workers/staff will be immediately punished, harassed tortured or transferred to other department. In the long run, the Management may tell such employees that their service is not required in the Organisation.

Sometimes, people knowingly or unknowingly work in such a way that its result affects the growth of the Organisation. The seniors, H.O.D or incharge, the Management as well as the concerned seniors never like such people within their department and the organisation.

Therefore, they would try to remove them from their path or from the company. In some cases, it has been found that if the accountant is authorised to sign the chequebook on behalf the Company, then it may prove very dangerous for the Organisation. Mainly in an Organisation, at least two signatories are required to sign the chequebook but for correction point of view, only one signature is required for the counter sign in the place of correction on the chequebook. A very wicked and wilful accountant can financially cheat the Company with his signature on the counter part/correction made on the chequebook, and make it in his favour.

If the accountant plans to cheat the Organisation, he can do so very easily. He can take the benefit of the poor rules and regulations or the loopholes of the organisation. The accountant can change the party's name written on the chequebook leaf and if he wishes, he can write his own name after making all the official entries of the instruments and himself sign on the correction of the chequebook leaf.

The Bank will make payment to the changed party name without any problem or verification. If the employees cheat the company in such a way that the matter comes in the eyes of the Management, the Management cannot tolerate such employees. They would immediately be terminated from their job in the Organisation. If anybody does anti- organisational activity in any way, his activities would certainly come to light one day and the Company/Organisation/ Management would terminate him as soon as the fact comes to light.

WORK ACCORDING TO THE INSTRUCTIONS OR JO SENIOR/HEAD/ INCHARGE KO HAI PASAND WOHI KAAM KARENGE

Nature is a great teacher and it gives us many lessons. The only thing is that we should learn to understand or uncode the answer of nature and learn from it. Everybody has seen a big river, with powerful water current. The main water current is so powerful that the current can gulp down everything coming on its way or in its direction. It can swallow everything without making the least of effort. On the other hand, we can also think from its opposite perspective. We will find that those objects or things which do not resist to flow with the main current will be carried very easily with it. If any particular object resists flowing in that main water current, the water current will use its power to engulf it but after some time, such objects are automatically thrown by the water current to the bank of the river and the objects, which did not resist to flow with the current, will be taken along with the water and will become a part of it. It is also true that it is very difficult to flow against the current. This applies to the workplace as well.

Generally, people love to keep parrots as their pet at home. They teach them to talk whatever they like or their family likes and after some times, the same parrot starts chanting the same sentences and names, which his master had taught him. Whenever he sees any person in the house, he begins to repeat the sentences/chants, which he had learnt. The master/head of the family/owner of that parrot feels very proud to listen to his banter. He feels very happy and loves the parrot very much.

Some people love to keep a dog at home as their pet as dog is a very faithful and obedient animal. The pet dog reacts according to his master's wishes. If his master gives him an order to sit down and keep quiet, the dog will sit without making any noise. Whenever this dog sees his master, he starts wagging his tail in expression of his love. The master likes his dog along with his actions and reactions, which is according to his choice. Therefore, he takes him out for a walk and talks about his good habits in front of his guests.

The same logic, applies at the Organisation or at the workplace. At the workplace, the managers /seniors/ H.O.D. or office in charge, generally, say nothing directly but they like those employees/workers who say yes all the time to their queries. There are some systems running in an Organisation in the Company's interest. Inspite of the Company's rules and regulations, the middle Management makes their own system to control the working of the workforce. At this situation, the middle management wants that their subordinates should follow their verbal instruction, statements all the time.

They desire/expect from their juniors that they should have blind faith on their concerned Bosses. If the boss tells them that a particular thing is wrong then the subordinates should believe that it is wrong without making any argument. They must always think that the boss is always right. They are never wrong. In other words, we can say that Management/boss/seniors expect from their subordinates that they should follow the wind direction, water current or office atmosphere and let themselves float freely as per the senior's wishes. They should never resist at any level, as they are not authorised to think but work, without opening their mouth they should work and have blind faith on their boss. (Just like the washer man's donkey, who has to obey the order of his master always)

The workers or employees, who follow these factors, will certainly be loved by the middle management and not by the higher management because sometimes the feeling towards the Organisation varies from the middle Management and the top Management or Higher Management. Middle Management expects from the subordinates that they should leave their mind at their home when they are coming to the office because it is not required at the workplace, as the middle Management will provide the mind to work according to their will.

Management thinks that their employees should work at their workplace, just like a horse that looks straight running on the road without looking at the left or at the right direction. They follow the directions of the road as their master directs them. The Master loves only those horses who do not give any trouble on the road. Similarly, Management also loves only those employees who follow the principles of the workplace/ dictats of their boss and do their work without seeing anywhere/anything, whether they are going in the right or wrong direction or in favour of the Company. The employees should work whether the work is in the Company's interest or not. It is not their job to think. They should work as per the desire of their boss.

If one works accordingly, they will definitely be promoted to the higher position. It is another thing that after getting promotion, these employees may be challenged in front of the top Management, as they are shocked to see such persons on higher positions. At the top Management, the feeling, towards the discharge of work is totally different and sometimes these promoted employees are adjusted as per their profile and responsibilities. The top Management may demote or transfer the undeserving and unqualified Managers.

TO RESPECT THE SENIORS / COLLEAGUES

Each human being loves to hear his own praise from others. Even THE Almighty God, also likes to hear praise from his devotees in the form of hymns shloks or chants. We try to praise The Almighty God in our prayer when we are in trouble. When we face problems, we usually go to the temple or to our place of worship to seek his blessings by praising HIM. We pray to him from the deepest core of our heart to give us His blessings. We even apologise to him for hurting or harming others knowingly or unknowingly. We pray to him for fulfilling our desires and if our prayers are true, God definitely gives us blessings and fulfils our possible desires as per the work and degree of devotion. At our workplace, the logic is almost the same for both the Almighty God as well as our seniors. Both of them are respected and we have to bow before both of them, because one of them, (God) has given us life and the other (senior) has given us (food /money/ remuneration against our labour / devotion/dedication/ ability or sincerity to our assigned work) our livelihood.

Both of them love appreciation and receptiveness. Both of them never open their mouth pertaining to which direction we should be taking but they only declare their decisions. They never tell us what is right and what is wrong. The workers/devotees will get the result as per their work/efforts done in any direction or as per their Karma. Similarly, the Management or seniors also say that their workers/employees will get result/benefits according to their work level/ devotions or dedication etc. or as per their Karma.

At the workplace, the Management/seniors/officer-incharge always expect from their juniors that they should give due respect to their seniors and colleagues. If we do not show them respect or if they feel that a particular employee is not giving due respect or ignoring any of the seniors or the Management, then it is possible that the particular concerned senior can punish the employee by any mode of punishment. At the same time, if we give them due respect then it is possible that the same seniors/ Management will give benefit to the concerned employees/ workers by giving promotion and increment.

If the employees have any problem with a particular Management/Seniors/Office-incharge, then at this situation, they should not stop paying them respect but they should give them more respect than before, inspite of their bad behaviour or their ill treatment towards the employees. If we behave respectfully, it is sure, that one day that particular senior will certainly change his mindset towards that particular employee and it is possible that at the time of appraisal of the employee, such seniors will give good remarks with the proposal of promotions/increment to the concerned workers.

Each human being is hungry for love, respect and appreciation. By appreciating other's work, we can easily get work done from them as the appreciation gives them encouragement and recognition to the work being done. If we work hard but no one appreciates us, then it is possible that the level of enthusiasm will decrease and as a result, more time will be taken to complete the assigned work.

For example, without appreciation of work, a person may take more time to complete his work but at the same time if the work is appreciated by someone, the person concerned certainly will be charged up and encouraged and will do his job with more care in less time. It means every person needs to be appreciated because in the process of appreciation the one who is showing appreciation shows his respect for him or her. On the other side, if we do not appreciate others, it means that, we do not know to respect others or acknowledge their good work.

When a beggar comes at our door and says, that God will give us blessings, power and money. The concerned person gets happy and gives alms to that poor beggar. The person gave alms to the beggar because he had shown respect to the person by making appreciation. It means the beggar had respect for the unknown person. Similarly, when employees like the beggar appreciate/respect their senior/Management at the workplace, the Management concerned will certainly bless them or help them in future.

Nobody will ask anyone to respect others. However, it is our duty to pay respect to all the seniors, whether at the work place or where we live in the society. In other words, we can say that if we do not respect others, the person may face several problems directly or indirectly. In general life, it has been observed that in many families, if the head of the family or the other members respect each other, then all the members of the family lead a happy life but if they do not respect each other and hurt them knowingly then it shows that they are not leading a happy family life. Their growth and prosperity will be affected by the disharmony.

Having the right value or sanskar is very important.From the ancient times, we have learnt that we should respect our teachers and elders. In school days if a student respects his teacher, he would definitely be a good student and get good marks. On the other hand, if he does not respect his teacher, he would not do well and not get good marks. It is sure that when we co-relate this situation with our workplace where we are working, we would get similar results. An employee, who respects all the seniors and talks with them very politely never, tries to hurt them under any circumstance. The seniors always like the concerned workers/employees. Such workers always get good appraisal remarks by their heads and their growth/ prosperity rate is higher than the others.

UNITY IN WORKFORCE TO GET A DESIRED RESULT / MISSION

The word "MISSION" is very important in our life. A small child grows with an ambition to do well in life and his parents always aspire that their child becomes an, Engineer/Doctor/IAS/ IPS officer etc, in his life. Therefore, they have to work hard to achieve their life's mission in the coming future. To achieve this, the parents provide all the required possible facilities to their children, so that they study properly and systematically and prove themselves in the competitive market.

During the School and College days' teachers and friends, help the weaker/poor students to study properly so that they could develop themselves and compete in the job market. However, the same person when comes to the office, the situation become totally reverse or different. In the office, there are many workers but most of them are good for nothing. If the same College friend is working here as the Boss/Superior at the workplace, the situation and relation becomes totally opposite from that of the school or college days.

In School/College days, friends help each other to get good marks in the examination but at the workplace, if one is assigned a specific work to be completed in a particular time, no one will come forward to help him or her. The superior/supervisors/incharge or even his own senior/ colleagues will not help or advice them on how they should do the assigned work. They will not even provide the means for doing the same. They will only observe how he is working and what mistakes he is making, so that they can point out his mistakes and highlight them in front of the Management.

I mean that for a healthy atmosphere in an Organisation there should be guidelines in place for doing each work. The boss/supervisors should guide their juniors. They should tell them the procedure of doing the work based on their experience, so that they could work easily with minimum mistakes. The colleagues should also help other colleagues in achieving /completing assigned work/ responsibilities. They should help each other without any bad intention. If a junior does any wrong due to lack of knowledge or experience, the seniors and colleagues should defend him and boost up his morale so that in the future, he would not repeat that mistake.

At the workplace, there is always lack of unity in doing any good work in the Company's interest. Unity is seen very rarely among the office staff, which is very necessary for the continuous growth of the organisation.

SELF-MARKETING

Market is a place where products are sold and the method, which we adopt to sell the product, is called marketing. Therefore, the people adopt various /different types of marketing strategies to sell particular products. In a Court, a lawyer sells his skill, ideas, specific knowledge/ arguments. A Teacher sells his knowledge, to the students, a politician sells his oratorical skill in his meeting/assembly and every political party sell their own philosophy to the public in their own way and try to convince them with their qualities.

On the other side, if we say that this particular thing is good, then we would have to convince others with all the plus points of such a product. Every day, we see new ads on TV which the producers, manufactures show or highlight on the television or radio. If they do not advertise their products/brands to the concerned market/people, their level of sale will be very low. Their business may collapse. I mean that marketing of a product is the most important factor for a product to be successfully sold and reach the people because out of sight is out of mind.

Similarly, a child cries, when he feels hungry. When he is happy, he may laugh and be busy playing. It means children also market themselves and try to convey their grievances without speaking anything. If the same child does not cry then, it is possible that the child would not get attention or food at the proper time.

At the workplace, we require many things to discharge the responsibilities or assignments and for this, we have to give our requirement for the same to the concerned department or people. If one person does not give his requirement to the concerned department then it would be very difficult to get the required things and for others it would be a problem to know the difficulties. As a result, the department/ person will have to suffer because they would not be in position to deliver adequate or proper output. At this situation, it is very necessary to point out the positive as well as negative things to the concerned department or person to get the required things.

In a nutshell, I want to say that at any workplace or in the Organisation, where we are working, it is very necessary to market ourselves. It means we should market ourselves in front of others. If we work for the Organisational benefit, we should highlight them in front of others seniors/colleagues at an appropriate time. We would have to put in their mind that we have finished the difficult work or what we have achieved was indeed very difficult. We should not worry about what people would think about our behaviour.

We should speak about our achievement to the people of other departments as well. We must project ourselves very well. Modesty is no more a virtue in today's times.

If we do not use such marketing gimmicks, then it is possible that other people will take credit and advantage of our vulnerability. The most important thing is the place of marketing and how we market ourselves or project ourselves. For example, if we are going to the market to buy woollen products, then we should buy woollen garments in winter or at a cold place. Similarly, if we have to market ourselves in the Organisation, about our achievements /innovation/new technique etc, then it is necessary that we should choose or target the right audience, the concerned seniors or department who would give importance to it. Finally, we should also try to market our image and our credibility in the workplace without thinking about other people. We should market ourselves in a positive way in the Organisation. For example, in an examination, some people get very high marks but when they face an interview, they are not selected because the topper could not market himself or prove himself in front of the interviewers.

For marketing, it is not necessary that a person has a good knowledge of the concerned subject but it is necessary that the person has a very good communication skill. This means how a person communicates his views / opinions, how he can convince others how he can hypnotise the person sitting on the other side is very important.

In various Organisations, there are some specific grade workers, whose only work is to show their face value in front of the seniors. They do not work seriously but always try to stand in front of the concerned seniors / Management at the right time. They try to show that they give more time in the Organisational work. They sit for late hours, so that the seniors/ concerned Management could know that they are very serious in discharging their work/responsibilities. This activity is also known as self-marketing. In today's, competitive market, it is necessary for everyone to work very seriously, honestly, loyally but along with the specific work, we should also know to market ourselves. For getting any official benefits, like promotion, increment or any benefit, it is necessary to have some quality in every worker for it is necessary to test them qualitatively.

(A) Duty First and Self Last:

The family is the first school of learning for a human being, where a sense of respect, love, give and take, recognition, language, behaviour, how to react, what is our responsibility, how to live in a society and so many virtues which cannot be described, are taught. This is the school where a sense of duty starts developing in our mind from our childhood.

Here we learn that duty is more important than self. For example, if we find that someone has met with an accident, then it is our duty to take him to the nearest hospital immediately than to think who that fellow is and what people will say. Helping the needy, feeding the hungry are some virtues, which we learn from our family/parents/society. The Organisation where we work is also a family. We should also treat it like our own family. When we will give them importance then a sense of emotional attachment will automatically develop in our mind, which will give an extraordinary energy to work.

When we consider our Organisation as a family and our Management as parents, then our grievances would reduce. We should take all the work as our own. Management of any Organisation also expect from their employees that they should have a feeling of a family. They should take all the responsibilities as their own and not as an official work or duty. Then it would not feel burdensome or troublesome.

At this situation, an automatic decision making power would develop in an employee along with a strong feeling of emotional attachment with the Organisation. Such people would come in the good books of the Management and would get lot of facilities. People would never say that this is not their duty or this work / responsibility does not come under their jurisdiction etc. If we want to eat a fruit from a tree, then it is our duty to look after the tree like the Organisation and it is also our duty to water and take care of the tree. Then only we are authorised to eat the fruits of our labour.

In our family, our aged parents/grand parents, desire from other members of the family that they should be taken care of first. It is just like an Organisation where the Management expects from their employees that, they should take care of the Organisation first. They should discharge their duties and then think about others things.

The employees who maintain this and give importance to such things, the Management definitely would care for them from time to time without any interruption or obstacle. Similarly, we also find in our family as a guardian/parent, it is our duty first to provide all possible facilities to our children and dependents than ourselves. During festivals, we should give gifts, clothes and sweets to our children and dependents first and not ourselves.

If, any mishap occurs in our family we on an instinct, do our best to save the family member or tackle the situation. Similarly, in any Organisation, the Management also expects from their employees that they should also have the same feeling towards the Organisation to tackle the problems or unwanted situation in the Organisation. On July 26th, 2005, there was flood in Mumbai, which was beyond the expectation of any person. The loss occurred in crores. Most of the employees were stuck in their offices.

During such critical situation, most of the employees had left the office as well as the portable equipments and had rushed to a safer place. They did not bother about the loss the company would incur. They were worried only about themselves and their family. Whenever such situation arises anywhere, our duty is to rescue other staff as well as the assets of the Company on which we are dependent. At the time of emergency, it has been observed that most of the workers leave the things as it is and they do not bother about the other colleagues and Company's assets. They rescue themselves first and flee away. They don't bother to remove the cash. An honest worker should not panic but use his conscience and discharge his duty. Likewise, when a ship starts sinking (Unfortunately) staff from the lower rank are rescued first. The captain of the ship is the last person to leave the ship. He makes sure that all his staff have been rescued.

In the same way, it is our duty first to save the Company's assets whatever worth it may have and the weaker staff from the panic situation than ourselves. Management likes such staff very much and at the appropriate time and situation, they give them award or honour them for their heroic deeds. We should all keep this factor always in our mind so that a feeling of responsibility would develop in our mind /heart in favour of the Organisation. We should give equal importance to our office and home, as both are equally important.

Family Life

The Management wants to treat their Organisation just like a family and their employees as family members. For example, when a girl after marriage comes to her in-laws family, her in -laws do not like to listen about her previous life or about her parents. They want that she should always praise her in-laws and appreciate their culture. If she fails to do the same, then her in-laws get unhappy. The family members try to harass her, and the family gets disturbed. Similarly, in an Organisation, the Management always desires that their employees should always praise their Organisation and not any other organisation.

The Management expects from their employees that they should think only about their Organisation and the Head of the Organisation. They should not take any leave; they should not bother about their own family. In some cases, it is seen that Management likes such employees who devote more time to their official work. The employees who are unmarried, bachelors, divorcee etc are in the good books of their Management because they have enough time to devote to their office.

RELATIONSHIP WITH EMPLOYEES

The employers want to develop a good and sound relationship with their employees .They want from their workers that they should take active participation in the Management problems and their decision-making procedures. The Management wants their employees to realise that the business is their own of which they are an integral part. It means the business, which the employer is carrying forward, the employer is not only the important participant but the employees are equally important because in the absence of them, it is not possible to run any business.

The Management expects from their employees that the subordinates or workers of the Organisation should follow whatever guidelines they make for their workers without fail.

The employer wants to see a good and healthy team spirit among his employees and achieve the desired goal. The Management also desires that the growth of the Organisation as well as of their employees should rapidly increase, that is why they invite their workers to participate in their decision-making process.

MEETING & CONFERENCE

The employer always desires that his worker should know each and everything about the Organisational rules and regulation, its merits and demerits and should participate in the decision making process. They should take initiative in the Company's interest and work sincerely but the employer never likes that the employees express their view in public meeting/conferences etc. In some cases, the Management deputes some people to observe the activities of the workers and pass on the information honestly. Such information sometimes helps the Management to keep the system in place. This system is very old. In ancient time Kings, also employed some Spies / Informers whose duty was to pass on the positive/negative information related to the public and the administration to the concerned King/Ministers etc.

FACE VALUE OF THE STAFF

In the marketing field, there is an eminent role of face value of any product. The producer/ manufacturers sell their product with the help of advertising the face value of the product in the market. They market their product by endorsing the product frequently on television or on radio broadcast, so that the public could recognise their product. As soon as the product disappears from the TV screen or from the media, the people/consumers forget the product. (Out of sight is out of mind)

Same holds true, in an Organisation. The Management gives importance to the face value of particular staff also. If the staff is not very good in working but always shows his face at the right time in front of the Management, then he succeeds in his self-marketing skill and he would always be in the good books of the Management. It means, the Management always expects from the staff that they should do their marketing within the Organisation. If a person is very good in working, and works very hard but does not do self-marketing, then he is a failure in the eyes of the management. The Management never asks any one to do their work or discharge their responsibilities but they desire that the workers should show their capability in front of the Organisation.

ARGUMENTS WITH SENIORS/JUNIORS

A healthy debate on any subject is very useful for any Organisation because with the help of the debate, one can exchange views. However, the Management never wants to listen to any type of argument within the Organisation, no matter how important an issue it is.

They like to listen to the healthy discussions on any subject, which gives importance directly or indirectly to the concerned H.O.D. / Management/seniors; otherwise, they do not like any discussion going on within the Organisation by any one.

IMPORTANT FACTORS FOR THE WORKERS

Everyone has some expectation from the other. The Management when employs someone at their workplace, expects that the coming workforce should have some qualities as per the requirement of the Organisation or situation. In general, when the Management recruits some workers for their Organisation, they expect the following qualities from them.

- Self-confidence
- Curiosity for Learning
- Ambition
- Fear of Failure
- Spontaneity / Promtness
- Patience / Forbearance
- Honest to their Work / Honesty
- Loyalty

SELF CONFIDENCE

Self-Confidence is one of the most important factors for a person to achieve anything or to survive in the Organisation. Without confidence, it is not possible to discharge assigned responsibilities in a scientific or logical manner in the Company's interest. It comes only when a person has full confidence on his work and he knows the merits and demerits of a particular job/ work.

The Management of any Organisation also expect from their workers/employees that their workers should have full confidence in their work field, so that they could work or discharge their duties/responsibilities in a specific period in Company's interest.

CURIOSITY OF LEARNING

Second important factor for success or failure in a particular field is the curiosity of learning or lack of it. In our opinion, no one is perfect. Small children are always curious to learn. They always question their parents and want to learn about a particular thing. The mother is like an Organisation/Management and the child is like a worker. Here I want to clear that the Management wants or likes to hear that their employees have the tendency or natural curiosity to learn about their assigned job. They should ask several questions about the assigned job from their concerned seniors, just like a child who questions his parents and tries to learn about new things.

AMBITION

Ambition is an inner power, which gives positive energy to a person to achieve something, which he/she likes. Without having the burning desire or ambition for achieving something, a person cannot make any progress in his life and his life may become very dull, un-productive, and the concerned person or worker may fall into depression and would stagnate.

When a worker will be so dull, his work will definitely suffer. He cannot be attentive, responsible or answerable to the assigned job. At this situation, The Management expect from their employees that each of them should have their own ambition, position in their Organisation. They should be positive thinkers, innovative, motivated etc and if they are in trouble, even then they should not express it to others because may be one person may be a motivator for the workforce while the other may be a de-motivator. They should always be smiling and be in a cheerful demeanour.

FEAR OF FAILURE

Fear gives a negative energy in the human beings and when fear is associated with failure then people hold back themselves from any risky work. They do not like to take any risk. It means that at such situations a person does not take any initiative in his work. Therefore, the degree of productivity becomes low. They do not get promotion or any increment, and the Company loses its profit. The Management expects from their employees that they should not have fear from the ups and downs or of any critical problem at the workplace. If the Organisation faces any problem, their employees should take active part to support the Company. They should give good ideas to their Management. They should participate in risky work in the Company's interest, so that the Management can have sufficient faith on particular workers / employees. They would surely give them adequate benefit at the right time. Therefore, we should work in such a way that one could win the heart of the Management and the seniors.

SPONTANEITY

During an adverse situation, every living thing first wants to protect itself from that situation. If we are walking on the road and suddenly a car comes in front of us, our first action is to protect ourselves from that mishap. If anything comes in front of our eyes, it automatically closes to protect itself. Reflex action is inherent in human beings.

In the Organisation/workplace, there are many workers working. Different workers have different temperaments and have their own style of working. Some complete their work very promptly but some take a long time to finish their work. Some workers take the responsibility from their seniors without knowing anything about that work as well as without thinking whether that work could be completed by them or not, but they take the responsibility from them. If some workers face any problem during their working, they try to solve it themselves without knocking the door of the seniors for their help.

The Management generally likes those workers / employees, who do their duty or complete their assignment in Company's interest. According to the Management, the workers / employees should themselves tackle the problems arising at the workplace without taking the help of any seniors or others. Some workers finish their work or assignment first and then they inform the concerned seniors or authority. If the work is good and liked by the higher authority, it boosts their morale, gives them self-confidence, and builds faith between the workers and the Management, which is very healthy for the Organisational growth.

The Management thinks that their workers should take the responsibility in the Company's interest and complete it promptly, as soon as possible. If they complete their assigned responsibility, the Management / concerned seniors feel very proud of them and keep them in their good books.

PATIENCE/FORBEARANCE

Everything takes its own time and the time schedule for each action or reaction is fixed. No one can change it. If, we plant a small mango sapling then we have to wait for some years to eat the fruit of that tree. If we will be in a hurry to eat its fruit then it is foolishness on our part. Nature always teaches us to have patience/forbearance in any situation. In spite of being in a hurry, a farmer cannot harvest before the time schedule of a particular crop. They have to wait patiently for the crop to mature. According to Revered Bhakti Poet "RAHIM" *work progresses slowly; no matter how much one waters the plants or waits for the fruits to be ripe, it will be ready only when its time comes. So one must learn to have patience.*

More or less the same logic is also applicable in any Organisation / workplace where we are working. Whenever a worker joins any Company, he has to do his job very honestly and he must have a lot of patience in learning the existing working system of that Organisation. It is not sure that the concerned seniors will give good remarks in the annual appraisal form without knowing anything about his work.

The Organisation is a public place because it has different types of people working together. They come from different backgrounds and have different temperament and endurance. We have to be very patient. Otherwise, we would be a total failure at the workplace. The Management of any Organisation expects from their subordinates or workers/employees that their workers should be very calm and cool. They should not be arrogant or should not have an egoistic nature. They should have the patience to learn new things therefore evolving new methods of working and to listen to the complaints and grievances of others.

Sometimes, the seniors get angry on the subordinates without any proper reason or without any fault. Sometimes, A does the mistake and the seniors give punishment to B, without knowing or making any enquiry. On the other hand, some times the higher Management gets angry on the seniors for their fault or mistakes and the concerned seniors release their anger on their subordinates / juniors without any fault of theirs. If such situation arises at the workplace, then the concerned worker should have patience. If the workers do not show their reaction on such situation, the Management would definitely like such workers because after some time the concerned seniors would realise their mistake and know the truth because ultimately truth prevails.

HONEST TO THEIR WORK / ORGANISATION

As we know, that Honesty is the best Policy. Workers working in any Organisation try to prove themselves of being honest and well-wishers of their Organisation. They think that they are the only well-wishers and honest employees of their workplace. Here, honesty is related to the work, decision, work distribution, appraisal of others, foresightedness towards the safety of the Organisation, promotion/increment of the workers, good behaviour with the subordinates, respect for others etc. Only monetary or financial honesty is not enough for any worker. It is only a part of their honest character. If a worker is very honest towards the financial transaction or in money matters of the Organisation but he does not work sincerely, then we cannot call him honest because honesty entails that a person should be honest in every respect for the Organisation.

The concerned seniors or the Management of the workplace expect from their workers that they should be very *honest towards their work.* It means that they should have their own sense of work. They should not be dependent on anyone or on even the concerned seniors. They should have enough knowledge about the assigned work/responsibility. They should have a clear concept or vision about the work and what procedure should be adopted which would be beneficial for the Organisation.

It has been observed that some of the seniors are found to be very partial towards some of their workers. Partiality sometimes proves very dangerous for the Company. In this case, some workers are found overloaded with the responsibilities while the others are totally free but they are working with them because of biased seniors' work distribution. The Management thinks that their seniors or responsible heads of the department should not be biased on any respect but they should be *honest with their work distribution.* They should distribute the responsibilities to the concerned workers according to their ability or skill, knowledge, education, position etc.

No one wants to *appraise the good qualities of the workers* working under any department, so that their morale could boost up. They only think about themselves and their group members whether they deserve it or not. If any worker does anything in Company's interest, the seniors should appreciate his qualities. They should be very honest in showing appreciation of others.

Most of the workers as well as the concerned seniors think only about the present problems of the Organisation and try to solve it. They do not try to think about any mishap or eventuality. Unfortunately, if some mishap occurs, they should know how to tackle it. They should be *foresighted.* They should honestly plan a program through which they could save the Organisation from any mishap or loss. (A disaster Management Cell should be created in all the organisations to tackle any kind of natural or manmade disaster/ calamity)

Apart from the above circumstances, at the year-end when the seniors make the list for *promotion and increment* for the benefit of the workers, they are very much biased. The seniors are very conservative in this regard. They do not give the priority of work done in the past by anyone but they give priority to personal relations with the workers, which is very harmful for the Organisation. Due to this practice, a genuine worker does not get promotion, increment, or any other benefit. They do not get any reward against their contribution in Company's interest but the others who had not even done anything; get promotion due to the partiality of the seniors. The seniors should be very honest and impartial in this respect.

Sometimes we have seen, *the behaviour of the seniors,* is very peculiar, which cannot be described in words. They do not think that all are working under one umbrella, whose ownership is associated with someone else, and not the concerned seniors. They are not the owners of that Organisation, so they should not treat their subordinates as their servants. I mean that the seniors should also be honest with their behaviour. They are not authorised to treat their subordinates as servants. We should respect all the seniors and their contribution. Similarly, seniors should also follow the same rule, so that they should also respect the work done by any subordinate working in any department.

Apart from the above qualities, if a person is honest in all the rest but not in *financial matters,* then it will be very difficult for him to continue in any Organisation. The Management can tolerate or forgive any mistake done by their subordinates but if they are involved in financial irregularities then no one would save them or cooperate with them.

TOUCH ME NOT

Management likes those workers who have the characteristic of a touch me not plant because as soon as one touches its leaves, it blushes and closes its leaves which is the reason it attracts people. The Management also thinks that whenever they ask anything to their employees under any circumstance, they should be willing to work and co-operate and should not have a rigid character but they should respectfully and willingly accept the challenge and responsibility *and they never like people having the characteristic of thorny or itchy bushes.*

TRANSPARENCY IN WORK

If there is transparency in work, adopted procedure or delivered instructions, the concerned work would be better. In general at the workplace, we do not find any transparency in the work procedure. If a person has been assigned to do a particular work, the person sitting on the next table does not know about that work, while both are working in the same department. Due to any circumstance, if the concerned person would be absent, the work would get hampered and the company would face a huge loss due to non- transparency of the work procedure. Therefore, the management expects from their subordinates that they should be transparent in their working and they should give correct information to their colleagues accordingly so that they should also know the development in the assigned work and can co-operate if need arises.

Only Proposal not Order

The management has a bloated ego because they are the supreme boss of the organisation. They are superior in every respect, whether in power, salary, or authority. So they know only to give instructions or orders. They like one way traffic in the management. In meetings they think that only they are authorised to express their opinion or views and others should listen to each and every word uttered, attentively.

In routine office work, there are several letters related to the day to day routine work, requirement or short term planning which the subordinates have to write to the seniors/ management for approval. In that letter if anyone by mistake, forgets to write the word proposal, then the management would make it an issue and would not pass or give the approval for the same because they think that their subordinates are giving them an order.

The management likes to be pampered and respected all the time by its subordinates. They cannot tolerate their shortcomings or misdemeanour. They desire that the subordinates can put forward any proposal with request but they despise taking orders from them.

❖❖❖

CHAPTER 10

EXPECTATION OF WORKERS FROM THE MANAGEMENT

Expectation, gives strength to a person to live positively. If we do not have expectations from anyone, we will become saints. If one person expects something then the other person too expects something from him. Expectation is mutual and reciprocal. One-sided expectation cannot be possible. A Mother loves her children and expects that her children should become good human beings and also care for her when she gets old. They should be good in studies, be disciplined, and should take care of their responsibilities. At the same time, children also expect from their mother/parents that they should also take care of them unconditionally. Then only it is possible to have a good relationship between them.

In our day to day life, when we hire a taxi for a particular purpose and expect from the taxi driver that he should know all the roads and the locations where we have to visit. The same taxi driver also expects that the passengers should not haggle with him and pay him as per the meter or the rate chart or that they do not take him to unsafe place and land him in trouble.

Sometimes we expect from our children that they should top their class without giving them any facility. At the same time, the children also expect from their parents that they should be provided with the basic requirements so that they can devote their mind and efforts to studies and be able to get highest marks in the class.

Similarly, if we have a car we drive it as per our requirement. We maintain the car by getting its servicing done on time but the same cars can conk off due to lack of a proper servicing and oiling or batteries getting discharged.

In the case of human beings, our body requires maintenance; otherwise, it will refuse to work properly. To maintain our body, we take balanced food and water to get energy and take medicines to protect ourselves when we fall sick.

In a nutshell, I would like to say or emphasise that both living and non-living things have expectations whether a Car engine or a human body. Everybody has expectations from their kith and kin, colleagues or fellow human beings.

The logic also applies at the workplace of an Organisation. As the management expects something from their workers, similarly the workers also have some expectations from their employers.

In General the expectations of the workers may be categorised into the following

- Adequate remuneration
- Proper Attention
- Time- Bound promotion and Increment
- Family atmosphere
- Job Security
- Recognition, appreciation and response of work
- Due Respect of seniors
- Fixed Working Hours
- Written responsibility
- Proper direction/instruction of seniors
- No public humiliation
- Freedom of speech
- Management should also listen to the problems of workers/subordinates
- No discrimination based on province or language

Everyone works only for his or her benefit. These benefits may be of different types. It may be in cash, kind or emotion. A mother looks after her child for her emotional fulfilment while a labourer works for his wages. A Mother cares for each and every small thing related to her child, which affects his/her, growth, and for this she works unconditionally. In the mother's case, the remuneration is in the form of satisfaction. However, either knowingly or unknowingly the mother, who loves and works for her child unconditionally, also expects from her child that her child should look after her in her old age. He should also support her emotionally and respect her. Even a beggar stands with expectation. It means each and every human being work for each other and expect something from them.

Similarly, at the workplace, the workers / employees work to meet the expenses of their livelihood and betterment but they also expect from their employer / management / seniors that they should also provide them with adequate remuneration according to their efforts, which they are providing to the company. Along with the proper remuneration, they also expect that their senior or management should pay proper attention to them and their work. They should also look at the available facilities given to them by the company and whether the facility is adequate for their requirement or not. If the facility is not adequate to their Work profile then it should be immediately upgraded or replaced, so that they could use their best of abilities in the company's interest.

Everyone works for their betterment and when it is blocked due to any reason or circumstances, and then they are not in a position to discharge their assigned duties in a systematic or desired manner. The involvement with their work gradually decreases and as a result, their names are not selected for promotion and increment. At this situation, the workers expect from their seniors that they should also see or make an analysis on different parameters, so, that they could be selected for promotion or increment from time to time in the Organisation.

The environment or a surrounding of any family plays a great role in the development of the individuals of that family. A member living in a balanced or clean environment may be more successful in his life than a member from a filthy surrounding or environment.

The environment of any workplace also plays a vital role in the progress or development of the concerned workers of the Organisation. For example, the speed and the efficiency of a car can be judged only on the road. If the condition of the road is not good/smooth/ is full of potholes then even a brand new car or even the costliest car cannot show its efficiency. If a road is crowded then a person cannot drive his/her car smoothly or it will take too much time to cover a small distance. More petrol would be consumed. The driver would get tired and drive his car in a bad mood.

On a crowded and busy road during hot and humid summer months if the car is not air-conditioned then the master sitting at the back seat would feel that the driver does not know to drive the car. The master does not want to know the situation of the road. This is akin to the environment of the workplace. Here I have tried to correlate the road condition with the workplace and the worker with the car.

People living in cold /places are more active and fresh than the persons living in a warm place. Similarly, a worker working in a private organisation might be more efficient in comparison to the Govt. Organisation because of the working environment and the condition of the workplace. The workplace of private organisations is fully air-conditioned and well maintained and most of the facilities are available for the workers by the management. The management itself takes pain to provide them with good working condition and environment so that the workers perform well and are able to use their best of efforts in company interest. Due to a good working environment, a worker of a private organisation gives more hours and dedication to the organisation in comparison to the Govt. Organisations where these facilities are not available.

The workers working at any workplace desire that their management should at least provide them good, clean and sound environment where they could easily be able to give more output as desired by the seniors. Along with the sound environment at the workplace, there should be a family atmosphere because it binds all the workers emotionally with each other and gives strength to the organisation for better output. At present days, most of the big corporate houses also try to adopt family atmosphere at their workplace so that their workers could give more output. When they would feel a family atmosphere then they would not bother to put in extra office hours. They would think that this work, (which they are assigned to complete), is not for the organisation but it belongs to them. They would try to give an emotional attachment / feeling in their work output with more integrity and dedication.

Job Security:

From childhood, we have learnt to live in different parameters and follow a discipline life, to secure ourselves from any eventuality. God has created a beautiful world for us and it is our duty to keep it safe as much as possible. We wear clothes; eat food and medicine to secure ourselves from any disease and we study diligently to secure our future. Similarly, today most of the people secure themselves and their family. Even their house, car or household goods are covered by insurance. I mean everyone tries to secure himself by all possible means.

When we start working, we try to secure our life and that of our family by taking suitable measures. Here people try to get a good job to secure their future but it is not possible for everyone to get jobs in the Govt. organisation. Apart from the Govt. Organisation, there are several private organisations, which also provide secured jobs. People working at any organisation expect from their management that their bread and butter, livelihood for which they are working and giving their valuable time and energy, should be secured. Most of the workers would not mind getting less payment but they expect that their income should be stable because their household expenses, children's future etc., depend on their monthly salary.

RECOGNITION, APPRECIATION & RESPONSE OF WORK

Nature has created several beautiful things on this earth which may be alive or dead but everything is recognized individually, so that people could recognise them by their name and if required could give their comments, and remarks. People are known by their own name in the society and people generally appreciate or criticize them because of their good or bad deeds. If a person, does anything against the society or humanity or commit a crime then he becomes a criminal.

In the organisation, each employee has his own employment code which the company has issued to him, to differentiate or recognise him at the workplace because it is possible that more than one person can have the same name and surname. Then it would be very difficult to differentiate between them. Similarly, at the workplace each worker has his own capacity and efficiency to work along with dedication and honesty. Not every worker can be a fraud, corrupt or shrewd but everyone has his own strength to discharge his responsibility. People generally working at any workplace expect from their head/ seniors/ management that their work, dedication or integrity should be recognised by the concerned seniors / department. They do not want to be a great leader but they think that their good work should be recognised and should be appreciated by the management in front their colleagues.

It is sure that if the work done by a worker/employee is not being appreciated by the respective department head or senior/incharge, then it will be very difficult to give a good remark at the time of appreciation for promotion or increment etc. If a worker gets punishment and it is highlighted in the organisation by the concerned seniors/head of the department or incharge. Similarly the good conduct of a worker should also be highlighted in the Organisation without fail. If a worker does any innovative work in the organisational interest, he must be appreciated by the organisation to boost up his morale.

As we are aware that the soldiers, paramilitary personnel are always appreciated for their good conduct, bravery and valour and they are presented with bravery awards which boost up their morale and emotional quotient. Every time, the worker does not expect a salary hike but expects recognition for his good work and that the seniors pat his back.

DUE RESPECT TO SENIORS & VICE VERSA

It is in our culture and values to give proper respect to elders, parents, teachers' relatives etc. When we pay our respect to the elders, they also reciprocate by giving us blessings and love which boosts us to give more love and respect to them. *Respect* is also an emotional food for human beings and it plays a great role in our life. Every person expects that his juniors should pay due respect to him.

At the workplace, all the seniors are like elders for us and we should give them due respect. Here the scenario is different. The seniors, in charge or the head of the department take their subordinates for granted that it is the duty of the juniors or the subordinates to pay respect or extend courtesy to their seniors without fail. Sometimes, the seniors are so egoistic that if due to any reason a junior could not pay his respect to the concerned senior or head of the department, he starts planning to punish or harass him. The seniors think that it is the duty of all the juniors to give respect to the seniors, whether the concerned seniors deserve it or not. The seniors do not bother about the status or image of any subordinate. They can insult their juniors at the drop of a hat. They do not care about who are standing around them. If a junior does any wrong or mistake then the senior fires the junior without thinking anything. At this situation, the juniors also expect from their seniors that if they have done any mistake and are guilty then they should be fired or insulted in isolation and public scene should not be created. It means the juniors also expect that their seniors should have some respect for their juniors. Then only it is possible for the juniors to pay due regards and respect to their seniors.

WRITTEN RESPONSIBILITY

The management recruits the manpower as per their requirement. In most of the organisations, the responsibility of each worker is fixed verbally. If anyone is hired for a specific job, the concerned person gives the instruction based on the local management to the newcomer that from today onwards the following responsibilities shall have to be completed by him. They give the instruction verbally and not in writing. As the instruction is not in writing so it is possible that the concerned person will commit mistake in discharging his responsibility because he might not be fully confident over his duty chart. There may be a huge communication gap. The worker may get confused about his responsibility, what he has to do or not, because the responsibility is not in writing. Due to this, his performance may get affected and he might not be in a position to satisfy his seniors or may not give the best of his efforts towards the completion of the particular responsibility.

At this situation, the workers simply expect from the management that the management should give them the responsibility in writing so that they could give them their best of efforts without losing the opportunity and communication gap.

PROPER DIRECTION/INSTRUCTION

It is very well known that the children who get proper guidance by their parents are more grounded and successful in their life than a child who is bereft of it. If anyone gets a proper guidance or has proper knowledge of the road, directions of a particular place, then such people reach their destination without wasting their time otherwise it takes a long time to locate the place. When a person has no idea about a particular place and he has to go there then uselessly he gets irritated in reaching the unknown location. The clarity in the direction of the destination saves several valuable things like, time, fuel, expenses and patience.

The same logic applies to the workplace of an organisation. Here also most of the seniors prefer to give verbal instructions or half-baked information to their subordinates, which creates confusion towards the completion of any assignment.

The subordinates or juniors working at any workplace also expect from their respected seniors that they are free to give instruction as per their desire or requirement but the instruction should be clear so that the subordinates should be able to give the desired result without wasting any valuable time and energy. Practically this does not happen at the workplace, so sometimes it gets very difficult for the subordinates to understand the assigned work to give the desired output.

ISOLATED PUNISHMENT

It is said that "TO ERR IS HUMAN AND TO FORGIVE DIVINE". No one is perfect and it is human nature to make mistakes. Everyone working at the workplace makes mistakes of which some mistakes are tolerable and some are not. Everyone has his own prestige and respect and no one wants to lose it at any cost whether he has or has not done any mistake. Even if one has committed a mistake, he does not like any person asking him about his mistake in front of other colleagues. Everyone knows that when a person is caught red-handed by the police in any theft case and is arrested, then also the criminal /offender expects from the Police that he should be manhandled or assaulted at the Police Lock-up/station and not at any public place.

Similarly at the workplace, the subordinates/juniors also expect from their seniors or management that if any senior or in charge plan to give punishment to any junior or subordinate, he must keep in his mind about the place, time and the concerned person. It means he should pronounce his punishment at an isolated place. If the senior wishes to reprimand his junior, the senior should call him in his cabin and reprimand him. He should not do so at a public place or in front of other colleagues.

FREEDOM OF SPEECH

Everybody wants freedom in his life. He does not like, anyone creating obstacles in his freedom. Right to freedom of expression is our fundamental right so we have the right to speak or express our voice or feelings in front of others. If we do not express our feelings then we may suffer from frustration and exploitation which would be harmful for our health.

In practice, at the workplace, there are several meetings and conferences taking place where all the respective representatives of all the departments are invited. The management tries to know the views of the workers on the new project or any new working system. They spend a lot of funds towards the meeting and conference in the company's interest. During the meeting, the management invites the workers to express their feelings or opinions on a particular subject or topic but it is very sad that when a worker or employee expresses his feelings in front of others, the organiser or the concerned management does not like to listen to his voice or suggestions. Thus, the workers are unable to express their feelings which directly or indirectly affect their performance. They start suffering from inferiority complex.

The workers or employees also expect from the management that there should be a transparent system in place and every worker or employee could express his feelings or they could forward their problems directly to the management in the company's interest.

Management should also listen to the problems of the workers/ subordinates

The head of the family or the parents listen to the problems of their children and give guidance / suggestions accordingly. In school, the teacher listens to the problems of his students and tries to solve them, so that the students of his class or school could do well and grow into an independent and responsible citizens.

Similarly, when one gets a job and starts working in an organisation with the hope that he would be guided by the seniors who would give suggestions and guidance to solve his problems (if any). In practice, at the workplace, it has been observed that no one bothers for others or one does not care for others.

At the workplace, the management plays a role of a guardian and the organisation of a family. The workers/ employees expect the same emotional attachment like their family or their school, where the parents or the school teachers were always ready to help and guide them. Here the situation is very different. No one (the seniors/incharge or head of the department) likes to waste his time to guide his subordinates. They even do not want to listen to the problems of their subordinates related to the assigned work. When a worker comes to his seniors with a genuine problem to discuss and the seniors do not take interest in listening, gives demotivation to the subordinate which directly or indirectly affects his work performance which in turn affects the growth of the organisation.

The workers expect that their seniors or management should listen to their problems, which they are facing at the workplace. It is not sure whether the concerned seniors are authorized to solve their problems but if they would listen to the difficulties being faced by the subordinates, they would not get demotivated and their work performance would not be affected.

QUALITIES OF SENIORS

Every coin has two sides. If the management has some expectations from their subordinates or staff then the subordinates or staff also have some expectations from their management. Similarly, if we expect some good qualities in the employers then the employers also have expectation from their employees or workers whom the employer employs because the growth of the company depends upon their positive output.

Every senior should have the following qualities to run the department smoothly and get the desired output with the help of the available manpower. In the absence of the following qualities, the person in charge for a department/division/section/Unit would not get success at his workplace. If under any circumstance, a senior dares to handle his department and the manpower without having the following qualities, he would face a terrible administrative problem at the workplace and in a short period, the management would certainly replace him from his position. The seniors should have the following qualities:

- Adequate Knowledge of their field
- Courage to take risk
- Be Consistent on their decision and behaviour.
- Communicate well
- Inspire and encourage others
- The capacity to listen patiently
- Stay Cool
- Be a role model
- Respect the juniors and seniors equally
- Be neutral
- Never condemn or insult anyone in front of others
- Fast and Judicious decision makers
- Have faith in collective effort
- Foresighted
- Understanding work value
- Punctual
- Self respect
- Honest
- Patient Listener
- And above all tons and tons of confidence so that they can lead the flock.

When one person hires a tutor for his child, the person first of all sees that the tutor should have good knowledge of the subjects he would teach and he has a good and sound educational background. He should have the quality to motivate the child to study hard, in such a way that he starts taking more interest in his studies. Similarly, at the workplace, the subordinates or the management also desire that their senior should have some defined qualities. Likewise he should have adequate knowledge of his field and should have confidence so that he could take up the challenges of the organisational growth.

In general at the workplace, seniors lack consistency in their decision taking, as well as on their behaviour. Their behaviour fluctuates like current/voltage. They are very unpredictable. If they have taken some decision then, they may change it in another moment. It gives a bad impact on the growth of the organisation. If they take firm decisions, the subordinates would discharge their assignment excellently but if the decision would change frequently then the motivation and the efficiency of the worker, would be affected directly. If the seniors do not communicate their direction/instructions correctly to their subordinates, then it would be very difficult for the subordinates to understand the assigned responsibility. Therefore, the seniors should have good communication skill and should be very confident.

In various organisations, the persons working on a senior position, have no patience or have no time to listen to the problems of the juniors. They do not have the inherent quality to encourage the juniors or to give them inspiration, so that the subordinates could perform their assigned job very well. The seniors are always in a hurry so they sometimes lose their patience and get very angry. They have less tolerance power, which is very harmful for the organisation.

Workers or employees working under such seniors, expect that their seniors should be a role model, having cool temperament and the patience to listen to the problems of their juniors. It is not necessary that all the grievances raised by the subordinates would be solved but the juniors only expect that if the seniors are not in a position to solve their problems, then they should have the patience to listen to their problems. By listening to their problems, half of the problem would be solved. It has a psychological effect.

Both the seniors and the juniors expect mutual respect from each other. At the workplace it has been seen that the seniors think that it is the duty of the juniors or the subordinates to pay respect to seniors and it is one-sided. The seniors do not bother to extend due courtesy to the subordinates, which gives a bad impact on the image of the organisation. At this situation, the juniors/employees expect from their respective seniors that if they are paying respect to their seniors then they should also reciprocate. Every right minded person has got self respect.

No one is perfect. Everyone does some mistake while working. When we work, we commit mistakes unknowingly. If we do not work then we cannot commit mistakes. If we commit mistakes, the concerned senior gets a chance to reprimand us. At this situation, the workers or the employees think that if they have done any mistake then the seniors are fully authorised to give them punishment but they should reprimand them in their chamber in private and not in the front of their colleagues because nobody wants to get humiliated in front of their colleagues or juniors.

The employees expect that their seniors should have the capability to take fast decision on any problem. They should have foresightedness, so that they could make plans accordingly in the company's interest and should have the capability to evaluate the work performance of their subordinates' neutrally or impartially.

Apart from the above, if a person is not honest then all the qualities are useless for him. Therefore, the person should be honest in every respect, with his subordinates, colleagues or seniors. I mean, the worker/employee thinks that all the seniors should be very honest so that they get inspiration to follow their footsteps and ideals.

❖❖❖

CHAPTER 11

LESSONS AND INSPIRATIONS

INTRODUCTION

God is our creator. He gives life to all the living beings on the earth. All his creations convey something or the other provided we know to un-code them. He always watches us and warns us about the events to be unfolded. So we need to be very watchful. However majority of the people ignore it or never try to unravel the mysteries of life.

In our family, parents are our role models while our teachers are our role models in the school. Similarly, at the workplace, we should learn from our experiences and take inspiration from the talented and learned seniors or subordinates.

In this chapter, I have tried to explain by several examples in our daily life, the happenings and the materials found around us without being noticed, to take lessons and inspirations from them, so that we could do our work more smoothly at the workplace and be able to understand the situation.

Nobody has the time to judge what is right and what is wrong, what one should do, or what one should not do. We should always open all our six senses at the workplace to know the situation. This chapter would help to understand the seniors, juniors' colleagues and their hidden characters or behaviour.

DO NOT HEAT THE MAGNET OTHERWISE ITS MAGNATISM WILL BE LOST

In any organisation, very few people have good knowledge, skill, and experience, and an enthusiastic approach, healthy attitude towards company's interest or welfare. All the above qualities attract the common people or workers of the organisation. Such people work very well, discharge their duties very neatly with less expenses and in time. In a very short period, such people get popular in the organisation based on their work and good behaviour.

On one hand such people start getting popularity in their organisation while on the other hand some people like the seniors, colleagues of the same department or in other department start keeping distance from them because they cannot digest their popularity.

Some of the seniors directly or indirectly make plans to harass the talented and highly skilled persons to defame or demoralise them, so that they could leave the organisation or change their good qualities. I mean that as the magnet is heated its magnetism is lost. Similarly, in any organisation, well-behaved, educated and skilled personnel are also like magnets and their quality is their magnetism. If a talented person /magnet is harassed/heated, the magnetism/good qualities of that talented person/magnet will be lost. So, the seniors should not harass their subordinates or juniors, so that their qualities or magnetism may not be lost due to their harassment and constant nagging.

INSPITE OF THORNS PEOPLE LIKE A ROSE FOR ITS BEAUTY AND FRAGRANCE

No one is perfect by nature and there are many merits and demerits in human beings as well as in other living things. We should take lessons from the nature. We can learn and take examples from nature, which can guide us in the right direction, and will give us the right perspective. If we minutely observe nature, we will see that at any difficult situation, nature is ready to guide us and show us the right path/direction and what we should do and what we should not.

We should not react suddenly on any situation but we should analyse the situation and then proceed forward. At any work place, there are various types of workers, having different nature, behaviour, temperament, capability to work etc., which may be totally adverse from our nature but we should not react instantly but we should listen to them carefully because everyone has some merits and demerits or qualities.

It is a known fact that the management does not want to listen to anything which is beyond their vision, opinion, and sometimes very harmful for the organisation. The higher management wants to listen to the voice of their employees but the middle management wants to suppress or does not want to listen to the voice of their subordinates under any circumstance. They think that they are the only managers, who are right and think for the upliftment of the organisation and who have the capability to think about the organisational growth. In practice, these managers are suffering from EGO. Because of which they cannot listen to any suggestions, whether in favour of the organisation or against it. It seems that one senior would say, that a particular worker, does not perform his duty perfectly and the higher management will have blind faith in him.

If anyone does any mistake knowingly or unknowingly, they will never forgive him or her and plan to punish him or her without fail. They will not have the foresight to see that there are several merits in a particular worker. If they punish him, the organisation may have to suffer heavy loss. The management knows that good and bad habits are inherent in the human beings. If any worker is frequently and regularly doing wrong then we should overlook his shortcoming, but appreciate his good qualities to boost his morale and let him know that he should give more attention on his good qualities instead of bad ones and gradually he would rectify his mistakes.

If a person is good at his work and inspite of having adequate experience, is making mistakes and not giving good performance, the management should not penalise such a worker but they should try to know the reason behind his consistent bad performance and the low morale. He may have official as well as personal problem. It may also be possible that at the work place some workers must be troubling him or not providing the right facilities to perform the responsibilities. If the Management would not listen to his problems, the worker would certainly leave the organisation, which may have a negative impact on the organisational growth. He may also try to end his life.

The management should try to know the exact quality of each worker and they should take advantage of their inherent quality but not of their circumstances.

Sometimes, due to the poor circumstance a good worker may not perform his best. The management should try to know the hidden circumstances under which his performance is deteriorating day by day and they should try to improve the existing circumstance for smooth working condition. In the context of rose and its thorns, we come to this conclusion that we should only see the good qualities of the employees but not their demerits because everyone has the combination of good and bad qualities, as we see with the rose. On one hand, it is an epitome of love, attractive, fragrant and a beautiful flower and on the other hand, it has several thorns.

LESSON FROM THE ENVIRONMENT

There are innumerable things on this earth, which gives us direct / indirect lessons to live and lead a good life. There are several things, which we should learn from Nature.

We generally go to school, college and other institutions to learn, to enhance our education and knowledge but there is one more institution, which is called our family from where we learn about love, bonding, sharing, sacrifice, patience etc that teaches us valuable lessons. At the workplace, where we work for our bread and butter, we should always be alert and attentive and be ready to learn right things. At the work place, there are several things in our surrounding which teach us a lot of lessons, on our behaviour and relationship with others.

CEILING FAN

We should watch the functioning of a ceiling fan hanging on the ceiling in a room. If, we observe it attentively, we would come to know how we should take instructions from our seniors, how to behave with juniors, how and when we should react on any situation. How, we should attract the seniors and how we should efficiently deliver the assigned work etc. Our keen observation would give us many answers on the hidden problems, of which, no one can give the right answer or suggestions or guidelines.

If, the fan is not functioning properly then we should take care of the fan and should try to know the reason behind it. If, it is repairable then we should get it repaired on an urgent basis or it would consume more energy and would not give adequate cool air. In the same way if a worker is sick, he cannot discharge his duty or work properly. If he takes some rest and medicines, he would be fit to work.

There is a very close relationship of this fan with the Manager and the subordinates working at any office or the workplace. Here the fan is like a subordinate, working under any senior and the person who switches on the fan, is just like our senior or management. Here the top or higher management is the main switch from where we get incoming current for this fan to function.

It depends upon the management whether they like the fan or the air conditioner. It is totally based on their decision. Sometimes, the management hires such workers whose remuneration is not very high but are necessary for the organisation.

At this situation the concerned management or seniors expect from these workers that they should work for the organisation whether it is beneficial or not but they should work only on the instruction of the management. They should work until the concerned management /senior do not give any further instruction to stop.

Through the regulator, we regulate the fan as per our requirement. Similarly, the Management/ seniors of the concerned department expect from their subordinates that they should also be under their control like the regulator of a fan.

They should not do anything more or less and do whatever is required. One should not do what is not concerned with that department or which the manager does not want. It means, the management/seniors want from their subordinates that they should not use their mind or extra effort to finish the work. If the senior desires to finish a particular work in a specific time period, they should do accordingly, which is akin to a fan. When it is switched off, it never revolts and stops working.

We should take a lesson from the fan and we should follow the instruction of our master/ senior/management/incharge, just like the fan obeys the instruction of its master.

Sometimes, a person switches on the fan and regulates it at the highest speed. If due to any reason, the fan does not accelerate its speed, the concerned person does not like this particular fan, because it does not fulfil his requirement. Then gradually he would try to replace this fan due to its slow performance or low expectation.

Similarly, when a management or a manager expects from a worker, a high degree of performance or a particular type of performance and if the worker fails to deliver accordingly, then the concerned management/manager, certainly would transfer the concerned non-performing worker to another department. They would never tolerate him. If they tolerate him and let him work without taking any action against him then, the company would have to face loss and the growth of the company; would be affected directly or indirectly.

For example, if the fan becomes defective, then it will not work properly and will never give desired output and if the fan will work, it will consume more electricity and the repairing cost will be higher. It may sometimes be almost the cost of a new fan. At this situation, the management will replace such fans or dump them in the storeroom where gradually the fans will turn to scrap.

If the manager fixes a pedestal fan in a particular direction but due to any reason, the fan turns in different direction, the concerned person will never like such defective fan and will get it fixed according to his requirement.

Similarly, in any organisation the management or concerned seniors have certain expectations from their subordinates on specific assigned work. They expect that their subordinates should deliver their responsibilities to them just like a ceiling fan, or pedestal fan delivers its assigned work as per the instruction of its master.

As, we fix the direction of a fan in a particular direction, the fan gives cool air only in that particular direction, or, if, the master fixes the fan in another direction the fan moves accordingly without fail. Similarly, the concerned seniors or management also expect from their juniors or subordinates that they should also do their duties or follow the instructions coming from their seniors like the fan, which obeys its master's direction to the T. If the workers deviate from their responsibilities and during the working hours would be distracted or look elsewhere, the senior or incharge would never like this. If the workers would not do their duties well, the concerned seniors would certainly transfer them to any other department and gradually, the worker may be ousted from the organisation in organisational interest.

In the Organisation, the management/manager/senior also sometimes behaves like the master of the fan. The master fixes a fan in a certain direction as per his requirement. Similarly, in the organisation or at the workplace the management/senior also gives a particular assignment to a particular worker to complete a specific work in a particular time. The management expects from their subordinates that they will not divert their mind from their main work. The master would never like his fan moving in a different direction inspite of being fixed at a certain direction. If it happens then the master would definitely replace the fan because, it does not fulfil the requirement of the master or it does not obey the instruction of the master.

If, some subordinate or workers do not complete their work in the fixed time frame, the concerned management/senior/manager would never appreciate such workers under any circumstance, because they have not done their work according to their senior's desire. In case of the fan, the master tries to replace that fan with a new one, so that the new fan can fulfil his demand.

Hence, the seniors/management/in charge, do not like such workers/subordinates because they have not done /completed the company's assigned job/work in a particular time frame or according to their boss's instructions. The management does not like such workers and gradually they try to depute them to some other place and recruit new staff for the same work, who can give better performance, in comparison to the previous ones. The management expects from their juniors that they should be obedient, loyal to the seniors/ management/ organisation.

Since, a new fan works more efficiently and there would be a less or negligible chance of repairing it. Similarly, a new employee / worker does not know the office politics, so they are very sincere in their duties and work performance.

They do not try to disobey the instructions of their seniors / management / manager. They always try to perform well, up to the satisfactory level of the concerned seniors. They think that they have to prove their ability, just like a new fan, which works, very smoothly. If each and every old staff perform their job/responsibilities well as the new worker does, the growth of the company will automatically increase.

That is why, the organisation, recruits new staff/worker instead of the old ones, just like the old fan which demands constant repairing and whose repairing cost gradually increases. Old workers sometimes give problems to the organisation, which seem unbearable/ unaffordable in company's interest. If we fulfil all the demands of the old worker or we repair the old fan, both are very costly for the company's interest. It would be better to purchase a new fan in less cost than the mounting repairing cost of the old fan. This is why the organisation prefers to recruit new staff. During the guarantee period the fan does not need any kind of repair which is similar to the probation period when the Company pays only the fixed stipend to the worker and they cannot demand more as per the appointment letter.

Thus, the organisation desires to recruit new people instead of continuing to work with the old ones. Old fans like old workers have old technique with them. They are not fully equipped with the new techniques or facilities. Presently, one can get technically sound people for a low salary while we have to pay more salary to old workers who are not technically sound or Tech-savvy.

It means, the old staff do not want to upgrade themselves with new technology as they age. It is more like the model of the old fan, which cannot be upgraded with the new remote control system. Therefore, the company wants to change them with new ones. At any situation, if the company offers to their workers voluntary retirement scheme which is mutually beneficial to the workers or who are facing retrenchment, should not feel bad, because the management takes the right step and looks forward to its future growth and profit. Here the management is not letting down its workers.

Inspite of having several merits and demerits in the old model fan or old employees, some of them are really good qualitywise not technologywise. I have a Philips Tape Recorder which I had purchased in the Year 1990 at Rs. 1800/- . Presently it is not in a working condition. Most of the mechanics have told me that this model is totally out of the market and Philips does not manufacture such models anymore. In spite of knowing that the tape recorder cannot be repaired, I am trying to repair it at any cost. I do not care about the cost of repairing because its quality is very good. Its sound quality is outstanding, which cannot be compared with any new model.

The same phenomenon is seen in some cases in any organisation. In spite of knowing that some workers are very old and do not perform as per the requirement of the Company, the management does not terminate them and let them work and they bear all their expenses and demands.

Some of them are really good, wise and experienced. Some of them are like an antique piece for the next generation to cherish. In the present days, there are several old model fans, which are working in the Govt. Organisations since a very long time. Inspite of having a lot of high-tech fans available in the market, the Govt. values the old fans due to the following reasons:

(Same holds true with the old Ambassador cars still being used in Govt. Departments inspite of having so many economically viable options)

- Old is Gold
- Sympathy / Emotional Attachment
- Loyalty
- Less repairing or bearable repairing cost.
- Having great experience.

When, we try to compare it with the workers/employees of any organisation, we would find that some employees/fans are very old in comparison to the modern ones but the management likes them due to their golden experience and emotional attachment which is generally not seen in the new ones. In present days, everything has become use and throw, hire and fire. It is the age of instant noodles and instant coffee. There is a total lack of emotional attachment. No one bothers about any one. Sometimes everybody knows that some employees are not performing well or are not competent enough with the new breed but the management keeps them only because of their experience. From time to time, they give valuable suggestions and guidelines to the management. As they are old, their demands are very few. They do not take unnecessary leave or give petty excuses. This is the reason they are liked by the management.

The management expects from all its workers that they should have emotional attachment with their company, where they are working. Management also aspires that they perform with their best of ability and they do not question the management on any issue. Their work is to deliver positively for the organisational growth.

Generally, the management /seniors /manager expect from their subordinates that they do not open their mouths. They should close their eyes ears and their own mind when they are working at their workplace. All these qualities are seen in the old employees and that is why the management likes them. Whatever the management expects from these old workers, are fulfilled by them without any interruption or questioning or hiccups.

SKY IS THE LIMIT

The ability of a human being is very closely related with their thinking capability and ambition. Ambition gives positive energy to the body and people try to react or act accordingly. If the ambition is not high then it would take a long time to complete the target and the person would get tired without doing much work. They would always feel very lazy. Their facial expression would be very dull and boring. Sometimes, it has been observed that the cells of our body become very weak and as a result, we fall sick. If the person is working in any office, and his performance is very poor, the management /senior/incharge is never happy with such people or workers who never deliver positively.

Our success depends upon the ambition/desire; we have, because it is ambition, which gives us positive energy in our life. We should take lessons from our surroundings. We should always think high. If we are living in a very poor condition and our thinking is like other people, then we will not progress but if at the same situation, we think that inspite of our poor condition, we have to get through the I.A.S. IIT, IIM etc. or other prestigious examinations, then it would be possible to achieve our target, subject to hard labour and right focus.

There are several examples in our society where people living in a chawl or slum with their poor parents, brothers and sisters get through the IIT,CAT,IAS etc. and other class I competitive examinations, which is very difficult to crack even for those leading a privileged life. It means that we should think high and take a lesson from the SKY and try to touch it because sky is the limit. Everyone is free to go beyond the Horizon.

Similarly, when we are working in our office at any post/cadre/position. We should always aspire to get a higher position / post in a positive not a negative way. If we think in a positive way then we will get positive energy in our body, which will give us the following:

- Learn new work.
- Patience

- Good Behaviour
- Listen to others
- Good grasping power
- Dedication
- Devotion
- How to win the trust of the Organisation.
- How to plan, make new strategy and how to complete the assigned target in a scientific and logical way.
- Involvement

The positive energy will change up our body, mind and spirit, which would help us to achieve the target. The management/ seniors expect from their workers/ subordinates that their workers should do their assigned work well in a logical and scientific way and it is only possible when the concerned workers would have the above qualities. These qualities are possible only when the people think positive and possess a high ambition.

It would even be better, if one takes inspiration from someone, who is working in a higher position, and takes lessons from him without any flattery, and try to achieve that position. They should get friendly with people who are more qualified, knowledgeable, experienced, well behaved and having high ambition, so that one could get inspiration to do well in life and be successful.

In our college life, we have seen, many students studying hard to compete the U.P.S.C. Which is the most coveted examination in India. They never think about Banking or State level competitions. In practice, when a student studies for the U.P.S.C. then the State level examination becomes very easy for them and they easily get through it. High level of thinking and positive attitude with sincere efforts makes one successful and helps crack such a coveted examination.

The management at any level in any organisation expects from their subordinates to have all the above qualities. Then only it is possible that they would be liked. They would never tell the junior or subordinate that they have the following merits or demerits. Nobody tells anyone that they should appreciate them, but they expect to hear a few words of appreciation about themselves. It is not necessary that everything should be in writing but it is required.

The same qualities are expected from a person in his own family. Today, the percentage of divorce, conflict between wife-husband, among brothers and family members are increasing day by day. Here, if, we assume the head of the family or the husband to be a senior/HOD/ management, then it would be very easy for any subordinate to have faith in his seniors or management.

The subordinates / juniors should not expect from their seniors that they should tell them what it right or what is wrong, what they should do or should not do. In the same way, our family would seldom give us right suggestions. We should not expect anything from anyone. When we are traveling in an aeroplane, our safety totally depends upon the pilot's expertise akin to our office, our H.O.D. or concerned seniors, who decide our well being. It does not matter what qualities impress or influence our H.O.D.

WINDOW

Window is a very important part for any house because without a window there will be darkness during the day. People living in dark and humid place, have to face lack of fresh air and sunlight to survive. As a result, the health of the concerned people will be affected and they will fall sick. Their mind and mental status may be unbalanced due to suffocation, lack of proper ventilation or lack of fresh air and sunlight.

Their thinking level may gradually deteriorate and this will affect their work performance too and when their work performance will be affected, their progress will be affected. It is like a chain reaction but of a different kind, so it is clear that window plays a very important role in our life.

Hence, window is not merely a window but it is a symbol of open mind and big thinking. It depends upon our perspective. I mean that people in their office or work place, should always have an open mind and all their senses should be opened and should take inspiration and look at the window as:

WINDOW:

- **W:** Wide thinking, Weak points, Welcome, Willingness, Winner, Wishful, Watch,
- **I:** Intellectual, Innovative thought, Indiscipline, Individuality, Intoxication, Issue,
- **N:** No Negligence, Neighbourly, Nostalgia, Notice, Note,
- **D:** Determination, Devotion, Discipline, Display, Displease, Duty first and self last, Distort, Dominate, Drag,
- **O:** Overall, Organisational thought, Optimist, Outstanding work, Overtake the procedure, Overhear, Outspoken, Overlook, Oppose, Objects, Obdurate, Obedient, Object, Obligation.
- **W:** Wind direction, Wisdom to think, Work is Worship

W: Wide thinking, Weak points, Welcome, Willingness, Winner, Wishful, Watch, Water

The Management also expects from their employees / subordinates that they should think not only for themselves but should also think for the organisation and its growth. Their vision should be wide. They should look at others as to how they are working, living and should learn from them. They should have an analytical mind, so that they can analyse their work performance, approach, availability of means to complete the desired target as per the instruction of their management or concerned seniors. As the MET Department from time to time forecasts the weather conditions and tries to alert or inform the common people about the weather so that they could take proper precautions as well as prepare themselves to tackle the rain, wind and thunder. Similarly, in any organisation, or at the workplace, the workers / subordinates/ juniors should also have the capability to read the organisational weather or working environment. It may be said that people should have such inherent quality, that they should guess the impending problem at the workplace due to the inherent sixth sense and they should inform their seniors / incharge / H.O.D. etc about the impending danger or problem.

They should always be prepared to face any kind of situation at the workplace due to any reason because, when we are working at our workplace, we have to face several hidden problems. Those problems may be personal or official may or may not be related to our work.

We should always be willing to do any assigned work. We should never think that a particular work, which our seniors or incharge have given us to complete, cannot be done by us, because such work does not come under our jurisdiction or in our department or it is not our responsibility. We should always be ready to do any assigned responsibility given by the concerned seniors. We should not ask them any negative questions and irritate them.

We should always think that our work performance is the best in the organisation and no one can beat us. If we have such spirit than a positive energy would help us to complete our work or to take up any challenge in the organisation or at the workplace.

We should have the ability to take any responsibility. We should try to generate work ourselves, because we may not have any work at a particular situation or time. Without having the desire to work, no one can complete their assigned work as per the desire of the organisation or the concerned seniors. Their desire to work will directly and positively affect their prospect of promotion / increment or other benefits.

One particular thing, which the seniors expect from their juniors or subordinates, is that they should have the capability or quality to watch the surrounding. They should know what is happening around them or at their workplace, so that they could be prepared to tackle the situation accordingly. By analysing the situation, anyone can guess the weak points or shortcomings of the work or workplace which they have to complete or where they have to survive.

Apart from the above, we should also learn from the characteristics of WATER. Everyone knows that no living thing can live without water. A person or any living thing can survive without water for one, two days or maximum a week but not more than that. Without water our body will not function and our body will get dehydrated and the energy of the body will start decreasing in such a way that it would will be difficult for us to breathe and one day we may die.

I mean that the workers in any organisation should adopt the role of water at their work place, so that the concerned worker like water, should become most vital for the organisation and their absence should be felt or missed. Then only such workers can get promotion, increment, or other benefits. If the work is not hampered by the absence of any particular worker, the management will take him for granted and they would not give him any benefit.

Our nature and behaviour should be very simple and flexible and we should be ready to face any circumstance and challenge and, we should always be in demand. We should not create any hurdle for the company. For example, if any big hurdle comes in the way of water, it tries to remove it from its path of flow and if that hurdle is not overpowered by its flow, it goes onwards leaving the hurdle at the same place. We should learn a lesson from it. In any organisation and at the workplace, there are several visible or invisible hurdles coming our way. We should not lose our patience or our temper to tackle them. First of all, we should observe the situation as to how big the obstacle / problem is? If the problem to be solved can be tackled then we should try to meet the challenge head on and remove the hurdle but if the problem is beyond our means, then it is better to leave it as it is.

We should not be rigid but we should be like water, taking the shape of the glass or the container in which it is kept. At the workplace, the management likes only those workers, who can take new shape. It means those who do not have their own identity. If they have their own identity, then it sure that they would occupy a prominent place and the management would have to provide special or proper space for them, but if a person has no specific ideas, identity, ego, thoughts etc, then the workers would fit at any place and every senior, management or any authority will like them, because they would be harmless and productive. They should also be like clay, which can be moulded into any shape or size depending upon the need or requirement.

If, we are harmless and have a cool temperament then, every senior, junior would like us and they would give their option to the management for the requirement of such workers. They know that such workers would be very faithful for the organisation as well as for the concerned seniors. They would never leak out any confidential information to any one; even if the person is associated with the top management.

We should also learn from running water, which is, clean, clear, dust free and bacteria free etc. For maintaining good and sound health, it is necessary that we should drink clean and clear water. Similarly, at the workplace or in an organisation the workers should also be very clear, clean and bacteria free i.e. harmless. Otherwise, the development of the organisation as well as of the concerned seniors, juniors or any worker will be hampered. They cannot get any promotion, increment or other benefit. If at any circumstance, the undeserving workers get promotion or other benefits from the respective management then it is sure that such benefits will not last for a long time or period. In a very short time, their original behaviour would come out in front of the others and the same person may be demoted.

In present times also, there are some people, whose character is totally clean and crystal clear just like the rainwater, or the Holy water of Gangotri. People swear by Gangajal (Ganges water) due to its purity and sacredness. The percentage of such clean workers is very less. There is a very small fraction of true workers. We should take a lesson from water and we should improve our conduct in such a way that no one could raise his or her finger on us or on our conduct.

Devout Hindus drink the holy water of Ganga when they are at their deathbed to rid them of their sins and life. It is however subjective. Water sustains life. It not only quenches our thirst but also maintains soil fertility and agriculture. We should not forget its good qualities. Similarly, the workers working at any workplace or in any organisation should save other people, colleagues, organisation, seniors, etc, without differentiating between them at the time of trouble, or a crisis, official or unofficial, on humanitarian grounds.

We should always be calm at any given condition or situation because cool temperament attracts others, while hot temper repulses them. No one comes close, to a hot object and vice versa. In this way, we should take a lesson from water and at our workplace or organisation or in front of any seniors, subordinates, colleagues etc. We should always be calm and keep cool. As keeping cool gives right direction and fruitful result. Nobody in the organisation likes their juniors or seniors getting hyper or angry on any situation and such action would reflect at the time of fulfilling their appraisal forms. We should also abstain from wishful thinking.

I: Intellectual, Innovative thought, Indiscipline, Individuality, Intoxication, Issue.

The concerned management or incharge / H.O.D. expects from their juniors or subordinates that they should have an intellectual as well as innovative thought. They should not depend upon the thought of their concerned seniors but they should have their own thought process towards their assigned work or hidden work. They should have the capability to work and complete the work without giving any problem to their seniors and they should complete the work according to their intellectual and innovative thought.

The seniors expect that their workers should not ask any questions on the work assigned to them but they should complete them as per the wish/desire made by their concerned seniors.

One thing more the concerned seniors or incharge never tolerate is indiscipline or improper conduct by their juniors, because if their juniors commit any indiscipline at the work place, the concerned seniors would be directly responsible for the same and the top or middle management would directly charge them for it and the concerned seniors would be directly answerable. Therefore, the seniors expect from their juniors or subordinates that they should not commit any type of indiscipline at the workplace, knowingly or unknowingly and maintain proper decorum.

The seniors also expect from their juniors or subordinates that they should always keep in mind that whatever work they are doing is for the organisation and not for any individual. They should work or complete any assignment, keeping in their mind that they are not working for themselves but for their organisation as the organisation is paying them to do the work. There is no concept of individuality at the workplace or in the organisation. Whatever one is doing, is totally for the organisation and not for any individual.

In general, everyone knows his capabilitys and his limitations, merits, demerits, good and bad habits, what is right or how one should behave with others but inspite of having all the knowledge, the seniors or juniors never like or tolerate any type of misbehaviour done by anyone anywhere.

Similarly, the seniors / Incharge to whom, we are going to report or we are liable to report to or under whom we are working, never like that their subordinates / juniors be indisciplined. It is possible, that the concerned senior under whom, we are working, may be the most indisciplined person of the organisation. Inspite of this, the same indisciplined senior also does not like that his subordinates or juniors be indisciplined in the organisation.

They never like any of their colleagues telling them that a particular worker, working in his department, is very indisciplined or he does not even know how to talk to his seniors or any reputed person in the organisation.

I mean inspite of having all bad qualities in the concerned seniors, H.O.D., Incharge, expect from their juniors or subordinates that they should always be very disciplined. The seniors also expect from their juniors that they should be very neat and clean in every respect in the organisation and no one should be given a chance to make any complaint against any of their juniors or subordinates, which they cannot tolerate, under any condition.

Apart from the above, the seniors also expect from their juniors that they should not raise any type of issue in front of the management, due to which they may have to face embarrassment or awkward position in front of any other persons in the company. The seniors expect, without telling anything to their juniors, that they should not raise any issue, to their concerned seniors and if the seniors permit them, then only they should raise the issue, whether the issue is in favour or against the organisation. They should not do it on their own.

The seniors expect that their juniors should not make any issue, which influences the concerned seniors. The issue should be such that the company would be responsible and not a particular person. If the company would be responsible then, the concerned seniors would not be held responsible for that particular issue. They want their subordinates to be extrovert but they never like that due to their extrovert nature the seniors should be exposed otherwise, they would be answerable for raising any issue. The senior is concerned about his own safety and not of the others.

N: No Negligence, Neighbourly, Nostalgia Notice, Note.

The seniors at every stage expect from their subordinates that they should be very obedient and deliver their responsibility according to the instruction given and, do only what their seniors desire. They should not neglect their work and instruction at any stage or under any circumstance. If they feel that there is some problem in completing the target or goal, the subordinates should inform their seniors but they should never neglect their instructions. The seniors do not want that due to the negligence of their subordinates their position would get awkward, as they are eventually answerable to the top management.

They do not want that due to the negligence of any subordinate, the company has to face problems or bear financial loss. It is alright if due to their own negligence, the company has to face financial problem but at the same time, they cannot tolerate that due to their subordinate's negligence, the company has to face any problem. If this happens, then the concerned seniors will take proper administrative action against the concerned juniors or subordinates due to whom the company had to face loss.

The seniors expect from their subordinates that the behaviour of workers working under their guidance should have a neighbourly behaviour with their colleagues or with other departments. They should not differentiate between their colleagues of the department, where they are working or with workers of other departments but they should consider them as their family members. The seniors can differentiate between the two departments or colleagues but they expect from their juniors and subordinates that they should not have any negative feeling for the workers of other departments or other colleagues.

It is true that the seniors require that their juniors working in their department or under their guidance should not feel home sick. They should be heartless and they should never try to express their feelings for their own family members. They should not talk about their own family members because they know that when their subordinates would talk about their family members then their dedication towards their assigned work would decline or they cannot devote themselves to their job. Their strength would decrease and as a result the output of those particular workers would not be as good or as per the desire of the management.

The seniors want that their subordinates should always talk about their organisation as a family. They should always think about its progress, how they could contribute in their company in the organisational growth. If the organisation would get profit or progress, the whole workers / staff would be benefited, so they should not openly express any feeling for their family members in front of them.

At the same time, the seniors also do not want to hear from their juniors or subordinates about the organisation where they were working earlier or where they were supposed to work. The seniors without making any noise expect from their subordinates that if they want to talk about the other organisation where they were working before, they should do so outside the office premises.

One thing more that the seniors want from their juniors or subordinates is that they should have full knowledge of the notice displayed on the notice board. Sometimes the concerned seniors also put a notice on the notice board. They expect that their juniors should appreciate or express their views / opinion about that notice.

Apart from the above, they desire that their juniors or subordinates should take note of each and every happening in the organisation and they should be fully aware of such happenings. If the seniors ask them about a particular happening in the organisation, the subordinates should be aware of it. Displaying notice on the notice board would apprise all the juniors and other workers of the happenings and important news and meetings.

One more thing that the seniors expect from their juniors is that whenever they call their juniors for any work, meeting or other related work, they should come with a pen and a notebook and should jot down the instructions which they may forget later on. As soon as the instructed work/ job responsibility is completed, they desire that their subordinates should inform them immediately.

They should not write on a lose page but on a proper writing pad. This way the seniors feel that their juniors are giving them respect. The seniors always desire that their juniors should give them due respect and they should work according to their instructions. Then only a healthy working relationship would develop between them.

D: Determination, Devotion, Discipline, Display, Displease, Duty first and self-last, Distort, Dominate, Drag.

Without having interest on the work one is doing, one cannot complete any given assignment. It means, for the successful completion of work there should be interest for that particular work and along with the interest, there should be determination, then only the work can be completed properly. Otherwise, the work will start but it may remain incomplete or be stopped in the middle. However, if one starts his / her work / assignment with interest as well as with determination to complete the work then no hurdle can stop them from completing their work. They would complete the task on time as desired by the concerned seniors.

It means the seniors desire from their juniors or subordinates that they should have determination as well as interest in their assigned work. They should also have devotion and work discipline to complete the task in a specific time period. The seniors also expect from the juniors that they should complete the assigned work according to the instruction given before.

One more thing that the concerned seniors, sometimes want from their juniors is that whatever work they do, should come forward in front of others. Otherwise, no one would know about those particular workers or his or her development or expertise. They should exhibit their work at their workplace so that everyone could be familiar with their work. The display of work should be in such way that it does not hurt or offend anyone. The juniors should first of all inform the concerned seniors about their plans.

The juniors cannot progress or grow by displeasing their seniors. We should not displease our seniors at any cost.

The seniors at every level expect from their juniors that they should follow the adage "DUTY FIRST AND SELF LAST". It means they should not give priority to themselves but they should give priority to their assigned work, which they have to complete. They should always remember that they are appointed at their workplace only for work, so they have to complete the work, under any circumstance. Duty comes first, and then other things follow.

For example, if workers assigned to complete work, which is necessary in the company's interest and at the same time, the concerned workers have their own personal or family problems etc. At this situation, they should complete their official assigned work first then only they should take up their family problems. Everyone should be clear in their mind that it is our duty, which gives us our daily bread. Therefore, we should first take up our duty and then think about our family or ourselves.

At the workplace, various types of workers are found. Some take interest only in distorting the fact and then they place it in front of the management or seniors, in their own way. In this way, a real / true culprit never gets punishment and it would be very difficult to know the actual problem of the workers, workplace or the environment where they are working. Some of the subordinates or junior or concerned workers misguide the seniors by giving the facts in a distorted way. Such workers are involved only in negative activities. In the initial period, they confuse the seniors but after some times, the concerned seniors come to know the facts through the whisper campaign. At this situation, the same seniors abhor such workers, who had in the initial period, distorted the facts before conveying it to the seniors.

The seniors never like such workers who lack honesty and integrity. They expect from their juniors that they should be crystal clear in their communication. They should not distort any fact but sometimes the same seniors possess the same characters, which, they do not mind at all.

At the workplace or in the organisation, some people are very dominating. Such people do not want to work, but they want to dominate other workers. They never want to see the progress of their colleagues. Such workers try to misguide them and try to distort their contribution before giving the information to the management. People with dominating nature become popular in a very brief period in any organisation and with their strong communication skill, impress the seniors and juniors in the entire department. Sometimes such workers prove very beneficial for the organisational growth but at the same time the seniors to whom such workers have to report, gradually start keeping at a distance from them.

They are stripped of all the responsibilities, which were given earlier to them. A day comes when the most popular person of the organisation has no work and when he is without his work portfolio, he is made to understand that his seniors do not want to see his progress in the organisation. It means the seniors are jealous of his popularity. In a way, his popularity hampers his progress.

I mean that if one is very popular in his organisation or department or at his workplace, it is possible that his boss may not recommend his name for promotion or increment. We should not be surprised to see this. It is the bitter truth. We should not feel bad or take it seriously when the boss does not give a positive remark on our creativity, devotion and contribution.

In an organisation, there are different types of workers in which some may be very fast or some may be very slow. Some people can take their decisions fast while some may take it very slowly or can never discharge their responsibilities in a specific period. They are always late in all the aspects. This characteristic is inherent in human beings.

People having such a characteristic, always try to create obstacles in the progress of their colleagues or organisation. They always try to pull the legs of their colleagues just to show their importance or smartness. The seniors, in the initial period, do not mind such behaviour of their juniors but after some time, when they come to know their true nature, they take action against them. One should not try to out smart others.

The seniors expect from their juniors or subordinates that they should not keep on dragging the ongoing work at the workplace because such behaviour directly affects the growth of the organisation, the brand, their reputation in the market.

O: Over all, Organisational thought, Optimist, Outstanding work, Overtake the procedure, Overhear, Outspoken, Overlook, Oppose, Objects, Obdurate, Obedient, Object, Obligation, One time one work.

It is human nature that the thinking of most of us is very narrow as well as confined to myself and not ourselves. This type of nature also affects our working style, performance, approach and self-progress. The appraisal done by the seniors are also very closely related to our thinking and productivity. The type of thought we have towards ourselves and towards the organisation, play an important role in our life. Some our us like to work only for ourselves while a few people give importance to the organisational goal and their achievements than themselves.

We should think first for the organisation for which we are recruited than ourselves. If there is any crisis where we are working, we should first try to save the organisation than we should think about ourselves.

Each and every senior in any position or having any kind of character, first of all expects from his juniors or subordinates that they should possess a big heart and wide thinking. They should not be narrow-minded and they should think about all the employees and workers. They should not differentiate among the workers, colleagues or department. Most of the seniors do not have such qualities but they surely expect from their juniors to be very broad minded, selfless and big-hearted.

The optimistic behaviour gives positive energy to every concerned worker. Their efficiency, dedication, stamina increases and due to these the output as well as the performance of the worker increases for the better and helps them to come in the good books of the management/ seniors. If a person is optimistic then it is sure that he will never say no to the seniors or the concerned persons. He will never deny to complete the given work or to take up any responsibility given by the seniors. Their work gradually becomes outstanding and the output increases.

Every senior, incharge, H.O.D. expect from their juniors that their work performance should be outstanding as well as their workers should be optimistic because when their workers would be optimistic they would never make any demand for any increment or promotion. Supposing on making any demand by the subordinates, the seniors tell them that they would get promotion and increment in the near future. Their faith towards the respective seniors and the organisation increases, only if they are optimistic in their nature.

The seniors never like that their juniors or subordinates overtake the procedure of the organisation or any system introduced by them. They expect that their junior should follow all the systems whether it is right or wrong, beneficial to the organisation or not. They should only follow the system devised by them. If anyone tries to overtake or modify the system, they get annoyed and give bad remarks during the time of appraisal.

They always act as a dictator and want every word or instruction be treated as a standing order of the company. No one should have the guts to challenge it. They should always obey the instructions given by the seniors. They should be very obedient. Sometimes some people, ignore or overlook the instructions, which the seniors never like. They want that no one should overlook any instruction given by the seniors.

Some people are very outspoken which gives them an edge or helps them to build their brand name within the organisation. In a few months, such people become, very popular in the organisation. The seniors never like such outspoken and witty persons. They think that their subordinates or juniors should not express their knowledge or comment on any topic or problems, without their consent, as they are in charge of the department.

It means no senior gives permission to say anything or to express themselves in any situation in front of others. Without the consent of seniors, the juniors cannot do anything. The seniors never like any person or workers who are outspoken or witty. If by chance a worker has such a quality and when working under the senior, the concerned senior tries to strip him from the responsibility and gives it to other workers, who are not capable to do the same. They do so because they are not outspoken. They keep to themselves and keep quiet.

It is often seen that most of the seniors have numerous meeting in the organisation without any rhyme or reason and give instruction to their subordinates to make plans for the presentation, for the betterment of the organisation as well as of the workers. The seniors think that plans or presentation whether it is right or wrong from the organisation point of view; their subordinate should listen and obey their instructions. They should not oppose their strategy or instruction or ask any unwanted question during the meeting which may give rise to awkward situations in front of the respective seniors.

One characteristic is found in all the human beings, which is called obduracy. In our own family, our small kids always force or compel us to buy a toy or something as per their interest. They always play and do what they like. Inspite of telling, them to stop playing and start studying, they do not bother and give a damn or ignore our instructions. Likewise in the organisation, some workers have the same characteristic like the child. They like to do whatever they want. They are not bothered about their senior's remarks.

If the seniors tell them to complete their work within a specific time period, the person definitely would not complete the work on time. If the senior asks him to come on a holiday to complete any work or during emergency, the concerned workers would try to make excuse for not being able to come or cite some false reason or try to ignore his order. The seniors will tolerate it once or may be occasionally but after some time the seniors would try to avoid such workers to involve them in any confidential or important work. It means the seniors or incharge do not want such workers who are obdurate.

They like such workers who are very obedient to their incharge, to their assigned work, seniors, and to their organisation. Every senior thinks that their juniors should be very obedient and they should behave like an obedient student. Then only they feel satisfied to do something in their favour. They want to make sure that their juniors deserve benefit.

They want that the workers should express gratitude to their seniors for doing them a favour. If anyone has done a favour for them, they should be highly obliged to him because there are very few people left on this earth, who think about the betterment of others. Therefore, if they have done a favour for their juniors, subordinates, they should be very much obliged for the same. The juniors should thank the concerned seniors immediately without fail and express their heartfelt gratitude.

If we have done something wrong, we should immediately accept our fault. If we have unknowingly done any wrong then, we should very diplomatically as well as politely convey the correct message to the concerned seniors. If there is any confusion created by some people to the management, seniors, we should, first of all accept our fault to satisfy the ego of the seniors but later on we should clarify everything to the seniors separately and let them know the fact.

It is very peculiar to observe that a computer takes only one instruction at a time. If we give more than one instruction, then it may be possible that the computer would hang or would give wrong message or give some sort of absurd message that we have done wrong. Similarly, we should also remember that when we are talking to any of our seniors, we should talk on only one matter or subject.

As soon as we start another topic or raise another problem, when the earlier topic is not completed, the concerned senior would get irritated and would get angry on the concerned person. It means, the seniors expect from their juniors that they should not raise irrelevant questions when the seniors are giving instructions to their juniors. When we fulfil one instruction completely, then only we should raise other questions, problems in front of them.

W : Wind direction, Wisdom to think Work is Worship

Like other natural things from which we take guidelines at our workplace, we should also see the wind direction, not literally but what is going on at our workplace. It does not give the actual meaning of the word. It depends upon us as to how we take the meaning or how we interpret it. Everything depends from person to person, as to how they react on any given circumstance. We should try to know what our seniors or management wants from us. It is not sure that they would say everything or would give everything in writing that they need the following things to be done. It is up to us how we read our senior's face. We should try to know what our management desires from us and we should do accordingly without creating any obstacle.

The workers can give their full output only when they are totally free from any responsibility or tension. They should have the wisdom to think, and are not bound to a particular work. When a worker gets freedom, then only his mind would work and would give rise to good and creative ideas in his mind and he would be able to achieve the required target.

Everyone believes in the power of the Almighty. He takes care of all of us. We pray to Him with all our devotion and sincerity. We try to please Him with our devotion, worship so that He can bless and fulfil our requirements, demands as soon as possible.

We avoid wearing shoes and do not want to do anything wrong which God does not like while praying. We become selfish in asking Him to fulfil our desires.

We take care of all factors, which please God. In the organisation or at the workplace, the factors are very similar. Here the seniors desire that their juniors or subordinates should pray not with flowers but with their devotion, dedication and work performance to please them. Sometimes we too act selfishly to attract their attention for our benefit.

They expect that their juniors should think their workplace to be sacred as a temple and they should worship their work and workplace. By doing such a thing, their seniors would be happy and would bless them with good appraisal or remark, which would be helpful for their promotion and increment etc.

In short, we can say that, if any one has any problem, we should try to know the reason behind that problem and try to solve them. Everyone working in the organisation should always try to know the wind direction of the management not literally but try to know the demand of the seniors / management or the concerned incharge as without having the knowledge of their desire, it would be very difficult to adjust / work in any organisation or in that particular organisation.

Apart from the above, if the problem is not adjustable, then we should look for some other job which indirectly the window of the workplace whispers in our ear. The management also expects from their employees that the knowledge level of their subordinates should be very wide. Their subordinate should know the entire development, not only about their own department but they should have a clear concept and knowledge about other departments, the organisational growth and all type of development going on in that organisation as well as at the workplace.

They should inform their incharge, seniors, H.O.D. of all the happenings from time to time without any delay. They should consider it as the part of their duty. If any one does not give information to the respective seniors the worker would never be liked by the seniors, inspite of having all the qualities, education, experience etc. They would never be promoted easily or in a routine way like other workers. Such workers would have to face a lot of problems at their workplace. Sharing information about the ongoing happenings at the workplace with the concerned seniors is the key to self-development. The subordinates should understand it automatically; otherwise, it would be very difficult to survive in that organisation in the long term or anywhere else by them.

We should take a lesson from the "window- grill. whenever we are working for the organisation, the policy, and strategy of the Company should not go out, in company's interest but it should be thoroughly filtered before disclosing it to any one.

WALL CLOCK

The wall clock teaches us to:

C : Catch the Opportunity

L : Be Loyal to the Management

O : Overwork, Outburst, Outlook, Oversee, Overcome.
Oneness, Omission, Officious, Offered, Offensive

C : Clever, Clear hearted

K : Knowledge, Keenness / Key / Know / Knock the door of Opportunity

At every stage and movement, nature is ready to guide us, whether we are deviating from the mainstream or not. *"TIME AND TIDE WAITS FOR NONE"*. There is no discrimination in the eyes of time and tide. It is fixed. Whether we work or not, time and tide does not wait for us, so we should not miss any opportunity coming our way. It is also said that "Time is Money". We should respect time, so that time can respect us. Time gives us the quality of discipline, which is necessary for any personal as well as organisational growth. Whenever we feel, disappointment at any circumstance, we should take a lesson from the WALL CLOCK and boost overselves to meet the challenges / obstacles coming in the way of our progress. We should boost our morale by taking the lesson from the clock as it continues working and tells us the time correctly. Likewise, we should continue giving our best to the company where we are working.

C: Catch the Opportunity

Opportunity does not knock at our door every time. We must make use of the opportunity no matter how different our work may be. If our inner sense is developed and gives us a hint that, we should not let go of the particular opportunity, but we should utilise it to its hilt. At the workplace, where we work, it is not sure that every day we would get an opportunity to prove ourselves. Due to any circumstance, the seniors/ management/ in charge suddenly might offer us a golden chance for a new beginning or a responsibility, which we should grab with both hands. We should respect the opportunity and try to perform with the best of our efforts so that the management would appreciate our efforts and recognise it.

Sometimes, the management finds that the concerned or assigned person for a particular work/job, is on leave and if the work is very important in the organisation's interest, then it is sure that the management would look for a new and responsible worker and assign him that particular work to complete. At this situation, if any one gets such an opportunity to complete a new assignment, he should respect the new opportunity and finish it with the best of his efforts. It may be a new beginning for him.

We should never utter, NO even, if it is beyond our capacity and knowledge, because such an opportunity does not come our way every day. Therefore, we should make use of the given opportunity to the fullest.

L: Be Loyal to the Management

"Clock" gives us the lesson to be "Loyal to the Management" and it is very true that the management also expects from their employees/workers that their employees should be very loyal to them. They expect / desire that the subordinates should think only about the benefit of the organisation. For example, when a new worker joins an organisation and if he starts talking about his previous employer or organisation, it is not liked. He should try to keep his previous work a secret.

When a girl gets married and if she brags continuously about her family or parents then, no one at her in-laws place likes this. Therefore, to gain faith, we should be loyal to our master. Without being loyal towards the organisation / family /spouse / seniors, we cannot be trusted.

O: Oneness, Omission, Officious Offend, Offensive

Oneness is unity and unity is strength. Work done collectively gives good result. Therefore, oneness is the most important factor to achieve a pre-planned goal. It is very difficult to achieve anything for a single person but the same may be very easily achieved, when more than one person is involved. People think that they are working alone but it is their mistake because they are never alone. More than one person, is directly or indirectly involved in a particular work to be completed. Oneness means being united and "United we stand and divided we fall." We should try to avoid any type of omission. The seniors expect that their juniors should not do any omission during their work handling or while completing their assignment. Being officious for any worker working in any organisation is akin to giving positive energy to the workers which generate interest to take up any responsibility or a challenge from their seniors. It is desired by most of the seniors that their subordinates should be officious to take up any challenge in their stride for the organisational benefit.

C : Clever / Clear Hearted

The letter "C" of CLOCK *denotes* clever as well as clear hearted. Being clever and clear hearted is very necessary for human beings. Without these qualities, we cannot get progress in any field as well as in our personal life, because both are such powerful factors of our life that it gives us directly an unmatched power of confidence and strength to work without fear of anyone. It makes us fearless and this strength of fearlessness gives us innovative ideas to work.

The seniors of any organisation like and support only those workers, subordinates or juniors working under them, who are clever and clear hearted who do not keep anything bottled in their heart. Those who can understand the fact just at a glance and in no time. If a worker takes more, time to understand the work or assigned responsibility, he shall never be liked by his seniors or incharge.

We should work continuously. If we do not know the work, we should continue to work without asking anyone about the job, as to how it should be done. The seniors only like to see their workers being engaged in their work, whether the work could be completed or not by the juniors, is beyond their jurisdiction. If the workers stay and work late hours, the seniors would be very happy to see them working hard.

They think that such workers who stay at their office late are very labourious and at the time of promotion, increment or any benefit, the senior, would automatically recommend these workers for the same.

On the other hand, if one went back home at a fixed time after finishing his office duty, the seniors would never like such workers. The senior always keep in mind that such workers are not flexible and have to go home on time, come rain, hail or thunder. They cannot be dependable workers.

K: Knowledge / Keenness / Key / Know / Keep / Knocking the Door of Opprtunity

The "K" of Clock also denotes something which gives us a very important lesson that we should develop our knowledge by reading news papers, magazines, journals etc, so that we could be familiar with new things, technologies which would give us an edge and help us in our productivity and efficiency of the work being done. By developing our knowledge, it would be very easy for us to devise more innovative methods to develop our skills and qualities. There is no age limit to acquire knowledge, as knowledge will widen our horizon in all the spheres.

We should try to diversify our ability and try to know about other work also, apart from our routine work, so that if any opportunity comes our way, we could switch over to that new responsibility /job. Simultaneously, we should always be ready to face any competition, challenge at any circumstance to achieve our goal. We should not stop thinking that this work cannot be completed by us. *Nothing is impossible; Impossible itself means I am possible.* We should not think negative at any cost or under any circumstance. If we think positive, we would get an inner strength, which would help us to boost our morale to perform better.

Overall, we should take a lesson from the CLOCK, thinking that every moment is very precious and we should not waste the precious moments unnecessarily but we should utilise them as much as we can.

Everyone should have keenness, which means the inner urge to do any work or learn something new. If a person comes forward without being asked or without being deputed any work, everyone would like him. Sometimes, while doing any common work, where not one is responsible but everyone is responsible and, if anyone comes forward to work at his own interest, then each and every one in the Organisation would like such a person and shall notice his initiative taking as well as keenness to work.

All the people like to support such people in any circumstance. More or less, the same logic is also found in the organisation or at the work place. If a subordinate or a junior does any work, without being assigned by any one, such workers would automatically impress everybody in the company and the concerned seniors. The seniors without any pressure would recommend such workers for promotion or increment or whatever benefit is possible.

One thing that is very important to understand is that, if a subordinate works in such a way at his workplace / department that he keeps most of the information to himself and reveals it at the right time to the respective or concerned seniors. All the seniors would like such subordinates. The seniors also like those persons who keep most of the organisational information and secrets confidential and reveal it only on the instruction of the seniors. Such workers never require any recommendation of their concerned department. The seniors recommend their betterment out of the way. Therefore, it is very bad to be a blabbermouth and keeping official information a secret is a very big virtue, which few people possess in the present days.

MIRROR : REFLECTS BEFORE YOU AS YOU ACT

All developments are totally dependent upon our attitude, thinking power, Action and reaction. It is up to ourselves as to how we take up a problem or how we tackle, a particular problem and what we learn or what lesson we get from it. If food is kept on a table then we would decide, whether we should eat that food or not. Nobody can force us to eat it. So, there are several natural living and non–living things, that give us lessons and guide us about the forthcoming problems, how to lead our life, how to work and behave in the organisation as well as at home and finally how to improve our work, skill etc.

We have all seen a mirror and have grown up looking into it. In the context of organisation, the mirror reflects a lot of things and teaches us various lessons.

These lessons are:

M: MOTIVATION, MINIMISE THE COMPANY'S EXPENSES, MAGNANIMOUS, MISBEHAVIOUR, MISAPPROPRIATE, MISCHIEF,

I: IMPROVE YOURSELF, IGNORE, IMPORTANCE, IMPRESS, INCONVENIENT, INDIFFERENT, INNOVATION,

R: REALISE YOUR MISTAKE, RETROSPECT, REPUGNANT

R: REFLECT BEFORE YOU ACT, RESEARCH ON WORK

O: OBJECTIVE SHOULD BE CRYSTAL CLEAR

R: REACT ON FAULT, REPENT, REPLY

M: MINIMISE THE COMPANY'S EXPENSES, MOTIVATION MAGNANIMOUS, MISBEHAVIOUR, MISAPPROPRIATE, MISCHIEF, MANIPULATION OF WORK/FACTS.

Every company wants to get growth / profit and it is only possible, when the expenses incurred in the day-to-day work at the work place of any organisation, is minimised in the company's interest. The concerned person working at his workplace, should think personally that the expenses incurred are his own and he should feel the pinch of it being spent heartlessly as if he has to pay or bear the expenses to be incurred in a particular project or work. The workers should feel that the concerned expenses are purely their monthly expenses, and the saving of a single paise would definitely affect their monthly budget. Then the concerned people will immediately reduce /curtail the running expenses, which may not directly affect the growth or output of the company but in the long run would definitely contribute to the profit of the company. Thus, the company would grow and if the company would grow, the workers working in that company, without any effort, would benefit in various aspects monetarily or otherwise. Once, the workers are financially sound, they would discharge their responsibilities with more motivation, dedication and sincerity.

The management thinks that the worker working at any level in their organisation should not spend unnecessarily. The Mirror also gives us the lesson that we should motivate our juniors so that they could get inspiration from us and they should complete their assigned responsibilities more efficiently. No one bothers to motivate others. One should get motivation first as self-motivation works as a catalyst. Self-motivation gives a positive energy to our body, which motivates us to work, in a very systematic way. There is very less chance of mistake in the work done by any self-motivated person because such persons think intensely before doing anything.

Most of the people like such people, who are very big hearted and have more space in their heart for others. His or her level of thinking is very big and in whose view, everyone is equal. He has love for all and not for the people in the higher position. It means, we should be generous at our work place. If we have been given an opportunity to benefit our workers, we should not have a narrow outlook but we should be magnanimous. We should help each and every person as much as we can.

Similarly, at our work place, there are some workers, who are very narrow-minded and they cannot think good or positive for their colleagues. They think only about themselves. If their juniors or subordinates are having any problems or they are facing other difficulties in their work assignment or they are not getting the required facility they do not bother at all or care for them.

Sometimes such people deliberately create trouble for their colleagues, so that they do not progress or get punishment from their seniors, on their failure of fulfilling the assignment. Some workers are found to be very narrow-minded and they cannot see the upgradation or progress of even their own colleagues or juniors or even of the people who work in the lower grade.

In general, the behaviour of workers at their work place is not satisfactory. They are so egoistic that they do not like to give proper respect to their seniors. They do not want to see or do not want to obey the instructions of their seniors. They always like to work as per their desire which sometimes gives a wrong impression to the organisation as well as to the concerned workers. Due to their egoistic nature, the performance or output of the concerned workers are sometimes found against the organisational interest. Such workers cannot think positively about the organisation. They always think about themselves, deliberately misbehave with other workers. They always knowingly or unknowingly try to hurt their colleagues.

Same kind of workers after sometime start making money by misappropriation of organisational funds. They start sitting late hours in the office or at the workplace, showing off to their seniors that they are the only persons in the organisation who are responsible and can save the money of the organisation. Only they can curtail the expenses in company's interest. In fact, such people always make plans in their mind as to how they can misappropriate the company's funds in their own interest. If they were authorised to give order for a particular quantity of article for the company, they definitely would order less or more material than required. If they were given an opportunity to work with civil contractors, they would take obligation in kind from the contractors for their own personal benefit.

At the time of preparing bills, they would definitely charge some extra money from that particular contractor and the contractor would put forward enhanced bill including the money he has paid to that person as commission.

They do not want to complete their assigned work but as they are bound to work or complete the target, so when they are questioned by their superiors or seniors about a particular given task, They start manipulating the facts or distort the facts, to make themselves safe. They give wrong information to the management or they give partial information to the management, which is in their favour, or they do not give the right or actual figure, because they know that if they would give the right figure to the management, then they would be questioned by the higher management. Therefore, it is better to divert the mind of the seniors and safeguard themselves.

In a nutshell, I would like to clarify that the management can tolerate slow working speed, less knowledge, less experience of their workers but they cannot tolerate misappropriation of money or anti-organisational activities of their workers. Similarly, the seniors can tolerate all types of weaknesses or drawbacks in their workers but they do not like their misconduct or misdemeanour.

I: Improve yourself, Ignore, Importance, Impress the Boss, Inconvenient, Indifferent, Innovation,

It is true that nothing is static in this world and everything is changing perpetually. If, we look at the working style of people at any work place, we would see many changes taking place. For example at the Railway Station, during the early days all the work was done manually which was a very lengthy, tiring as well as time taking. However, people were working because such a system was in vogue those days. Gradually time changed to Computer Age and the same system became computerised which became much easier and faster. Before the telecom revolution, trunk calls were booked to make long distance calls, which took a long time. But now with so many options, we can talk to any one sitting in any corner of the world, in no time. I mean that as the technologies are changing, the workers should also change themselves and they should also learn new technologies and use new and modern gadgets otherwise they would have to face a lot of problems at their workplace.

Sometime ago, our accountants were making accounts manually but today they use Tally programmes for the same work and with the help of that they do the same work more efficiently, effectively and accurately. Each and every organisation likes to appoint such accountants who have the knowledge of computer and Tally, because with the help of Tally programme they can prepare the balance Sheet or any other required report in very less time.

Some of our colleagues even today do not have the knowledge to operate the computers. The management likes those workers who have full knowledge of computer operations or have knowledge of advanced techniques used by the young and the new generation.

It means, we should try to improve ourselves or we should learn the new techniques by all means. We should give importance to other workers, colleagues and others who have more knowledge than us. The persons having such qualities are liked by all the seniors and management. There is no age limit to learn something new and interesting.

One more thing that the seniors never want to see is their juniors or subordinates ignore their instructions. They do not bother whether it is right or wrong. They think that their subordinates should obey their instructions blindly in front of others but if there is anything wrong in their instructions or if it will have adverse impact on the concerned seniors, they expect from their subordinates that they should inform them in private about the particular project or instruction and not publicise it.

They want that their subordinates should always give importance to their personality, knowledge and position whether they deserve it or not. They always want positive answers from their subordinates, juniors or colleagues.

Sometimes, people want to impress their boss by doing anything bizarre or going to any extent. If the boss wants to listen to the weak points of others, the subordinate without hesitation fulfils his wishes. In the initial period, they may convince their boss and get promotion, increment and other benefits but after sometime, the same boss does not like such subordinates. They come to know of their bad character and other weak points, which is not beneficial for the company or the organisational interest.

There are a few characters in the organisation whose main work is associated with giving trouble to others. They are the trouble shooters. They always plan to cause inconvenience to their Boss, subordinates, and colleagues or to other departments. The seniors never like such workers. We should also avoid such people and also if any one tries to give trouble to others we should convince them not to do such activity because by doing so, they would never get promotion, increment or any betterment. In any case, if any senior by mistake, proposes their names for any type of benefit, they would fall into trouble. Therefore, it would be better to maintain distance from such pests in the organisation.

If we do anything new and innovative work at our workplace, our rivals shall also appreciate us. We should always think of working in innovative ways for the organisation, and then only, we can survive in the organisation. We should always think that we all are the workers of our organisation and we are not the owner of that company. We should not forget the reality/ truth.

R: Realise before you act, Realise your Mistake, Retrospects, Repugnant

No one is perfect in this world. Everyone has some good and bad characteristic inherent, which cannot be changed easily. However, it is not possible to change it but it can be improved in a positive way. At the workplace, no one has full confidence over his or her assigned work. Any systematic work procedures always give a right answer or right result. However, we are human beings. Everyone knows that we should drive our car from the left; we should not overtake from the left side, if anyone is overtaking, then he should alert others by honking, so that any accident can be avoided. Similarly, at the work place, we know the right procedure to give good results but sometimes, we do not follow it, make mistakes, and give justification for the same.

It has been observed that most of the people react on any matter without thinking about its result or without knowing anything about the fact. People commit different types of crimes without thinking of its results. They do not think what the reaction will be and what will be their side effects. Sometimes in the office also workers react on their seniors without thinking of its effects. If people would think for a while, before committing any wrong or anti social activity, their conscience would never allow them to do such activities. People themselves can be a good judge, who can decide what is wrong or what is right, what work is suitable for the organisation or which work would affect the organisation adversely. Unfortunately, workers do not listen to their inner voice or to their conscience.

Here the management also expects from their juniors, subordinates workers that if they would think for a while before completing or before starting their work, then it is sure that most of their problems would be sorted out without taking any help from others. Their performance would thus improve and they can achieve their target or goal without fail.

In a another example, when we dress up for any party or any other occasion, we try to see our face in the mirror, as to how we are looking and if we find any fault, we rectify it immediately. Then only we go out for the party or elsewhere. Similarly, at the workplace, the seniors or management also expect from their subordinates that they should also visualise their work to be completed in their imaginary mirror and then they should proceed. If one would follow such rules, their performance as well as their output would definitely increase and such workers would get promotion or increment or other benefits without fail.

In a general case, any senior or management expects from their subordinates or juniors that if they make a mistake, knowingly or unknowingly, they should accept their mistake immediately so that there should be no misunderstanding between the management and the workers, seniors and the juniors etc. If we say sorry for any mistake committed by us immediately to the concerned seniors, the seniors would forgive our mistake and would not take any action against us.

The seniors expect from their juniors that if they have done any mistake, they should think over that mistake and try to find out the reason behind it, so that in future it could not be repeated.

One very important factor in our life is that, we should not betray others, at home, at the workplace, in the organisation or outside the organisation. It is difficult to forgive, others for their betrayal. Similarly, we should not disobey the decision taken by any seniors on any strategy whether the decision is in favour of the organisation or not. If the colleagues or the company disowns any employee, a negative force engulf him, which would make him vengeful. As a result, the dedication, attention towards the assigned work of the concerned worker, working at his work place would decrease and directly affect his forthcoming promotion and other benefits.

Any senior or the management at any level cannot tolerate repugnance, aversion done by any of their juniors, subordinate or colleagues. If any one does such a thing the environment of the workplace or the organisation gets affected. The concerned senior or the management would definitely take proper action against such persons. It means we should care for all the other factors which affect the organisational branding, prestige, image etc, otherwise it would be very difficult for any worker to get promotion, increment or continuous growth. If the workers do not think about the reputation of the organisation, then the concerned senior or management would transfer the concerned worker to a remote area or kick him out of the company.

O: Optimistic, Objective Should Be Crystal Clear

Nobody knows what would happen in the next moment and no one can stop the happening because it is the Almighty who controls nature and our existence. There is nothing in our hands but we should always be positive which would give energy to our body. There are two types of energy, which generate in our body. One is called positive and other is negative energy. Hence, the optimistic thought is associated with positive energy while the pessimistic thought gives negative energy to our mind as well as to our body.

It is up to ourselves as to what type of thought we would like to develop in our mind. When we know that there is nothing in our hands and we also know that positive thinking gives us a lot of energy to work then it would be better if we always be optimistic so that we shall get positive energy. The energy associated with optimistic thought would help us to perform our duties in the best of our efforts in a scientific and logical way.

It has been observed in the organisation that when the workers do not get their due promotion or increment, then they start looking for another job. They do not have the patience to remain in the organisation or to face their seniors. They do not want to be optimistic and as a result, their credibility decreases in front of their concerned seniors. They do not know that there is some genuine problem from the management side. They think only about themselves. If they look into the eyes of the organisation, a lot of their problems would be solved.

I am narrating a true happening in an organisation. The so-called management or middle management once made a promise to their workers that in the next month all the workers would get an increment. Some workers who wanted to leave the company deferred their decision.

They thought that the management would fulfil its promise and they should rely on it. Their positive thinking or optimism increased but their labour and company's turnover decreased. After two- three months, the management did not bother to give them the raise. Therefore, the workers again started leaving the organisation due to the false promise of the middle management. It means that the optimism of the workers as well as of the organisation gives a direct or indirect growth to the organisation and vice versa.

The concerned seniors also expect from their subordinate and juniors that they should have faith on the management. They should be optimistic, and not pessimistic because there are several decisions which are beyond the jurisdiction of the seniors or middle management. Therefore, the juniors should have the patience to work sincerely. Promotion and increment would definitely follow if they discharge their duty honestly.

Apart from the above, we generally observe on the road or in traffic that the movement or speed of an auto-rickshaw with passengers and without passengers is totally different. An auto-rickshaw with passengers follows the traffic rules and takes the right way with specific speed but on the other hand, the speed varies in the auto-rickshaw without passengers and it does not follow the traffic rules. The reason behind is that, the auto rickshaw having passengers has a right and clear objective. He knows where he has to reach. He has the objective of passenger safety and reaching their destination. When seated with a passenger, the auto-rickshaw driver follows the traffic norms systematically.

The efficiency of the auto-rickshaw driver increases which boosts up his morale. On the other hand, the rickshaw, which is empty running on the road without any passenger, the way of driving, is totally different from the other because the objective is not clear. Here the direction is not clear and hence the efficiency will decrease. It will consume fuel without giving any output.

In the organisation too, if a worker has a clear objective, responsibility, time frame, punctuality etc.he can easily put in the best of efforts in company's interest and he cannot afford to sit idle. He shall always try to contribute more to the organisation and as a result, such a worker would get the desired benefit. On the other hand, if the objective is not clear, the workers cannot utilise their efficiency in the organisational interest.

At the workplace, in most of the organisations, the objective towards any specific work is not clear. The objective is vague or in double meaning and we have to be very alert in discharging our duty. We observe that if we have to complete the work in favour of the company then the objective towards our assigned work must be clear. In case, the objective of any assignment is not clear from the management's side or the concerned senior is himself confused in a particular case, then at this situation, the workers should themselves take their own decision and make their objective clear and finish the work.

After that, they can make the time frame, schedule, strategy towards completion of work, budget, requirement if any, etc for their assigned work. Then performance or output can be measured otherwise it is very difficult to measure the work done by any worker.

CALENDAR

To get success in any field, it is necessary to have punctuality in our life and daily routine. Without being punctual, it is not possible to get success whether in the office or in the general personal life. Punctuality gives us a positive energy to work more logically, systematically and scientifically. If we make our work schedule and try to implement it in our life then it is sure that our work performance would increase automatically and would have less error or mistake.

A Calendar gives us the direction to handle the favourable or unfavourable circumstances in the coming future. In the office, we should also make a work schedule, routine on which we should work, except for the unavoidable circumstances. If we do our responsibility and discharge it properly, it is sure that our senior, management or the incharge under whose supervision we work, would be very happy and they definitely would appreciate our work.

We should take lessons from the Calendar, which hangs on the wall at home or the at workplace without disturbing others. The calendar does not force anyone to take lesson from it but it is up to us as to how we see a particular thing and under which circumstance. If one thing is better or useful for one person then it is not necessary that the same thing would also apply to others. It is up to their thinking as to how they take or visualise certain things in life.

If we take the calendar in a positive way in our life then the same calendar would give us the following insight, which may be very useful in achieving our goal, target or dream for which we all are working.

C: Creative mind, Careless, Caricature, Catch, Commanding, Collective, Comparison, Communal Talk, Complaint Of Others, Congratulate, Confident, Consistent Behaviour Etc.

All the living beings are very creative. In our daily life, we see a small ant or a small honeybee working tirelessly and not wasting their time but being very creative. Honey Bees are found busy in preparing their hive and collecting pollen for making honey. Each person has creative mind and thought process. Every person has his own idea of working and living. In the organisation, there are also different kinds of workers having different types of minds with different creative ideas.

People are always found engaged in something or the other, as GOD has given us the most beautiful and creative mind. We should not misuse the same. We should not make fun of anybody's creativity, whether it is official or otherwise. Such behaviour will give a bad impression among seniors, management and colleagues.

During duty hour, we should not sit idle but do some work, and our behaviour must be very good so that it could easily captivate the seniors, management as well as our colleagues. We should not take any capricious decision, which could create any problem for the organisation later on or give a bad impact on the image of the company. During office hours or while we are working, we should try to be cheerful, maintain silence and do not make the environment clamorous.

As the clamorous environment gives a negative energy to the workers which directly or indirectly gives adverse impact on the performance of workers while calm, silent and cheerful environment gives a positive energy to the workers, by which the performance of the worker increases. Management, in charge, seniors always think that their subordinates should perform their duty in a better and scientific way, so that the company could make progress. When the company would get progress, the workers associated automatically would get better remuneration, benefits which would improve their life-style.

Whenever, we work at our workplace, we should not show carelessness in the working procedure. We should first of all think properly on any assigned work, which we are going to complete. We should make plans, strategy, checklist the procedure, so that the mistake could be minimised. Due to the carelessness, the impression of the seniors on any juniors or subordinates gives a bad or wrong impression on their mind, which reflects at the time of their appraisal for promotion, increment or any type of betterment. Therefore, we should always take care of ourselves as well as of the company assets used by us. We should generate an emotional bond between the workplace, work and ourselves as well as with the equipments on which we are working or using.

Some workers are very cheerful by nature and laugh at the drop of a hat and they very effortlessly impress their seniors, colleagues or other persons at the workplace. In the beginning, their colleagues take it very easy and enjoy their company but in the long run, same colleagues do not like their cheerfulness. Thus the impression of such workers gradually decreases and the in charge or seniors do not want to assign any serious work or any important work to such people who never take things seriously. In the bargain, they lose good assignments.

The seniors do not trust such workers and when the seniors lose trust on any worker then it is very difficult to forward his name for promotion or increment. It means, we have to understand that all our activities are watched by our seniors at various points, which more or less are co-related with our betterment at the workplace. Therefore, we should always give proper importance to each and everything. We should not make fun of any colleague and senior. We should give them proper respect, inspite of knowing that all the concerned seniors and colleagues do not deserve the same but as we are all working under them or working with them, we should give them due respect.

All the relationships, whether in the family, at the workplace or anywhere else, are closely related and inter-dependent. We are social animals and there are different types of people living in the society. Some are very good-natured and have very good behaviour, character etc while some are totally different. One's thinking capability or level is associated with the relationship between other people and things. The level of sentimental relationship also directly or indirectly affects the work performance of the individual. This sentimental relationship may be between the person and his assigned work or with the subordinates, seniors or colleagues etc.

This sentimental relationship and its affects vary from person to person and the circumstances. Sometimes it gives good result or sometimes it affects adversely.

If a person is very sentimental, he may take wrong decisions at workplace, which might have adverse impact on the organisational growth. It is good to be sentimental but at the time of decision-making, we should think from our head and not from the heart. If we think from our head or use our mind, the decision taken will be logical and beneficial.

In the organisation, many workers hold obligatory posts. Most of them are close relatives or friends of the first family of the organisation or of the respected seniors. At this situation, if such a worker does any wrong, then it would get very difficult for the concerned seniors or incharge to take any action against him. If the seniors do not take stern action against him then the organisation, would lose and if they take action then the concerned worker as well as the concerned seniors who are taking action, would lose. The condition becomes very critical for the respective seniors. We should always take the decision in the organisational interest not in the particular worker's interest. If we take correct action, everyone would support us otherwise in the long term, the person, who is responsible for taking the action, would lose. Our action should not be based on awe or sentiment but it should be neutral and in favour of the organisation.

At the workplace, we find that few workers are doing nothing. They simply sit idle or they do not want to do anything but they like to command others, in such a way that they are the only persons in that organisation, who care for the company while others do not bother or have any sympathy. Such persons always try to escape from taking any responsibility but they do not refrain from giving suggestions to others. These type of persons or workers generally are very egoistic and self-centred. They do not bother for others. They want their fragile ego to be satisfied but they do not care to give respect to others. This type of nature gives wrong message to the workplace and vitiates the atmosphere.

In practical life, not a single worker would like his senior commanding him or the seniors also never like that their own subordinates, juniors or colleagues dominate/command them, whether the command is right or wrong. Nobody likes it in a democratic setup. If any senior gives instruction to his subordinates in a commanding way, the potential of the concerned workers reduces. Their motivation level as well as their performance level also reduces. The senior should not expect from his subordinate that they would always give them the desired output. It is not possible that they would be cent-percent successful. On the other hand if, the same seniors, give instructions very politely and very diplomatically, the same subordinates will devote more time and finish their task with their best of efforts. They would never bother about the extra hours given by them to complete the assigned work. It means, that the seniors and the management does not like that instructions should be given to the subordinates, juniors in a commanding way because it degrades their morale and gives a bad impact on the image of the organisation. Whenever we are given any opportunity to work in the organisation or at the concerned workplace, we should always do the work collectively because united we stand and divided we fall.

In the organisation, no one can complete the work without taking help of others. There is a collective effort, which gives positive result and good performance. The seniors and the management always expect that their subordinates should put in collective effort to complete the assigned work. It means a good collective effort can give a very positive and good result. It also means all the concerned subordinates involved in that particular job get credit and if a particular senior/incharge is appreciated by the management, the senior / incharge should also take the name of others or share his appreciation with the ones who had given their support in getting the good result. Otherwise, it gives a wrong impact on the support staff. If we get an opportunity to do something for others, then we should not miss the opportunity at any cost and we should work for the deserving people.

We should not make any comparison at the workplace related to the salary, benefits and the facilities provided to particular workers. There are different types of workers working in any organisation, having different pay structure and other perks, while they are working in the same cadre. If anyone makes comparison related to the salary in front of any senior, the seniors never like such talk and they don't approve of this in front of others but they definitely want information on this topic and they love to talk on this topic privately. They do not want to talk or discuss on this topic publicly. We should always care about maintaining proper decorum.

Some workers are very talkative. They cannot stop talking for a single moment. They blabber all the time. They talk unnecessarily without any reason with their colleagues, juniors or sometimes with seniors. They do not know what they are talking or remember what they had said to others and they speak without any rhyme or reason. Due to this nature, other persons working at that workplace get very annoyed and irritated as their continuous one-sided talk which creates disturbance and affects their work performance. Their concentration is disturbed and they cannot use their best ideas while working. If, the seniors do not give any warning or they do not tell them anything, it does not mean that the seniors have not noticed their blabbering. They reserve their comment and use it at the time of appraisal of the concerned workers. When one talks continuously without having any specific topic or uselessly with their colleagues, juniors or any other persons working in the organisation, it is possible that the direction of the topic would turn towards politics because, Politics is such a topic, which has no end. It is open for discussion endlessly and in this way, one can use unparliamentarily or obscene language at the workplace which is strictly forbidden.

If, we know which Political party our colleagues support, then it would be very easy to pull their leg through the discussion. When we discuss on Party and Politics, then after some-time, the situation of the workplace may turn very unpleasant. The workers may not like to see the face of their own colleagues because their colleagues may be supporters of the opposition party.

We should always avoid talking or discussing communal talk. We should not be narrow-minded as we have been brought up in a secular atmosphere and live in a secular country where all the religions are equal.

The management or the seniors never like such discussions due to which the situation gets vitiated. It gives rise to the birth of Union in the organisation as well as on the workplace, which is very harmful for any organisation. It destroys the harmony of the company and it directly or indirectly decreases the growth of the company. No company can get desired output if the workers indulge in trade unions. The management never likes any union in their workplace, so we should keep ourselves away from office politics.

Some people are engaged in backbiting their colleagues, seniors or juniors. We must remember that if we try to pull the legs of others, our legs would also be pulled without fail. As no one is perfect and everyone has some weak point in their working style. If we try to pull the legs of others, we should always be prepared to face the consequences. This way most of our energy would be wasted. When our energy will get wasted unnecessarily then our output would be affected and we would not be able to perform or satisfy the seniors with our best performance. No seniors expect their subordinates or juniors to waste their time and energy backbiting and gossiping. In exceptional cases any senior may like it for a while but after sometimes the same senior would dislike such habit of the juniors as they assume that if such juniors can talk about the secret of others then it is very much possible that the same junior can talk about their secrets as well. Therefore, it would be better to maintain distance from such workers.

Thus, we should never talk rubbish about others working in the same place, same organisation etc. If we do so, we would be held responsible to tarnish the image and brand of the company. Such anti organisational work, activities are punishable and people should abstain from such activities.

If any worker of our organisation does any good work in company's interest, the concerned seniors, juniors or incharge should forward their names to the concerned authority for reward. We should appreciate them as well as their work in front of all or at least where the concerned workers are working. If we would make any appreciation of their working system or work done, they would be charged up and they would work more in a systematic way, so that their seniors can get the opportunity to appreciate them.

We should never fail to appreciate our juniors, subordinates, colleagues and others so that a sound and harmonious environment could be formed in the organisation as well as at the work place, where we are working. If we would follow such a thing, then our confidence level would increase and we would always try to take higher or bigger responsibility. Our working style, thought, planning, implementing power etc, would develop for getting a higher position.

If the workers are very confident about their assignment then the confidence level of the concerned seniors would automatically go high. For any work whether at the work- place, in the organisation or while driving on the road, we need high confidence and concentration. One cannot drive even his own car if he lacks confidence and concentration. No one can work in the organisation, if the person has no confidence. Even in Parliament, Assembly, the speaker should have full confidence to preside over the house otherwise he cannot function well or cannot take any right decision. We can give better performance if we are self-confident. With more confidence, we can achieve whatever we want.

The behaviour of any worker, seniors, colleagues play a very important role in their personality development or in the development of the general image. There are some workers in most of the organisations, who do not have their self-identity. Inspite of having all the qualities of a manager, if a person changes his statement from time to time, then his juniors would not have faith upon such a senior because he changes his stand or statement as per the situation. In this connection, the workers, colleagues, subordinates or senior should have a consistent behaviour or stand on any subject. They should not change their view according to the situation. They should be firm and determined.

Generally it has been observed that if any statement is going to create problems for any person, or if the seniors observe that the concerned management is getting angry with their verbal statements, instructions given to the juniors, subordinates or other workers, then the concerned seniors would suddenly change their stand and would refuse to acknowledge that they had given any instruction or statement to anyone on any subject because it does not come under their jurisdiction. It means, we should learn that our behaviour at the workplace or in the organisation should be consistent. It should not fluctuate.

If our behaviour fluctuates, then we would lose our faith in front of our juniors colleagues and directly or indirectly, it would affect the growth of the organisation. Our credibility would get questioned. But our consistent behaviour would boost the morale of our workers, colleagues and they will give more time and energy to their work. They would automatically get motivated with their seniors consistent stand or consistent behaviour. They would always rely on such people and would think that someone is out there in their support.

A : Absent, Accelerate, Accept, Affection, Agitation, Alert, Alcohol, Almighty, Ambitious.

The letter "A" of the calendar, gives us the inspiration to be motivated and be in high spirits if others get promotion, benefit etc and we are deprived of it. We should think that we are not the ones to assess our work ourselves. We cannot judge our own performance. If one thing is good for us, then it may be bad for others. We cannot assess ourselves whether our work was beneficial for the company or whether it helped the company in its economical growth.

Our duty is to perform well or work sincerely on our assignment but the concerned seniors as well as the colleagues, workers and the rivals, official colleagues can judge our performance very well. If any worker, colleague, senior always criticises our work done, but appreciates our work in front of others then we should feel that our work is up to the mark or is satisfactory. Such thing can only be possible when we are regular in our work, and without any valid reason, we are not absent from our workplace. We should not be absent without getting prior leave sanctioned by the respective seniors. If due to some reason, we are unable to attend our duty we should inform our seniors immediately with the specific reason as to why we are not able to attend our work. Then only it is possible that the concerned seniors would have faith upon ourselves. The seniors desire similar conduct from all their juniors. This way important work does not remain pending and can be finished without being dragged for too long if the concerned staff is on leave.

We should always follow the order, instructions of our seniors and complete our assignment in the scheduled time frame with the best of our efforts. We should accept all types of instructions or orders coming from the seniors, without having any hesitation, confusion or thinking otherwise. We should accept the challenge. Even if it is known that the particular job or assignment is difficult to complete on time, or it may be beyond us. We should accept it without telling anything to the concerned seniors. If we feel any difficulty in working, we must consult each other or the seniors and get help from them but at the time of delivering the assignment, we should keep our mouth shut. If we follow such methods then everyone would co-operate with us.

Whenever we have free time we should help, our juniors, colleagues or whoever need them. Other colleagues too should not hesitate in asking for help, if they are unable to do a particular work, so that the work could be completed on time. We should use new methods so that the assigned work could be completed within the time frame. The concerned seniors or management think that their subordinates or juniors are clever and know time management and that they would guide themselves with their own methods and accelerate their work without having any instruction or guidance of the seniors. They want that their subordinates should not ask any work related question. They should be familiar with all the new working methods and if the seniors ask them to demonstrate their method, they can do so happily.

They want that the work done by the junior should be done with love, emotion and dedication. They should show or feel that they are doing the job but are working for themselves. It should look like that they are not working for the organisation but for themselves. When a person does his job with affection then he can be self-confident and motivated to tackle all the challenges coming his way.

One thing that is very important in our life as well for any organisation is getting agitated. Such an action is totally banned in the organisation. It provokes the workers against the organisation for anti organisational activities. We should not resist from discussing on any topic with the seniors or we should have healthy arguments with the seniors on any topic. If the concerned boss approves our assignment, we should follow it. People would be very happy to follow our example. In any organisation, if any worker or subordinate gets agitated in front of the management, people would never be happy in that particular organisation or at that workplace. It means we should not go against the system or swim against the current.

We should always be alert and have knowledge about the development and changes going on in the organisation. We should try to learn new techniques introduced in the organisation. The seniors think that their subordinates should have every kind of knowledge and know the rules and regulations so that the level of the mistakes could be minimised to fulfil the assignment. We should not deviate from our target whether it is for our organisation or for ourselves.

In general, the habits of the people working in any organisation are more or less the same. They love to mislead themselves by not doing their assigned work properly. They love to spend their time as they wish. They do not bother about the organisational rules and regulations. They think that they are fully authorised to do anything without prior approval. They do not bother what the others think about their habits or what the juniors or colleagues think about them. Most of the people love to drink. The story of the persons assigned to work in the night shift is totally different from the persons working during the daytime. They do not listen to others and they think that they are the knights of the night.

Due to such thinking, most of the people working at night shift consume alcohol and after that they start gossiping about other colleagues in the workplace. The environment of the workplace gradually deteriorates and simultaneously, the output of the individual as well as, of the department depletes. Such information, comes to the knowledge of the higher management or the concerned seniors in very less time that such workers working in so and so department working under so and so seniors are not following the rules and regulations of the organisation and taking drinks during their duty hours.

Any senior or the management never likes to see that their subordinates defame the name or image of the organisation. We should ourselves understand our limitations and always avoid doing such unlawful activities in the organisation, otherwise, it is sure that it would be very difficult to get any promotion or increment or any type of benefit. We should always have self-respect. Then only others would respect us.

What God is to temple, parents are to family and management is to the organisation, all are equally important and supreme. We cannot get anything without their permission or approval. As we usually go to the temple and pray to God for our well-being and forgive our sins and mistakes. Similarly, at the workplace, the subordinates, juniors also assume the concerned seniors as their Almighty. For example, if a worker works very diligently in the interest of the company but if the concerned seniors do not want to give proper response, reaction or weightage to his work or performance, then nobody can help it. The concerned worker would be ignored and would never get the proper reward for his job. As God loves to hear his praise in the form of hymn or prayer, similarly the seniors at the workplace, desire from their subordinates that the juniors should always implore or whine (girgirana) in front of them for assistance or any kind of help.

If we are very good workers, good performers, well behaved, it is not sure that we shall get promotion or increment or any betterment from the organisation/management. It all depends upon the decision of the concerned seniors. Without their wishes, we would never get anything. It means we should act according to their likes and dislikes. If we want to work in any organisation, we should follow the rules and regulations of that place; otherwise, it would be very difficult for anybody to survive there. As the rough translation of a Hindi saying means while living in water, one cannot have enmity with the crocodile. So it is wise to be on very good terms with one's senior or boss as they are stronger and mightier.

L : The letter "L" of the calendar gives the following lessons which are very important as well as necessary for our progress.

- Labourious,
- Leadership
- Forward Looking
- Ladder,
- Laminate the work with emotion to shine,
- Laugh at others work,
- Legal,
- Liability & liable,
- Liberal & flexible,
- Livelihood,
- Loopholes.

It has been observed that when the workers after sometime, do not progress and their life becomes very unproductive, their performance gradually deteriorates and negative feelings are generated in their mind, which prevents the workers from progress. At this crucial or critical situation, the letter "L" of the calendar teaches us that we should not think about what we have done wrong, any mistake or any negative thing for the organisation but we should look and think forward, try to make amends and make ourselves perfect workers. We should prove ourselves as being labourious and always try to lead at the workplace. It means we should always think that we are the head of our department.

Apart from this, there are several things or messages, which we should learn from this letter. No one can get anything without continuous labour in the required direction. Everyone says that they are giving the best of their services in their organisation but they do not get the required or desired position or reward. There is a very close relationship between the degree of labour and the direction in which the labour is applied. If, we labour hard without having the right or clear concept of the assigned work. And without defining the procedure and planning, it would be very difficult to get the desired result inspite of our hard and continuous labour. We should have full knowledge about the work, which we are going to do.

There are some fixed steps, which we have to undertake to complete any assigned work in a desired way. If anyone ignores some of the steps to get a quick result, the result may be defective. So we should not miss any step or we should not skip the procedure or do not take shortcuts. Whatever we do, should be presented in good shape. It means, the presentation of our work done should be very neat and clean, so that even a junior level worker could understand it.

If there is any drawback in our work, we should present the work in such a way that the weak points should be concealed for the moment, when the seniors or concerned persons are having a look at it. Nobody can claim that his or her work is always perfect but it does not mean that we would not do our best to complete our work.

Some workers have a jealous nature, owing to which they never appreciate other's work done. They do not do anything but they enjoy by making fun of others. They are there only to criticise them so that the concerned workers get demoralised and demotivated and the next time they do not try to do any work. If we are the true workers of our organisation, then we should never laugh on our colleagues or make fun of their work. If we continue doing it, then it would have a bad impact on ourselves, due to our criticism or making fun. The seniors never like jealous workers.

Very few workers find themselves very happy or problem free, in any organisation. It means everyone has to face some problem at their workplace, which they have to tackle. Some workers are so aggressive by nature that even while having some minor problem, which can be solved amicably by talking together or mutual understanding, they resort to legal assistance or take outsiders help to solve the problem. The seniors think that if any one has any problem at their workplace due to their colleagues, or seniors, whether it is technical or administrative, the concerned workers should consult their seniors or incharge to solve the raised problem. There is no need to take outsiders or legal help. Legal help is the last option to be adopted by any one. No senior in any organisation wants to tarnish his or her organisation brand name in the Court. So it is better if the problem is solved mutually and amicably and the case in not dragged to court.

The purchasing power has changed drastically in the present times. We can purchase any thing by cash, or by other mode of payment but true people are very rare on whom one can have faith. It very difficult to find them in this world. It is not impossible but it is difficult. There are various instances in our society or organisation, where one was deceived or backstabbed by the servant, friend, relative or colleague on whom the person had faith but was sadly deceived or ditched by them. In the organisation also, there are different types of workers working, who seem to be very close to the organisation but in a real sense are of dubious nature.

They can go to any extent if they come to know that there is some scope of benefit or to earn underhand. The workers then start misusing the funds, services and brand name of the organisation, or start anti organisational activities. In a real sense, any senior of the company who has a little sympathy for the Mother Organisation, shall not leave such workers without punishing them for their misdeed. On the other hand they like only those workers who are honest or sincere on whom they have faith, trust or they believe that these workers in a real sense work for the company.

The workers should not in any way be a liability to the organisation. If a worker does not do his duty properly or does not deliver the required performance in the fixed time frame, due to which company has to face problems or they have to pay penalty. We can say that such workers are a liability for the organisation. Some workers are being appointed on a very high salary but they do not do anything, because they are ornamental officers of the company. No person can make any complaint against him because no one will listen to anything against him, as he is very close to the first family. Therefore, such workers are very much a liability for the organisation, as they do not give the required output to the company. On the other hand, they are a financial burden on the company.

In general, any incharge, senior, H.O.D. never like such officers. Inspite of the above, some workers who are not associated with the first family or hold obligatory positions, also sometimes do not deliver their assigned responsibility in a proper manner or desired time frame. In some organisations, there are some people associated with the Union. In practical sense, they do not want to do their assigned duties but they expect their promotion, increment or other benefits like other workers, which cannot be possible. The concerned seniors of such workers do not like those people / workers belonging to the Union. They know such people can only create trouble for the organisation and nothing else. So they should not associate themselves with such Union workers, otherwise, it would be very difficult to get any promotion, increment or other benefits from their immediate seniors. However, everybody knows the office Unions become a big headache for the Management.

At the workplace, we have to tackle different types of people and their problems, which may be genuine or may be fake in the eyes of the management, but we have to tackle all of them. The workplace or the organisation is a type of public place, where we have to interact with different kinds of people having different type of temperament, nature, behaviour etc. The position of any manager, H.O.D, or Incharge sometimes become very critical and awkward. Whether they favour them or go against them, they would always be held responsible for their stand or approach. During tackling awkward situation, one should become diplomatic and flexible. Being rigid would prove to be a disadvantage for them.

At such a situation, we should not have a rigid stand but we should adopt a flexible stand, which suits all. In the organisation, there are several rules and regulations to run the company smoothly but sometimes we should close our eyes, if the instructions are coming from the seniors, because if anything goes wrong, the concerned seniors would also be responsible or answerable. We would have a valid point to say that the particular senior had given instructions to do such a work, then why should we take tension for it. We should work but we should be flexible and diplomatic according to the situation. By being diplomatic, one can avoid unpleasantness and bad blood.

At the workplace everyone has his own responsibilities, strategy and target, where one has to perform his best to get the desired or assigned goal. Some people do their job enthusiastically and they enjoy themselves during their work but on the other hand there are some workers in the same place who work only because they have no other option. It means such workers do their job because it is their necessity. Here there is no emotion in their performance. For example, when a guest comes to our place, we try to give him comfort as per our capability. The guest feels very happy to visit our family, because we serve our guest whole-heartedly. At the same time if we do not serve our guest wholeheartedly, the same guest would not enjoy our service or hospitality and would not want to be our guest in the future.

At the same time, the seniors or incharge or the management of any organisation expect from their juniors or subordinates, that they should do their assigned job, responsibilities emotionally and wholeheartedly because action speaks louder than words. The activity of any worker, working at his workplace should be written on his face, which can be read by everyone. When the workers would work at their workplace with concentration and depth, then they would come to know about the weak points of that workplace, organisation, systems, strategy, which could be rectified for better performance in future. So they can start working afresh with new vigour, innovation and right approach.

If the workers find any drawback or any weak points, they should inform their concerned seniors through which the weak points could be put forward to the higher management. It is not possible for any senior to know every happenings going in the organisation or at the workplace. The seniors are not directly associated with the workplace and their problems. They do not have to face any problems of the workplace. Therefore, the workers are the main source, from whom the seniors could know of the weak or plus points of the organisation.

This is the reason the seniors want that their subordinates should inform them from time to time about the happenings of the organisation or the workplace. If any worker follows this strategy, that worker automatically comes closer to the concerned seniors while others cannot. Once, the worker comes close to any senior, the senior gives good remarks on his proposals, appraisal while others may not have such a chance.

E : Energy, Earnest, Enthusiasm Execute

People working in the same routine job for a long period, start getting monotonous. When the people feel seriously that their life has became monotonous; their working energy level starts getting low. They cannot even think about their own family life, how to work, and what method to be adopted to get the best result at their workplace. They start forgetting even the basic etiquette and manners, which is very necessary from home to workplace. They do not take any interest in their assigned work anymore. They do not want to execute any instructions laid down by their seniors, management or in charge.

They do not want to listen to any instruction of their seniors. Thus, the combination of all these demerits directly affects their performance and they become very lazy and lethargic. When a Senior, Incharge gives them some specific responsibility to complete in a specific time frame, such people are mostly unable to complete it as per the requirement of their boss but in any case if they complete the assigned job, then their performance level would definitely deteriorate. Management does not like such people and gradually starts keeping at a distance from such workers. If the post of such a worker is obligatory, then the management would definitely pay his salary but would gradually withdraw most of the power given to him and the person working at a high position would be without any power, authority and like a first class prisoner or a bird trapped in a golden cage.

At this stage, management expects from their lethargic lazy and bored workers that they should boost up their morale by taking a lesson from the letter "E" of the word calendar. We should always be energetic by getting self-motivation. It comes to us by thinking positive or by taking everything in a positive way. If our seniors give us any sort of punishment, we should not take it negatively or feel vindictive but we should take it positively and think over our demerits and why the boss gave us punishment. The cause or reason should be removed or rectified on an urgent basis because it affects the individual's self-esteem.

We should always try to learn about the new things, new changes and happenings at our workplace or in the organisation. No one should come to us and say about any new happenings but it is we, who have to investigate the ongoing things. No one is bothered about others but we have to care for ourselves. Then only can we survive in any organisation or at any workplace.

If the seniors give us any instruction or assignment, it should be executed at the earliest possible time. The concerned seniors would be very happy or be satisfied by knowing that their instructions are implemented or executed. If the said project or instruction gets stuck later on, they do not mind but in the initial period, it should be commenced.

We should not mind any ups and downs going on in the organisation as well as in the respective department due to any reason but we should make ourselves most energetic, enthusiastic and must work earnestly.

N: Never feel weak, Navigator, Neglect, Nagging, Nepotism, Nervous, No- word, Novelty of work

In general, life is not a bed of roses. At every step, we have to remove the thorns or obstacles. Everyone wants to have wealth and prosperity, promotion, recognition but it is not possible that everyone can achieve these things. It means every one cannot achieve all their desires or they cannot fulfil all their wishes. There are several hidden circumstances, situations on which the fulfilment of our desires depend. Every person, working in the organisation at any position want that they should also have a big post, fat salary and timely promotion but practically, it is not possible. Though some of the workers in any organisation are found to be very sincere, dedicated, skilled and knowledgeable but unfortunately, they do not get a proper response from the organisation, management or from the incharge's side. They think that they are neglected from the mainstream of the organisation.

At this situation, we can take some lessons from the letter "N" of the word Calendar, which would be very helpful at such a stage. We people should never think that we are not capable for any particular job or it is not possible to complete such assignment within a specific time frame, by us, but we should take all the responsibilities without thinking otherwise. No one is perfect. We should first try to do the complicated work. We should never think that our knowledge is weak under any circumstance. If we really do not know then we should consult our colleagues, seniors or concerned department to learn the ropes.

If we do not know about a particular thing, then we should not say it openly to any one that we do not know such a thing but meet the concerned people separately for the same. We should take interest in that particular work and try to learn.

As we know that no one is perfect, whether in the organisation or in the society or in our own family. More or less everyone has some drawback and this is the characteristic of human beings otherwise no one would respect others and the progress would be totally blocked. For example, God has given us only five fingers on each hand. God has super power and He creates us but God has given five fingers of different length, because they are required to make a fist, which denotes strength, power or stamina of an individual. Therefore, whatever God has given us, is based on some logic and has a specific purpose. Wouldn't our hand look awkward if all the fingers were of the same length?

We should not have indifferent attitude under any circumstance owing to any reason. We should always think that we are powerful or the strongest workers in this organisation. Whatever we are doing is correct and according to the requirement of the management. Then only it is possible that we can complete our assigned work, otherwise it would be very difficult to do any work properly.

It is also seen or observed in any organisation that all the workers are engaged in their own assigned work and no one has time to do other work or to observe the work of our colleagues.

We do not bother about their status or difficulties. But if we have some spare time then without hampering our daily or assigned work, we should spare some time for other persons or colleagues or to help the needy, without thinking that we are doing a favour for anybody or are guiding them but we should navigate them towards the right direction. If we help the needy workers then God would certainly help and guide us.

We should not think that such persons are junior to us or this does not come under our jurisdiction, or his salary is very poor in comparison. Such mental state of a person is very harmful for the organisation as well as for the worker. Due to such mental state, one neglects his own colleagues or juniors. If this comes to the knowledge of the management, it immediately takes action against such persons, whether the person is working in any prestigious position or not. As the management never likes, that its brand or image is harmed due to any statement given by the seniors or the workers.

If we want to get respect from our workers, juniors, subordinates or colleagues, then first of all we have to respect them without feeling otherwise. Everyone has different character, behaviour and endurance power at the workplace. If due to any reason, (official or unofficial) or owing to any unavoidable circumstance, we get angry on our colleagues, juniors or subordinates, we must always remember that we never use obscene or abusive language at the workplace and we should not nag any of our colleagues on any subject because it creates difference between the colleagues, seniors, juniors or subordinates, which is very dangerous for the growth and progress of the organisation.

One thing, which is very common in any organisation or at the workplace, is undue patronage of relationship. It is the weak point of all the common people that they support their own relatives or kin. They want that their own relatives should get the job and not the others. They prefer to give promotion, increment or other betterment to their own kin working in the concerned organisation, whether they are working at a lower cadre or upper grade. They do not want to punish their kin, working in the organisation, even if they do any anti organisation activity. Nepotism should be avoided at any cost if we want to see the organisation prosper. Merit should always be preferred.

First of all, they want to rescue the concerned relatives from their problems. Some times every one comes to know that the senior is giving open shelter to his own kin working under him or under others. The management never likes such things because it gives a sense of frustration, demotivation to the workers. We should not do such activities, which give a wrong message to the workers as well as to the higher management.

We should develop self-confidence, by doing the right job at the right time according to the requirement of the management. If due to any reason we feel nervous, we cannot perform our best. We should develop our skill and knowledge as much as possible which would boost our self-confidence and when one has self-confidence, he would never get nervous.

The concerned management always watch the level of our confidence, dedication and will power. The management likes only those workers, whose confidence level is very high, who never get nervous while performing any tough task or responsibility. The management, before giving any big responsibility to any particular person, tries to make sure of himself or herself pertaining to the level of confidence of that particular worker. If they find their level of confidence is adequate and as desired, only then they would give them any big responsibility, otherwise they would never give them any responsibility whether big or small.

There is no time as such for an opportunity to come our way. An opportunity can come our way anytime and anywhere. Any seniors, incharge, management can give opportunity to any one, if only we are prepared to take that opportunity. We should not lose it at any cost. Inspite of having no knowledge of the work, experience or specialisation in the required work, people get several opportunities to do a specific work for the management, only because the concerned workers never say NO to the seniors or management and have self esteem and confidence.

The management does not want to hear NO from any subordinates, juniors or senior workers. If we are sure that such work is not suitable or beyond our jurisdiction, knowledge or capacity, then also we should not say NO to the management that we would not be able to do this particular work as we do not know or we have no knowledge about it. First of all, we should grab the opportunity with both our hands. After that we should decide how and what to do or how to proceed.

There should always be novelty in our work or while making a new system for the Organisation or for the workplace where we work. If we try to bring novelty in our work, then we must have clear intention and the best of interest for the company. Then everybody would help or co-operate with us to complete the work. The message would automatically be forwarded by our hidden well-wishers to the higher management because no one can say anything against or condemn a good or novel work. Every management tries to find out such persons from their inner work force to bring about new changes in the organisation.

D: Dedication, Devotion, Daring, Decorum, Decision, Discrimination, Distort, Dressing, Discipline

In general, workers working in any organisation hesitate to raise any question against the faulty systems, norms, rules and regulations, or anti organisational activities done by any one. All of them think that the problem is not theirs to raise or speak against any harassment done by any person of the organisation. When a worker realises that anti organisational and unsocial activities are going on in the organisation. They feel that they are so helpless that they cannot do anything against them. Then their energy level as well as enthusiasm gradually begins to decrease which affects their performance level directly.

The management does not like such people, workers whose performance is very poor or who want to escape from their responsibilities. After some time, these people are unable to take any decision because of their low confidence level. At this situation, we should ourselves learn to tackle the situation because no one from the management or the seniors would come to teach us about the right things or what is right and what is wrong. Therefore, we should develop our inner sense and let our conscience guide us.

Each and every assignment is very difficult to complete. It cannot be completed without dedication and devotion towards the completion of the assigned work. Whatever assignments we workers are getting from our respective seniors at the workplace, needs dedication and devotion to get it completed. It needs strong mental and willpower to make different strategies, methods, planning to complete the assignment. We should devote our time along with our own interest in the assigned work. Then only it is possible to complete our work. If any one does not give required time and interest to a particular work or assignment, then it is not possible for anyone to complete it. Lack of interest makes one dull and devoid of mental strength and persistence.

We should not think about the outcome or result of any work to be done. We should not think whether it could be completed by us or not, whether we have the capacity or capability to complete it. One thing we should always remember is that we are working for a particular organisation because the organisation is giving us remuneration for our time and labour. We should always think about the company's interest more than anything else. We should always be ready to work through thick and thin in company interest, without having any fear. We should be daring enough to take up any challenge. The management has no objection, if the subordinates take any decision in the company interest, but they only desire that before taking any unanimous decision they should be informed properly and timely or should be taken into confidence.

On the other hand, the daring nature of an individual who is ready to take up the challenge is very fruitful for the organisation but we should not bypass any senior, or the company's norms, rules and regulations or we should not neglect or disobey any system of the organisation, which is necessary. If it is required to take any decision in the absence of the authorised person of the company, then it is our duty to take a telephonic consent from the concerned person or authorised person and should also apprise him of the situation. If the workers adopt such strategy, then the management would like the concerned workers, who take such decisions wisely when such circumstance or need arises.

The management likes such workers, who take their own decision in taking the confidence of their concerned seniors because ultimately the senior will be held responsible for the merits or demerits of the systems or for any mishap. In this situation, it is possible that when we inform our seniors about the happenings or situation, the concerned seniors will give us the right guidance, suggestions based on their experiences and show us the right direction.

Sometimes, during the preparation of CR or the annual appraisal report of the workers, the H.O.D, incharge wilfully makes discrimination against some dedicated workers and tries to demotivate them. The management does not like or tolerate such activities of their employees. Sometimes the, workers inform the happenings to the management in such a way that the truth of the fact is totally distorted. For a few minutes, such activities can impress the incharge but in a few days, the management comes to know the real facts and they punish the distorters. In this way we come to know that we should not distort the facts because we would be held guilty as a culprit for punishing innocent workers.

The teacher gives good remarks to the students who come to school in neat and clean uniform and behave well because it gives good message to other students. Similarly in the organisation or at the workplace we should come to our office in neat and clean and well fitted clothes and behave well with all the seniors, colleagues, subordinates or the people of other departments. We should be very polite and should not hurt other's feelings. The management can tolerate a worker, if he is weak in knowledge or skill but they cannot tolerate any worker if he is in-disciplined.

It has been observed that the workers who have given long service to the organisation are very old employees. Sometimes they take their seniors, systems of the organisation for granted and give unwanted statements about the organisation, seniors, colleagues etc, to any third party, in the presence of others. The management strictly hates such workers because of their misconduct, misdemeanour and lack of decorum.

The letter "A" denotes: Articulate, Advice, Advocate, Argue, Admirable, Admissible, Adopt, Aggressive, Against, Apology, Approval, Arrogant

Generally, workers do their job, work but they never try to know what they had done, whether their work would give positive results to the organisation or not. Maximum of our workers do their work more or less similarly. They do not want to analyse their performance. They do not make any self-assessment on the basis of their past performance. Sometimes, they do such ridiculous work, which makes them miserable and creates awkward situation for the company.

At this situation or circumstance, we should take lessons from the letter "A" of the calendar to normalise or tackle the anti organisational activities raised at any workplace.

Whenever we feel that we are in trouble or we are not able to perform a particular assigned job due to any reason, we should take advice from our seniors. It is not necessary that the seniors would be concerned with our own department but it could be from any other authentic source too. Here the cadre or official position should not come in between. It would create mutual understanding, if we take help or guidance from our seniors. Most of the seniors feel very proud if other workers take advice from them. In addition, owing to the interaction the seniors will get news of their colleagues, seniors etc or would come to know of the loopholes of other departments. The seniors also feel very happy or proud, if the advice seeker is a female staff. The seniors would most probably free themselves from their important meetings and assignments, if the lady staff seeks little time for discussion on any official or un official issue. We should talk to our seniors on any problems only after the lunch break or in the evening after office hours, because before the said period, they should not entertain anyone as they should complete all their meetings and assignments before entertaining any of the juniors whether male or female.

One thing, which irritates everyone is when any one starts an argument on any official or unofficial subject. Everyone gets disturbed and all the workers get angry due to such activity. One should always tone down his voice even while speaking bitter truth to avoid unpleasantness.

In the office, or at the workplace, or in the organisation, every person has his own thinking, feeling, likes and dislikes which varies from person to person but it is very common that no one likes to hear arguments specially, when a junior or a subordinate starts it on any subject or topic with their seniors. Inspite of having close relation with their subordinates, the concerned seniors would never like their subordinates, juniors, argue with them on any matter, whether it is in the company interest or not. We should always restrict ourselves, from talking too much without any reason. This logic is not only suitable for the workplace but it is applicable for the entire place, whether it is school, college, any gatherings, or our own family. We should have the strength to control our anger because it leads our life towards certain destruction.

We should make sure that we appreciate our colleagues, whether they are good or bad whether their behaviour is tolerable or intolerable but we should appreciate their work done. When we appreciate their work, they would be motivated and automatically their performance would improve and when their performance would improve the growth of the company would increase. When the company would rise, the seniors would recommend their name for promotion, increments. Without adulation or flattery to the seniors, everyone would progress as action speaks louder than words.

We should always remember to be happy and content with whatever we have. If we are poor financially, we should prepare our mind as well as body to accept the difficulties due to it. It is not necessary that everyone has a good boss, is in his good books, or is liked by him or the work is according to his liking. It is very rare when a person gets the job, department according to his knowledge, education, and interest. If by chance anyone gets such a job, the person is very lucky. Everyone should accept their assigned job, work, responsibilities given by their seniors; otherwise, it would be very difficult to survive in that organisation, or department. Every day the situation and the condition changes. We should not be aggressive or excuse ourselves from any difficult situation, but we should learn from them. If we would minutely observe the situation, it would give us several valuable and golden guidance to tackle any adverse situation. We should not show our aggressiveness on anybody on any situation but we should work peacefully.

We should minutely think over what our seniors demand from us. It is not necessary that the seniors would disclose all their wishes, but we should learn to read between the lines. If any senior asks us to support a particular worker, subject or to adopt a particular system, even if the outcome of that system is not favourable for the organisation, we should handle it diplomatically. We should appreciate the system designed by the seniors; otherwise, it would be very difficult for us to survive at the workplace under them.

If we have to work with the seniors in a particular organisation, then it would be best to throw the word "against" out from our dictionary. We have seen several examples in the organisation, where the management dumped all the persons, workers who had raised their voice against the proposal of the management. If we do any mistake knowingly or unknowingly, then without thinking or consulting any one, we should apologise to the concerned person or the management.

The seniors think that any work should not be done or implemented without their consent. It is very easy, if we take approval for the work to be done from the concerned seniors prior to starting the work. The seniors would be very happy. They would think that the workers, subordinates are giving them due importance and it is better to be in good terms with them. In our family too, whenever we have to do any new work, we generally take permission from our parents before starting the work. If we work without taking prior permission for the same from our parents, they would get angry. Similarly, in our office, if a worker does any work without taking prior permission of the concerned seniors, the management would get angry or they may take disciplinary action against him for the same. Therefore, it would be better to take the required permission, for safety sake.

We should not be rude or arrogant under any circumstance because we are nowhere in the hirerchy or we have no existence in the organisation then why should we increase our blood pressure (B.P.). If the seniors ask us to do a particular work, we should do it immediately because in the organisation, there are several types of work which are not necessary for the company, but we have to do them , as it is necessary for our survival. Therefore, we should not be arrogant. Simultaneously, we should not assault or insult our seniors under any condition. We should never forget that we are after all, mere workers of the organisation. We are only giving our service to the company for which we are being paid and we do not have any right to assault or insult anybody, whether in the organisation or elsewhere.

For example, In the School or College, we have seen that there are some students whose main intention is to pull the leg of the teacher, just to impress their own friends (mostly girls) sitting near them in the classroom. Similarly, in the organisation, there are few subordinates or seniors, whose main interest is to insult their seniors or juniors without any proper reason. In both cases, it is very harmful for the concerned workers, seniors or for the organisation.

If any one does, such activities, the concerned seniors would never propose their name for any benefit. Therefore, we should pay our courtesies or regards to our seniors as well as juniors. Everybody expects that they should be given due respect. It is reciprocal.

The desire for respect or courtesy is one sided for the concerned seniors. For healthy work atmosphere courtesy should be extended from both the sides. It should be mutual. Then only a good working relationship can be developed and the organisation can grow faster. Mutual respect is very necessary irrespective of age, cadre or gender.

R: Recognition, Readiness, Realisation, Research, Revenge, Reasonable, Rebel, Revolution, Refuse, Regularity, Reliance, Religion, Regards, Respects, Routine work, Ruthless.

Every one works for his own benefit, betterment and expects something from the other end. There are several objectives in our life, which compel us to live decently and, to earn otherwise, it would be very difficult to survive. This objective gives us a positive attitude and energy, which helps people to work more. For example, if we come to know that our seniors, bosses are present in their cabins and they may call up, as and when they require. Thus, we may become very conscious, serious about our work, task and be ready to face any query or question raised by them. This is because we know that the boss will give recognition to our work done or efforts made for the organisation.

But on the other side, if we know that our boss, Incharge is out of town and would not come to the office on a particular day then generally we leave the office before the office closure without giving any reasons or on the pretext that we have some urgent work in the market. This is because, we know that if we would sit for a long time after office hours no one would come to see or observe our efforts or work or no one would come forward to appreciate our work or give recognition to our work done. It means we all work at our workplace only to get recognition. The management, incharge expects from their subordinates that they should work diligently in their presence as well as in their absence. Their work should not suffer in any case.

In general, it has been seen that the workers are not prepared for any mishap, unscheduled work or any emergency, which causes great damage to the organisation. People start working when their boss or incharge ask them to do or prepare a particular report. They cannot prepare any situational required report, with self-guidance. The boss can ask to present any type of report, any time without prior information or schedule. The management thinks that their subordinates are already prepared. They already have done their homework, or they know the requirement of their boss. This is why they demand any unscheduled or unexpected report from their subordinates. At this situation, if the workers are not prepared accordingly then the position of such workers would definitely get awkward in front of their seniors or management. Therefore, it is our duty to maintain a MIS report or we should always be ready to face any situation and we should be ready to provide any report to the concerned management without fail. If the workers fail to provide the required report to the seniors, the image of the workers would suffer and become very bad in front of their seniors. The seniors also judge us as to how much prepared we are so we should have an immaculate record keeping, providing all the information.

The power of seniors should not be taken for granted. If any senior does any favour to any worker, working under him, the worker must realise his power. Similarly, if any worker has done any mistake, or he did not fulfil the instruction of his seniors or he had hurt his seniors or colleagues, which caused misunderstanding between them, the concerned worker should realise it and try to get it rectified on an urgent basis or say sorry without hesitation.

We should always search within ourselves or try to assess ourselves as to what merits and demerits we have and what wrong or right we have done for the company. It should be clearly known to us. We should analyse our work done and try to rectify the mistakes. We should never forget the one who had favoured or helped us in the past. We should try to reciprocate one's kind gesture positively without letting them know.

In the organisation, there are various workers working under a particular senior at a common workplace. Everyone has his own power of endurance. Some are very hot tempered while some are very cool. Some workers are always planning to take revenge from a particular worker, which gives a wrong message. We should not take revenge from anybody be it any senior or colleague but if anyone is giving us trouble or disturbing us, we should work more diligently without thinking otherwise, but think only about our work and its betterment, so that through our work, we could take revenge on any person. If one does extra work beyond anyone's expectations, then definitely the company would grow and the concerned workers would get promotion, increment or other benefits while the others would not.

Most of the workers in the organisation do not know how to give proper answer to any query or questions raised by any senior. If the senior asks to give the answer of "A", as "A" is wrong as per a particular senior. Then everybody would start saying that it is wrong, but if the answer or logic of any senior is not suitable, then it is our duty to provide a reasonable explanation along with suitable examples, with carefully framed sentences to convince him about the truth, without hurting him. The management also knows or is familiar with the facts but they desire that their subordinates should have a clear knowledge that they could manage the critical situation by giving reasonable explanation to convince their seniors. Some of the seniors, inspite of having enough knowledge of the facts or happenings, do not want to come forward but they want to convince the concerned seniors or workers through their worker's reasonable statements. Sometimes, the seniors do not want to say anything to anyone directly due to some reason. At this situation, they take help of their subordinates or colleagues to pass on the message through the reasonable and logical statements of their subordinate.

Some workers are very aggressive by nature and get angry even on a small objection. Their endurance is very low due to high blood pressure and they do not think anything before talking. They generally use unparliamentary language even with their seniors, colleagues, workers. Any opportunity from the management or from outside can come at any time without knocking at the door. It does not wait for any favourable situation or condition. Everyone is authorised to forward one's name for the forthcoming opportunity. Even a lower cadre person could get the best opportunity provided they forward the name of the workers to the management.

It is necessary to control our behaviour, temperament and statements. Otherwise, inspite of having good knowledge, skill and experience, it would be very difficult for anyone to make use of the best opportunity offered by the management, because the management does not want to tolerate the aggressiveness or rebellious nature of their workers, subordinates at any cost.

Due to the high handedness of any worker, the concerned worker generally knowingly or unknowingly refuses to follow the instruction of his incharge, H.O.D. without thinking of the repercussions. The seniors do not want their instructions being refused or ignored by their subordinates. In the organisation, everyone is working under a specific in charge or supervisor. If a worker follows the instruction of his seniors, whether the instruction is fruitful or not, it does not matter. The image of the concerned worker would be very high in front of his seniors if he never refuses their instruction but when due to any reason if the same worker refuses to obey the given instruction, the image of the same worker would turn bad in front of the same seniors.

It means the management at any cost does not want their instructions to be ignored or disobeyed by any of their workers in their organisation. We should not refuse any instruction coming from the higher management, whether the instruction damages the image of the organisation or not.

Regularity at the workplace plays a very important role at any workplace or in the organisation. Inspite of having good knowledge, skill and experience in a specific field at their workplace, if the concerned worker is irregular or is frequently absent without giving prior information to the concerned senior. The management does not like such workers or they do not want to boost them up by giving them a good opportunity, financial or otherwise, who are irregular in their attendance at the workplace. They like only those workers, who are very punctual and regular. The management does not like anyone's irregularity, because it shows their irresponsible behaviour or unaccountability on the given assignment. The irregular workers are not very faithful for the organisation or they cannot be reliable for the management, as they do not know about the day-to-day activities or happenings at the workplace. A person would be reliable, accountable faithful in the management's point of view, only when he is punctual and regular in his duties. So, if anyone wants to get promotion or increment or wants to conquer the heart of his seniors or the management, he should be very regular and punctual and always be physically present in front of the management or the concerned seniors.

We live in a secular country and we respect all the religions or faith equally. The workers should remember that the discussion on any religion or faith within the organisation or at the workplace is totally banned. We should not waste our energy in irrelevant discussion because in an organisation, there are persons who practice different religions, but are working together. At the workplace, their religion is only work and their thinking is for organisational growth. This is the religion for all and there is no scope for other religion other than this. The workers should always remember that they are working in a particular place and due to their discussion the environment of the organisation could be polluted or so it would be better to avoid such discussions as far as possible.

If the workers have all the good qualities but do not have etiquette and manners, and do not know, to respect their seniors and are un-courteous, then, inspite of having good qualities, no one would like such people. Because, respect and proper courtesy is very much required by the management as well as by the individuals.

Everyone knows that snakes are very dangerous and poisonous and can take the life of a person in no time, but the snake charmer can control them by giving proper instruction through their BEEN (Wind Instrument used by the Snake charmers). We can win over our naughty, stubborn and unruly kids by talking and convincing them on their manners by being very patient, polite, and respectful irrespective of their age. We must think that though we have given them birth, we should respect them and not hit or abuse them.

Similarly in the organisation there are several seniors or workers who have different temperaments, nature, behaviour but we have to work with them as well as tolerate them which can only be possible when we give them a smile, due respect and proper courtesy inspite of their suspicious nature. By doing this, it is possible to win the ruthless heart of our seniors, incharge because it is true that some of the seniors have a very bad and cruel attitude, which is very difficult to comprehend. They only want respect and courtesy but they do not want to give respect to their subordinates, juniors, which should be reciprocated. It cannot be one sided. One would not become small by giving respect to his juniors; on the contrary he would get more respect.

We should always guide ourselves with our own set of rules. First of all, we should complete our daily routine work, and then we should think about other things. We should never dump any work for the next day but it should be cleared on a day-to-day basis, as tomorrow never comes. Files should not pile up on our desk and we should not ask our juniors to complete our work. We should never disclose office secrets to anyone no matter how close he is.

MANGO TREE

It is human nature to learn from Nature as well as from wise people who have more experience. Nature always teaches us the lessons of life but people always overlook it due to their daily workload unwanted mental tension, fatigue or lack of awareness.

If we see a Mango Tree or any other tree, which bears fruits, never harms anyone. People always, try to take benefit from those trees. People stand, sit or take rest under the shade and enjoy the cool breeze but they never think about that tree and take any lesson which the tree wants to convey. If we think about that tree, we would get many lessons, which we cannot get from elsewhere. The Tree tells us about the seniors and juniors as well as about the duties and the responsibilities, which we generally do at our workplace.

It also tells us how we should tackle the bad situations when all the seniors, boss and colleagues turn against us. How we should treat them and how we should remain patient and calm. We have seen that a tree laden with fruits lowers its branches automatically and bends downwards and tries to touch the earth. People come and pluck the fruits, which are at their approachable height, but the same people do not disturb the fruits, which are distant from them or are out of their reach. However, when there are no fruits in the trees the branches are in their normal position. Therefore, it is said that learned and wise people are like fruit laden trees. They are very humble and are closer to the roots or are very realistic.

People always give their support to humble and true people like the branches which bow down with its fruits or tries to touch the earth. In spite of having high value in the market the true worker does not bother about his positive points. We should also apply such logic in our Organisation. If seniors or H.O.D. have vast knowledge , power they should bow downwards, be polite and soft spoken as well as be helpful to their subordinates or workers working under them or working in that Organisation.

If they do so, the worker working under them would feel very satisfied either during favourable or adverse situations. On the other hand, the seniors having full power and authority without having soft nature and negative attitude towards their subordinates or worker working under them, would prove dangerous for the Organisation.

In most of the Organisations, as soon as some people get power they change their behaviour. Such changed behaviour is very harmful for their subordinates and the Organisation. The seniors should take lessons from the Mango tree, which bows down when its branches are full of fruits. The tree never eats its own fruits but it is for others. Therefore, the seniors should be selfless and their behaviour should be persistent in all the situations.

If we have something and we want to use it for the betterment of others, we should do it without thinking otherwise. We should always remember that a good opportunity comes only once in a while and is like God's gift. In the Organisation, if anyone has been given power, they should utilise their power in support of the workers and Organisation. The seniors should also take lessons from the Mango tree, which always bows down, when its branches are full of fruits. It gives us cool air, calm, peace, sweet fruits and protects us from the heat of the Sun, apart from giving abundant oxygen for breathing.

SANDAL WOOD TREE AND SNAKES

In the Organisation or at the workplace, if our seniors are not good-natured or their behaviour un-consistant, who always abuse their staff and dislike them. The workers do not know what step, methods, technique should be applied to please such seniors because all their benefits depend on their recommendation. The worker would not benefit, if their seniors would not give right remarks to the concerned workers. Nature is always ready to give us lessons without charging us anything but we never give importance to them. We should always try to take lessons from Nature and tackle the problems coming in our daily life, whether at our workplace or at home.

At our workplace, there are various persons having different nature, temperament, thinking ability and level of patience. Some Head or seniors are found to be very bad for their employees. People have no idea, how to tackle them. At this situation, we should not be disappointed but we should take lessons from Nature. One should remember the facts of sandal wood trees and the poisonous snakes. Here if we presume all the seniors to be snakes and the workers workings under them like the tree. The sandalwood tree attracts the poisonous snakes owing to its fragrance, does not get poisoned or gets affected by its venom. The sandalwood paste is used for Puja and religious rituals but the venom of the snake does not affect its virtue. Therefore, we must keep on working without being affected by our venomous seniors.

We should attract such seniors with our good work, good behaviour and patience without being aggressive and work according to their desire. If we do our work according to their liking, it is sure that such seniors would definitely change their attitude and come closer to the workers as the snakes come closer to the sandal wood tree due to its fragrance. We should obey all their instructions good or bad, without thinking otherwise. One day such a person would definitely change his behaviour and attitude. We should not react on any of their comments. We should become indifferent to their adverse comments as well as compliments.

PLEASE KEEP SAFE DISTANCE

Everyday when we cross the road or while commuting, we see a message written on the rear of transport vehicles: *PLEASE KEEP SAFE DISTANCE.* Most of the people read this adage but do not give it any importance or try to understand the meaning, behind its writing or take lessons from it in their lives, whether at home or at the workplace. This message is really a punch line for our life. We can interpret its meaning and try to follow it. These key words may be used in several stages of human life like:

- Human Relationships: At Home and at the Workplace
- Electronic System
- On the Road

Relationship: A relationship can be between:

- Friends
- A teacher and student
- A wife and Husband
- The Seniors and Juniors
- The Servant and Employer
- The Management and the Employees
- The owner of the Company and the Workers
- A specific distance is required to see anything otherwise it cannot be seen.

ELECTRIC CURRENT

In electricity, there are two poles, one is positive and the other is negative pole. The two opposite poles are useful only when they are separated with a minimum distance but when due to any reasons, these two poles break the barricade and come together a bright spark comes out which creates darkness. It means, it should maintain a minimum specified distance for functioning smoothly and good performance.

TWO VEHICLES ON THE ROAD

When we drive a vehicle on the road, we should keep and maintain a minimum distance between two vehicles. If we fail to maintain the required minimum distance, there is a chance of the vehicles colliding and an accident taking place. It can be avoided by keeping our vehicles or maintaining a safe distance from other vehicles. Here, we also learn that if we have to run our vehicle very smoothly, then we should follow the traffic rules and regulations, to avoid any mishap. This logic is applicable to our different relationships in life as well.

For example:

Friendship : Friendship is a very sweet bond between human beings. Friendship can be between two or more people. This sweet bond exists irrespective of our social status, caste and creed. Lord Krishna and Sudama had a sweet bond of friendship. It can be between two families also. Each friend should regard and give space to each other. Friendship would develop only when friends would keep a safe distance in every respect. As soon as they break the minimum required distance between them, i.e. start interfering in their personal life, the friendship turns sour.

Teacher and Students : A different kind of relationship is also seen between a teacher and a student. Several factors are required to maintain such a bond. Students should have a lot of respect and regards for their teacher. The teacher should reciprocate by teaching and loving them irrespective of them being rich or poor, highborn or lowborn etc. If they do not maintain distance between them or become too familiar then the relationship will not last.

Wife and Husband : In the case of a wife and a husband, there is a secret and sweet bond but this secret bond is very fragile and can easily break, if wife and husband do not trust each other or do not give space to each other. Both of them should respect each other's feelings and emotions, which is only possible when they maintain a safe distance from each other. As soon as they lose trust, stop respecting each other emotionally or otherwise, the bond snaps.

SENIORS AND JUNIORS

In modern society, it is seen that people working in a small or big Organisation, develop friendship with their juniors/seniors colleagues very quickly. They take their lunch, smoke, and drink together. They think that there should be no difference between the juniors, seniors and all of them are friends. When they become friendly with their colleagues, they stop respecting each other and gradually they start fighting on small things. They have less fear of their boss and seniors. Thus, the productivity of the Organisation gradually decreases.

On the other hand, we can say that there should be no friendship between two or many workers of any Organisation, working at a common workplace. Such friendship is unproductive for the Organisation as well as for the individual. Of course, they should be cordial to each other.

At this situation, Management expects from their employees that they should maintain a safe distance from their seniors. They may not say a word but their inner feelings warn them from time to time that they should not be familiar with their junior staff, as we all know that "Familiarity breeds contempt." One should learn to read between the lines.

WHEELS AND THE BRAKE PAD

It is a very apt example of keeping safe distance from the Management or others, to run the organisation smoothly. We have seen wheels and their brake pad. There is a very close relationship between them and both should be of good quality to run the car smoothly. In one's absence, it will be very difficult to run the car or to keep it under control. The vehicle can run smoothly on the road, only when there is a safe distance between wheel and the brake pad. As soon as we push the brake peddle to minimise the distance between them, the vehicle gradually becomes slow and ultimately stops.

Similarly, in any Organisation, the relationship between the Management and the workers/employees is a very important factor for the growth of the Company. Their mutual relationship, co-ordination, understandings, courtesy etc. is very necessary to run the Organisation. For rapid growth of the Company, it is necessary, to have a good relationship between the employees and the employer. It is only possible when both of them give due respect to each other, by listening to the instructions carefully and implementing them accordingly in Company's interest. For the smooth functioning of an organisation, it is required to keep a safe distance or to maintain a safe distance between the employers and the workers. If one does not maintain the required minimum distance from the each other, then there may be unwanted disturbance, misunderstanding, tension, disrespect for each other, misuse of funds, sources etc. which would directly or indirectly create obstacles for the Company to run smoothly. Therefore, we can take lessons from the wheel and the brake pad of a car.

SPECIFIC DISTANCE TO SEE ANY OBJECT

We can see an object only if we maintain a safe and minimum distance. If the object is far, it becomes invisible due to long distance. In other words, inspite of having, good qualities a very loyal, faithful and honest worker for the Organisation, should maintain a minimum safe distance from his employers or the Management. The Management also wants to maintain an adequate distance from their employees. Inspite of having good relations with the Employees, they never like that their workers interact with them except for some exceptional cases or on formal occasions.

All the above-mentioned examples give us valuable lessons to imbibe at our workplace. We should strictly follow all the rules and regulations and should implement them in our general life. If we would follow them, it would be very fruitful or beneficial for both the workers and for the management or seniors. If any worker desires to get promotion increment or respect at his workplace he should follow the above principles without fail otherwise it would be very difficult to maintain a sound relationship with each other.

If a person works in the same Organisation, where his college friend's father is the owner of the company. At this situation, the owner's son desires or expects from his college friend that he being a worker / employee should also maintain a safe distance from him, because there is a huge gap between their status and position. The employee should never flaunt his friendship in the company, as it would demean their friendship. Friendship is very valuable and fragile. It should be cherished but should never be misused.

❖❖❖

CHAPTER 12

PROGRESS OF EMPLOYEES OR WORKERS

PROGRESS OF EMPLOYEES OR WORKERS

Progress of any Organisation not only depends upon the dedication or qualities of their workforce but it also depends upon their seniors and their qualities as well as their dedication. Any Organisation can get the adequate or desired progress or growth, if its seniors, H.O.D. along with their workers give best of their efforts in the Organisational interest. Apart from their dedication, it also depends upon the physical health, age group, capability, decision-making power, likes and dislikes of the seniors as well as of the common workforce of the concerned Organisation.

Similarly, development or progress of human beings also depend upon their power of thinking. As we know that, the human beings think through their brain. Here we can compare the activities of brain with the seniors of any Organisation.

For a while, we can assume the seniors as our Brain and workers as the body parts. In this situation, our body reacts according to the message received from the brain. Without receiving message from the brain, not a single part of our body can move or react. Our body parts first take instruction from the brain and then as per the instruction, they function or make any movement. A healthy, educated, dedicated, enthusiastic, person has a sound brain in comparison to an unhealthy person. A common healthy person can think better than an insane person, while both may have similar physique. A normal and healthy person can give better performance than an unhealthy person. This is because of his sound brain capability, power of analysis, thinking power etc.

It means the complete positive or negative activities of human beings depend upon the health of the brain of the concerned person. Similarly, the progress or downfall of any

Organisation directly depends upon the mental status and health of the brain of the concerned Management / Seniors/H.O.D.

If any Company is not getting the required or overall estimated result, the employees are not responsible for this but the concerned seniors and the middle Management are. The employees or the workers cannot do anything without getting any instructions from their concerned seniors. If the concerned seniors are not giving proper instructions to their subordinates then how can anyone expect positive output from their subordinates or the overall progress of the Company?

Sometimes, in certain Organisations, the Management tells their workers that as the Company is not getting profit, they are not in a position to provide them betterment or better salary in comparison to the market. Here the subordinates are not responsible for the non-performance of the Company. The workers had worked as per the instruction of their seniors. Here only the seniors are responsible, as adequate instruction was not given to the subordinates.

In another example, if someone hires a labourer for his personal work at home and does not give him proper instruction about what he has to do. The labourer will sit idle without completing the work because the person, who had hired him, had not given him proper guidelines. If work suffered and the master had to face some financial loss, then the hired labourer is not responsible but the person who had not given him proper instruction/guidelines is fully responsible for the loss.

Similarly, in the Organisation, if the Organisation is not getting the estimated return in terms of business or progress, then in such a case the concerned Manager, Management are fully responsible and not the workers. Inspite of their best efforts they are not getting proper benefits, because of their seniors and the concerned managers.

It means inspite of having all the good qualities, the worker, his progress, benefit depends upon the quality of his seniors. If his seniors would have a sound brain, the subordinates would get the best of everything within the Organisation otherwise it is not possible.

OLD BOSS AND NEW BOSS

As we know that, nothing is fixed but each and every thing is working at its own pace. Only dead things have no movement but when we think about them in an other way, we would find that there is also movement in the dead or stagnant thing. There is a movement under the earth crust and under the ocean floor, which we cannot see by virtue of which we get fossil fuels and petroleum products, but some activities are going on continuously which we sometimes, feel during the earthquake, tsunami and volcanic eruptions. The only thing is how we perceive it. It all depends upon our keen observation. Due to the movement of our body, we are getting energy to work. We take in fresh air from our surrounding and sometimes, if we do not get fresh air, we go out to get the required air to breathe otherwise, we may fall ill and would not be in a position to think or do anything. This situation is very much similar to the activities held in any Organisation.

It has been seen that if the H.O.D., or the boss is changed or transferred and new Boss/ H.O.D. Comes to handle the division or department. The growth of such Organisation, automatically goes upwards. As the new boss, has his own strategy, views, ideas, working procedures and the ability to think. He would try to introduce a unique system for the Organisation and as well as for the workers.

The workers would also try to impress him by doing a lot of work and would show their dedication, devotion and integration.

In this way, the growth of the Organisation along with the employees would automatically increase in such a way that monopoly, cronyism groupism, which may sometimes, become very harmful for the well being of the Organisation, decreases.

Workers would also get benefits by their new boss by getting increment or promotion because the new boss does not have knowledge about the existing systems, behaviour of the workers, as well as the working environment of the Organisation but the old employees have. Such old employees would try to hypnotise him with sycophancy, flattery and the boss may favour them accordingly. It all depends on how he reacts or takes it.

In some cases, it is also possible that if the new boss had already decided that he would leave the Organisation in a certain period of time due to some specific reason, then it is possible that such a boss, may think that if he is leaving this Organisation then why not do some favour for the existing workers, working under him.

They would never create any obstacles on any project or any proposal of any employee. The behaviour of such a boss suddenly becomes flexible and he would try to upgrade them.

MISMATCHED PORTFOLIOS

In an several cases, it has been observed that the management prefers to assign a mismatched portfolio to their workers or subordinates, so that they do not perform well in their assigned department and they could boss upon them. Although it is against Company/ Organisational interest but the immediate management or the authorities always prefer to adopt this strategy to control the workforce and keep them in check.

In another way, we can say that the management wants from their employees that they should work in such a department, which is beyond their capacity, interest and experience. They know very well about the merits and de-merits of this strategy but inspite of this, they adopt this, so that they can handle or control the workforce in their own way. By such strategy, the main losers are employees because inspite of having good and adequate skill and experience they do not get their due. The work is one sided and they are not able to get due progress. Due to the strategy of the management, the workers do not get proper and regular progress in their work. This is a very common practice. Around 90% of the workforce is affected by it.

It is observed that a manager/ workforce, skilled in a particular subject/field, can discharge his assigned responsibilities in a very scientific way. He can prepare a new strategy to work smoothly, which may give a very rare chance to the seniors to point out his mistake or comment on his non-performance. But the concerned in charge, seniors, in spite of having required knowledge make him work in a different department, so that they could point out some mistakes from his work and harass him easily. This is the reason that inspite of fulfilling all the criteria, a worker cannot get promotion and increment on time.

Sometimes, the Management gives the responsibilities to such a person, who is not interested or does not know anything about the assigned job/responsibility, which he is going to handle. Due to some unavoidable circumstance, management gives him full co-operation, so that he can learn more about that particular assigned job. Management may provide him some extra facilities to learn and handle the new job/ assigned responsibility.

The person concerned, devotes his maximum efforts to discharge his responsibility/duty in the most systematic and scientific way. He may gradually prove himself as the bonafide worker of his Company/department. However, when he proves himself as one of the best employee/worker of the Company, the same Management is afraid of such an employee, as they think that such a knowledgeable worker may, one day point out their weak points and may raise his voice against the weak system or the loopholes in the Company. As soon as the management feels that they may face some loss due to such an honest worker, the concerned seniors immediately change his existing portfolio, give him a new assignment, and ask him to prove himself once again by throwing a new challenge. The morale of the worker is shattered beyond repair thereby leading him to depression or frustration. They may also transfer his credit to some of their near and dear ones.

Thus, the worker is back to square one from where he has to start from scratch. The new head of the department would tell him that, as he is a new worker of this department, so first he has to prove himself. This way, he will not get any benefit, inspite of doing good work in Company's interest. It will take a long time for him to get an upgradation.

FAIL TO PROVE THEMSELVES AS BONAFIDE WORKERS

We know that man proposes and God disposes. There is nothing in our hands. Inspite of having all the facilities or amenities, we sometimes fail to complete a work. Inspite of our plans and strategy we are unable to complete that assignment due to some unforeseen problems.

Similarly, at the workplace of any Organisation, many people face some problems. The concerned seniors or incharge give instructions to complete a particular work but they never take pain to give a briefing or information about that job or the procedure, so that it could be easy for the workers to complete it. They think that their duty is only to give instructions and to take action against them in case they fail to complete it.

The following factors are responsible for their failure at the workplace.

- Lack of Self Involvement
- Lack of Clear Concept
- Errors
- Less Working Hours

Lack of Self Involvement:

The seniors at the workplace want a high level of involvement from their workers in any assigned job. As without having inadequate involvement in any assigned job or project, may lead to failure towards the Organisational goal. If a Company or Organisation gets profit in their business, the main strength is their involvement from the first day of the inception of the project. For example, if a child gets good marks in his class, it means his parents take interest in his studies and they are totally involved in their child's welfare. Otherwise, it would not be possible.

It means, in other ways, it can be said that the Management wants that their workers should take keen interest in their work responsibility/ assignment etc, because without their involvement, the progress or the growth of the Organisation is not possible.

A coach of any game like football/cricket expects from his players that they should take keen interest in their game. They should get fully involved in the match otherwise; it would be very difficult for them to win the match.

Similarly, at the workplace, it has been observed that the workers working under the guidance of any senior or supervisors do not involve themselves much with their personal work, as is required. They work just for the heck of it. The workers first think about their personal security and if they find that it is alright then they do not involve themselves in the assigned work. They get complacent. If they know that on their failure, or their lack of good presentation, the seniors sitting as the head cannot do anything against them, then inspite of having every knowledge/skill, the workers do not involve themselves in their assigned work.

Since the workers sometimes do not show their involvement in the Company's working procedure or generally make themselves aloof /distant from the existing systems, guided by some seniors/head of the department. This is the reason at the time of recommendation for promotion, increment or betterment; the concerned seniors do not consider their names for the same.

Lack of Clear Concept:

Lengthy and unclear or confused guidelines hamper the progress of the Organisation. It means the instruction given should be crystal clear. A clear instruction takes a short time to give a good result and vice versa. The Management expects from their workers that they should do their job or discharge their responsibility in a systematic and scientific way. It means the employees should divide their whole work in different segments and time schedule for different project/work, so that they can involve themselves completely to give good and satisfactory results.

The Management expects a quick result against their assigned work from their workers, which is not possible without splitting their jobs/responsibilities/assignments into several small segments. The workers should first review all projects/work/assignment with full involvement and do their job enthusiastically. However, unfortunately in most of the Organisations, generally workers are not found so responsible with their work because they have no clear instruction as well as a clear concept of their assigned work. This is the reason the concerned workers cannot deliver their duty according to the desire of the concerned seniors or the Management. Because of their lack of concept, they cannot give the desired result.

Mistakes:

The workers working in any Organisation are directly or indirectly observed by the Management. The Management always keeps an eye on all the employees as to how they work, how they react on any system or any instruction, how they deliver their duty, how they perform and to what degree is their dedication, whether they are working honestly or not. There are few workers generally, officially assigned to oversee this and report to the concerned Management accordingly. This type of system is very useful for the growth of the Organisation, subject to it not being biased or misused.

The Management observes every mistake/error committed minutely by their workers/employees and simultaneously they also observe their good work, attitude and enthusiasm. They also observe their smallest point of error. People think that the Management has forgotten their small errors done in the past but they are wrong. They have every detail in their record or in their mind.

It means it is advisable for the worker or employee of any Organisation that they should not do any mistake knowingly or repeat their mistake, which they had done in the past. They should not give any point to the seniors, so that they can take action against them.

Less Working Hours:

In general, the workers do not complete their work during working hours but they spend most of the time in meeting with the seniors or other people or doing useless things. Sometimes, it is in Company's interest and sometimes it is not. Most of the workers start working in the evening, sit in the office for late hours, just to show the Management that they are the real and dedicated workers of the Company, and are very dutiful. The Management also gives importance to such people. They do not want to know the impact of such workers on the Organisation but they support such employees without knowing their intention.

If a worker works in the office, with full dedication and leaves the office just after office hours, then most of the seniors do not like such activities. They believe that the worker should stay in the office until their seniors leave the office, which is sometimes very difficult for the subordinates to maintain, because the subordinates come to the office according to their schedule from distant suburbs/places but the seniors come to the office according to their convenience and leave the office accordingly.

At the time of making appraisal for the subordinates, such seniors review all these points too. They review on their late working hours and also consider it. This is the reason, sometimes; the genuine workers do not get promotion and increment but the superficial workers get it.

WHEEL BALANCE

The wheels of a car/vehicle should be balanced for smooth running. If we ignore it then it is possible that our vehicle would start troubling us. If the wheels of the vehicle are properly balanced or aligned then the expense on the maintenance of the vehicle would be low. Similarly at the workplace, for the progress of the workers it is necessary that there should be a proper balance, or alignment coordination among the colleagues, assigned work and the respected seniors, otherwise inspite of having all the qualities, a worker would not get his due.

ZODIAC SIGN

Everyone knows that the fate of any individual depends upon his date, place, time of birth along with his ZODIAC SIGN. Normally when a person decides to get his children married he tries to match the horoscope of his children with their prospective partners. If their horoscope does not match then it is assumed that the pairing will not be auspicious. The relationship between the wife and the husband also depends upon their ZODIAC SIGNS. If their Zodiac Signs are favourable to each other, then their family life would be very good and peaceful. On the other hand, if their zodiac signs do not match with each other then it would be very difficult to lead a happy and peaceful life.

Similarly, whenever we start a new work, business or any project, we emphasise on its date of inauguration, which depends upon the auspicious Muhurat, Lagan, or auspicious date, time, direction and month. The Priest assures the concerned person about the date and time to start the business as good and auspicious for that particular business or project or for his Zodiac Sign and lagan.

Similarly, at the workplace of any Organisation, progress of the workers also depend upon the co-ordination of their Zodiac Signs and their concerned seniors, supervisors, in charge or the Management or the decision maker. If their Zodiac Signs are favourable for each other, then there will be no problem between them. They would lead a normal life and would have continuous progress in their career but on the other hand, if their Signs are not favourable then it would be very difficult to maintain a balance in the relationship between them or to survive in that Organisation.

I have used "Zodiac Signs" in a practical sense. It means the progress of the workers depend upon the combination of Zodiac Signs between the workers and the concerned seniors. If the combination between the seniors and the workers match, then the progress of the concerned worker is definite and sure. The worker would get recommendation for promotion and increment or other kinds of benefit otherwise it would be difficult. This is the reason some people's career reach the sky in their chosen field or vocation while others are not so lucky.

It has been seen that if the concerned seniors are peeping Toms and the workers too are similar, the senior would definitely like his workers and he would recommend their name for promotion or increment, even if the workers are worthless and do not deserve the same.

On the other hand, if the senior is abusive but the worker has adverse nature, then it shows that their zodiac sign does not match and he would never get promotion or other benefits. If the senior is very honest and principled then he would like only those workers or subordinates who are honest and sincere. Here the seniors would give promotion or increment to the honest and sincere workers along with the deserving ones.

In a nutshell, I mean that for the betterment of any worker, the character, behaviour, likes-dislikes, mentality, knowledge, skill, background, education, loyalty and the personal relationship should match with the concerned seniors, otherwise it would be very difficult to get promotion or increment or any benefit at the workplace under any circumstance.

It can be explained by another simple example. An organisation appoints a group of Management Trainees in a particular year. Some of them do very well in their career while for a lucky few, their career propels like a rocket, touching the sky. They become the top officials of the company by dint of their luck and efforts, but here their zodiac signs too play a very significant role in their upgradation. Some may be very unlucky and would stagnate thereby falling into depression and frustration leading to utter despair and doom. This has been cited from my personal experience.

From a particular batch of the top notch B-schools or the IITs, everybody's career takes a different course. Some excel while some lead a hunky-dory life.

❖❖❖

REFERENCES

- Principles Of Management-" Dr. Varma & Agarwal
- Elements of Personnel Management and Industrial Relations- Pradeep Kumar.

QUESTIONNAIRE

CHAPTER: 02

A BRIEF NOTE ON THE MANAGEMENT

Questions:

(1) Define the various types of Management.

(2) Explain the various functions of Management.

(3) What do you understand by the Middle-order Management and explain the functions of Middle-level Management.

(4) What is Supervisory Management?

(5) What is the importance of Planning, Coordination, Motivation, Organising and Controlling in a smooth running Management?

CHAPTER: 03

THE ORGANISATION

Questions:

(1) What do you understand by Organisation? Explain.

(2) What is Line Organisation? Explain its merits & demerits.

(3) What is the difference between Line & Staff Organisation?

(4) Explain the merits & demerits of Line & Staff Organisation.

(5) Explain the various functions of Staff Organisation.

(6) What do you understand by the present days' Organisation? Explain its qualities & characteristics in your own words.

CHAPTER: 04

A BRIEF NOTE ON THE PRACTICAL MANAGEMENT

Questions:

(1) What do you understand by the Practical Management? Explain by giving examples.

(2) What type of instruction do the workers receive from their seniors?

(3) Without having any facilities, how does a person complete the assigned work?

(4) What is the difference between theoretical Management & Practical Management? Explain in your own words.

(5) What is the importance of Practical Management in ones career?

(6) Explain the various problems which one has to face during the completion of an assignment in *your* own words.

CHAPTER: 05

MANAGERS AND THEIR TYPES

Questions:

(1) Define the various types of managers found in any Organisation.

(2) What do you understand by Street Manager and what are the characteristic features of a Street Manager?

(3) Write note in your own words about the confused Manager.

(4) What do you understand by a Termite Manager and what are the reasons of their development in any Organisation?

(5) Write a note on a Jealous Manager. Why is the boss jealous of his subordinates?

(6) Describe the merits and demerits of an indifferent and Grey Hound Manager. How are they useful for an Organisation?

CHAPTER: 06

A BRIEF NOTE ON THE BEHAVIOUR OF THE MANAGEMENT TOWARDS THEIR WORKERS/EMPLOYEES

Questions:

(1) Why does a senior usually ignore the contributions of his subordinates?

(2) What are the reasons behind the ill behaviour of the seniors?

(3) Why a boss never tries to upgrade his talented subordinates?

(4) Why a Head of the Department does try to misguide or mislead the Management?

(5) What are the factors responsible for the work presentation?

(6) Write a short note on the reasons of useless gossip.

(7) What is the relationship between a kitchen knife and the workers in an Organisation?

(8) Define the word discrimination and explain in your own words its merits and demerits.

(9) Why workers do not want to respect their seniors? What are the hidden reasons behind it?

(10) What do you understand by Positive & Negative Energy in the point of view of the Practical Management?

(11) Why does a subordinate have less respect for his senior?

(12) What are the reasons of demotivation & how does it affect the performance of a worker?

(13) Why Organisational faith of the worker deteriorate & explain its different aspects with reasons?

(14) Why do seniors/management only give instructions & do not want to listen to anything? Give a proper reason on the practical management's point of view.

(15) What are the factors responsible for the work presentation?

(16) Why a senior does not want to listen the word "NO" from his subordinates?

(17) Why dissatisfaction develops in a worker, while he may be a good, dedicated, honest, skilled & labourious worker of the Organisation?

(18) Why a worker does not raise his voice against the seniors and keeps his mouth shut, inspite of knowing that his question is beneficial for the Organisation?

(19) What are the factors responsible for the sadistic Nature of the seniors?

(20) Write a short note on work presentation & explain its demerits & merits?

(21) Explain the positive & negative affects of Divide & Rule policy?

(22) What do you understand by the terrn "Topi Transfer"?

(23) Write a short note on "I am the senior you are not".

(24) Is groupism among the seniors or workers in an Organisation, useful or not, Explain it in your own words?

(25) Why honesty is ignored and dishonesty is rewarded at the workplace?

CHAPTER: 07

WORKERS AND THEIR BEHAVIOUR

Questions:

(1) What measures are adopted by the workers to divert the attention of the concerned seniors from their weak points?

(2) Everyone wants to do supervisory/liaison work at the workplace. Explain in your own words.

(3) In general the seniors take credit themselves and discredit their subordinates. What are the reasons behind it? Explain with suitable examples.

(4) Explain the types of workers generally found in an Organisation.

CHAPTER: 08

RESPONSIBILITY AND BEHAVIOUR OF THE MIDDLE MANAGEMENT

Questions:

(1) Explain the various responsibilities and behaviour of the Middle Management of an Organisation.

(2) What are the responsibilities of the Middle Management towards the top Management in Company's interest?

(3) What are the responsibilities of the Middle Management towards their subordinates?

(4) What are the responsibilities of the Middle Management towards the Image or Brand of the Organisation?

(5) Explain the behaviour of the Middle Management in general towards their Company.

(6) Explain the behaviour of the Middle Management towards the subordinates.

CHAPTER: 09

EXPECTATIONS OF MANAGEMENT FROM THEIR WORKFORCE

Questions:

(1) Explain the various expectations of the seniors, Incharge, Head of the Department from their concerned subordinates.

(2) Write a short note on "Do not take it for granted"?

(3) Write a short note on "Duty First and Self Last"?

(4) What are the important factors of workers which are required at the workplace?

(5) How does one get promotion & increment?

(6) How can a person win the faith of his ill behaved seniors?

(7) What are the reasons behind an ill behaved senior?

(8) What do you understand by the dual personality at the workplace? Are such people dangerous for the workers or not? Give reasons with examples.

CHAPTER: 10

EXPECTATION OF WORKERS FROM THE MANAGEMENT

Questions:

(1) What are the expectations of the workers from the Management?

(2) How does the environment of the workplace affect the progress of an employee?

(3) Explain the reasons for which a person works in any Organisation?

(4) What are the ideal qualities of a senior?

CHAPTER: 11

LESSONS AND INSPIRATIONS

Questions:

(1) Explain" Do not heat the magnet otherwise its magnetism will be lost".

(2) Inspite of several thorns people like roses for its beauty and fragrance. Explain it in practical management point of view.

(3) How do you learn from the Environment? Explain.

(4) Explain the different lessons which we get from the Wall Clock.

(5) What do you understand by "Catch the Opportunity"?

(6) What lessons do we get from the Mirror?

(7) What do we learn from a Mango tree in general life?

(8) What do you understand by "Keep safe distance? Explain with examples.

CHAPTER: 12

PROGRESS OF EMPLOYEES OR WORKERS

Questions:

(1) What are the factors responsible towards the progress of the employees?

(2) What measures should we take, if we are not promoted for a long time?

(3) How does a zodiac sign work in the progress of a worker?